EMERGING AS A TEACHER

Robert V. Bullough Jr,
J. Gary Knowles
and Nedra A. Crow

London and New York

First published 1991
by Routledge
11 New Fetter Lane, London EC4P 4EE

Simultaneously published in the USA and Canada
by Routledge
a division of Routledge, Chapman and Hall, Inc.
29 West 35th Street, New York, NY 10001

British Library Cataloguing in Publication Data
Bullough, Robert V. *1949–*
Emerging as a teacher. – (Investigating schooling).
1. Teaching. Professional education
I. Title II. Knowles, J. Gary *1947–* III. Crow, Nedra A. *1951–* IV. Series
370.71

Library of Congress Cataloging in Publication Data
Bullough, Robert V., *1949–*
Emerging as a teacher / Robert V. Bullough Jr, J. Gary Knowles, and
Nedra A. Crow
Includes bibliographical references and index.
1. First year teachers–United States–Case studies. I. Knowles, J. Gary,
1947–. II. Crow, Nedra A., *1951–*. III. Title.
LB2844.1.N4B83 1992

ISBN 0–415–03862–6
ISBN 0–415–07040–6 pbk

371. 1—dc20   91-13639
                                                       CIP

EMERGING AS A TEACHER

There i ... job and
actually ... chers in
their fir ... earch of
a worka ... hart this
progres ... ved with
childre ... r in the
classroc ... extensive
observa ... actors in
the exp ... ceptions
which n ... to make
their gr ... ult.
　The ... ing and
those i ... g of the
journey ... lp more
experie ... develop-
ment. I ... cation a
founda ... in which
probler ... ed in the
develop
　Rob ... tudies at
the Un ... rofessor.
J. Gary ... Iichigan.

INVESTIGATING SCHOOLING

The aim of this series is to scrutinize those everyday aspects of schooling which have tended to be taken for granted and to treat them as objects for investigation and study. The series will include two major sorts of books: the source book in which a single author or multiple contributors look at various 'givens' in the social construction of schooling and secondly, research methods texts which show the teacher or student how she or he might continue such investigations.

To Larry, Nancy, Marilyn, Barbara, Heidi and Kay

CONTENTS

PREFACE

Emerging as a Teacher was written for a variety of reasons: like other educators, we derive much of our satisfaction from our students; we feel good when our students do well. As teacher educators, we derive pleasure from having our former students develop into powerful and effective teachers. But, unfortunately, as pre-service teacher educators we rarely have had the opportunity to discover whether or not our work has borne the desired fruits. It was, therefore, in part to see how some of our former students fared as teachers that we undertook the research upon which *Emerging as a Teacher* is based. Furthermore, as we have worked to develop interesting and responsible teacher-education programmes over the past few years, we have necessarily come face to face with our own and the field's limited knowledge about teacher development. It is self-evident that the more we know about how students become teachers, and the factors that influence their development, the better able we will be to forge teacher-education programmes that are genuinely educative. We believe that *Emerging as a Teacher* will prove useful to teacher educators as they – as we – think through the complicated problems associated with teacher-education reform. We also were motivated by the desire to assist beginning teachers in their quest to forge satisfying and productive teaching roles. In this regard, over the past few years, we have found case studies to be a powerful instructional tool for helping beginning teachers to think usefully about teaching, themselves as teachers, and their professional development. Finally, we should admit that we undertook the project as a means to do something that we each enjoy thoroughly, and that is talking with teachers about teaching. We feel especially fortunate in that the six teachers whose stories are reported here, who are now friends, were so willing to talk openly about their work and to let us into their lives. It is to them that *Emerging as a Teacher* is dedicated. They have taught us much for which we are grateful.

We owe additional debts of gratitude: we wish to express our appreciation to the families of the six teachers. We were acutely aware that the time spent with us was time that often would have been otherwise spent with family. Given the pressures on families in the first year of teaching, this was no small sacrifice. In addition, we appreciate the support given by Professor Ralph Reynolds, Chair of the Department of Educational Studies, that enabled us to complete the case studies. And we appreciate the helpful and occasionally long conversations we have had with our friends and colleagues, Professors Andrew Gitlin and Don Kauchak of the University of Utah, and Professor Paul Klohr of the Ohio State University. Finally, we are grateful to Professor Ivor Goodson for his early and continuing encouragement of our work.

In researching and writing *Emerging as a Teacher*, Professor Bullough is responsible for chapters 1, 2, 5, 6, 7, 8, 9, and 10 while Professor Knowles is responsible for chapter 3, and Professor Crow for chapter 4.

Robert V. Bullough Jr
Salt Lake City, Utah

ACKNOWLEDGEMENTS

Portions of chapter 7, 'From expert to caring adult' appeared originally in the *Journal of Curriculum and Supervision*, copyright 1990, and are here used with the permission of the Association for Supervision and Curriculum Development. Portions of chapter 2, 'What am I?, What am I doing here?', and chapter 6, 'Teacher is nurturer', appeared originally in *Qualitative Studies in Education*, copyright 1990 and 1991 respectively, and are here used with the permission of Taylor and Francis, London.

1

SETTING THE STAGE: ORIENTATION AND ORGANIZATION

Recent reviews of the teacher-socialization literature (Crow, 1987; Knowles, 1989; Zeichner and Gore, 1989) point to several weaknesses. First, comparatively little is known about the actual process of socialization as it is experienced and takes place during pre-service training and into the first few years of teaching; second, in the quest for cause and effect relationships, much of the research has seriously oversimplified the socialization process; and third, little attention has been given to the interactive nature of socialization, particularly interaction among biography, beginning teachers' preconceptions about teaching, and the teaching context. Respecting the later point, Weinstein (1989: 53) accurately describes the situation when she states that '[teacher-educators] have paid scant attention to. . . students' past experiences or to their implicit theories of teaching and of learning to teach'. In sum, surprisingly little is known about how a person becomes a teacher, although this is essential knowledge if teacher-education reform is to produce more than window dressing.

We were acutely aware of these gaps in the literature when planning and conducting the research reported in *Emerging as a Teacher*. Nevertheless, *Emerging as a Teacher* is obviously far from being an adequate response to them; a single book could not hope to remedy the situation. Our intention is more modest, that *Emerging as a Teacher* will help illuminate the early phase of the process of becoming a teacher without omitting too much of its complexity, and that the cases and interpretations presented will usefully and accurately portray the central role the beginning teacher plays in his/her own socialization, *understood as a process of learning to participate in a social group*, and, more broadly speaking, professional development.

1

With these aims in mind, one of the early tasks faced was to come to an agreement on a theoretical orientation that would be responsive to the interactive and, we believed, very personal and complex nature of socialization and development, and that would enable authentic interpretations both useful and interesting to teachers and teacher-educators. The agreement that resulted drew upon insights from diverse sources, and represents an extension of earlier work undertaken in the Educational Studies Department, University of Utah (Bullough, 1988b, 1989a; Crow, 1987; Knowles, 1989). The sources included symbolic interactionism, and, mindful of Goodson's (1988) caution that symbolic interactionism has tended to emphasize situation at the expense of biography, recent work on the role of metaphor in thinking, and a rather loose conception of schema theory. Each source will be considered in turn.

SYMBOLIC INTERACTIONISM

Despite falling on hard times, symbolic interactionism, particularly as represented in the work of Herbert Blumer (1969), remains an extraordinarily fruitful approach to the study of social action (Hargreaves, 1986). It offers a set of premises that are compelling, representing what Hargreaves (1986: 148) deems its 'appreciative capacity', as well as a set of methodological clues that are particularly appropriate for the project at hand.

Blumer (1969) succinctly states the premises upon which symbolic interactionism rests:

The first premise is that human beings act toward things on the basis of the meanings that the things have for them. Such things include everything that the human being may note in his world – physical objects, such as trees or chairs; other human beings, such as a mother or a store clerk; categories of human beings, such as friends or enemies; institutions, as a school or a government; guiding ideals, such as individual independence or honesty; activities of others, such as their commands or requests; and such situations as an individual encounters in his daily life. The second premise is that the meaning of such things is derived from, or arises out of, the social interaction that one has with one's fellows. The third premise is that these meanings are handled in, and modified

2

through, an interpretative process used by the person in dealing with the things he encounters (p. 21).

Accepting these as working premises shaped our research agenda and informed our methodological deliberations. The first premise requires that careful attention be given to meaning and meaning-making. On the surface this may appear obvious, but it is not. As Blumer observed, and as Hunt (1987) twenty years later reminds us, social science research rarely attends to the 'inside'. Instead, human behaviour is treated as a product of abstract and reified forces that, in Blumer's words, 'play upon human beings' (p. 3), constraining and directing human behaviour. Given this premise, our task was to identify research methods and establish relations that would enable us to uncover and understand the meanings central to beginning teachers as actors in ever changing situations (Blumer, 1969: 51). In turn, we would gain insights into beginning teacher socialization and development.

The second premise acknowledges that meanings arise 'in the process of interaction between people' (p. 4). They do not exist 'out there' in things – things do not impose meanings on people – nor are they inherent to humans. Hence, meanings 'as social products, as creations that are formed in and through the defining activities of people as they interact' have a history (p. 5); meanings are historically grounded and fluid. These characteristics of meanings are extremely important to the study of teacher socialization, underscoring the importance of attending not only to the meanings beginning teachers bring with them into teacher-education programmes, or into the first year of teaching, and how meanings change, but also to their interactional, situational (context matters!), and biographical origins.

The third premise, that meanings are used through interpretation, is extremely important to the direction of this study. One implication of this premise is that up front we had to accept that no two persons, despite sharing similar contexts, would understand those contexts – or make them meaningful – in precisely the same way; socialization and development are profoundly idiosyncratic and personal; in effect, persons socialize themselves, they are not 'socialized'. Researchers cannot, therefore, uncritically impose a preset cluster of concepts and categories to give order to the interactions and situations being studied. Ultimately, the concepts and categories that are used to organize and present the researcher's understanding must speak sensitively to the subject's life experience and understanding. The meaning of particular events and experiences, therefore, must be illuminated by the teachers themselves and acknowledged as their own; and they alone can verify the validity of the data analysis and the interpretation that form the basis of the stories that are told. Of this, more will be said shortly.

There are additional implications of this premise that arise because of the nature of interpretation which involves an internal, generally unarticulated, conversation. This internal conversation involves two steps, according to Blumer:

> First, the actor indicates to himself the things toward which he is acting; he has to point out to himself the things that have meaning. . . . Second, by virtue of this process of communicating with himself, interpretation becomes a matter of handling meanings. The actor selects, checks, suspends, regroups, and transforms the meanings in the light of the situation in which he is placed and the direction of his action. Accordingly, interpretation should not be regarded as a mere automatic application of established meanings but as a formative process in which meanings are used and revised as instruments for the guidance and formation of action (p. 5).

Thus, because of the internal conversation, the interpretation of meaning, and the behaviour linked to it, is always forward looking and purposeful. But, more than this, and in a way somewhat different from what Blumer asserts, through this process the person actually forms the situation of which he is a part.

Taking this premise and our expansion of it seriously required that we not only needed to identify, as best as we could, the significant objects to which the beginning teachers attended but especially to the meanings used to form the situation itself, and to the origins of those meanings. Moreover, we needed to attend to how meanings changed over time and to why they changed. Methodologically, then, part of our task has been to gather data that captured the episodic and evolving nature of meaning-making over time. Ongoing collection of descriptive accounts of how the teachers saw and thereby made their world, observations of actions taken on things, and records of how they talked about those objects and changes in how they talked, were essential data sources.

An additional point needs to be made respecting the nature of interpretation: it is the possession of a 'self' that allows the internal conversation to take place; it is having a self that enables the individual to interpret and act on the world and, in turn, to be acted upon. As Blumer puts it,

> Nothing esoteric is meant by [the term] 'self'. It means merely that a human being can be an object of his own action. Thus, he can recognize himself, for instance, as being a man, young in age, a student, in debt, trying to become a doctor, coming from an undistinguished family and so forth. In all such instances he is an object to himself; and he acts toward himself and guides himself in his actions toward others on the basis of the kind of object he is to himself (p. 12).

Our conception of self, Blumer further asserts, has its origins in seeing ourselves as others see us. This is accomplished through a process of 'role-taking', a process by which we assume the position of the other. This source of data common to us all, informs our internal conversation about the kind of person we think we are. For teachers there are many such data sources which often act toward teachers in contradictory ways which have profound importance for beginning teachers who are seeking to negotiate a teaching role, or *a set of relationships and understandings that, when taken together, define 'teacher.'* It is to students especially that teachers turn to in determining who and what they are – their 'professional identity' (Pajak, 1986: 123) – but administrators, colleagues, parents, and the 'press', among other groups, all play important parts. By interpretating the actions of these 'objects' the teacher makes them more or less meaningful and then, based upon the interpretation made, attempts to establish a more or less appropriate line of action to attain a desired end.

There are, however, multiple selves, an inner or core self, and a 'situational' self: 'much of what constitutes our 'selves' is situational, varying with context, [but] we also have a well-defended, relatively inflexible substantial self into which we incorporate the most highly prized aspects of our self-concept and the attitudes and values which are most salient to it' (Nias, 1989: 26). It is these

5

two selves that enter into the inner conversation noted by Blumer, an 'I' and a 'me'. In *Emerging as a Teacher* we are particularly interested in the situational self, self-as-teacher, but this self can be understood only in relationship to the inner self which is the 'core of both person and teacher' (Nias, 1989: 79).

Each of Blumer's three premises speaks to the interactive, reflexive process involved in self-formation. From the perspective of our interest, the concept of self-in-formation is pivotal. Consider: the beginning teacher enters a teaching context and tries on and tests a conception of the teacher role as a self already formed – a substantial self – but still forming. This 'teaching self', as the kind of object the teacher thinks he or she is at that moment and in situation, is composed of a cluster of meanings that are tested and adjusted reflexively in response to meanings derived from interpretations made of the actions and statements of students and others within the context by way of pursuing a desired pattern of action. This is inevitably a conflict-laden process wherein the teaching self and the meanings attached to it and the actions that flow through the interpretation of the context, reside more or less uneasily alongside definitions put forward and acted upon by others sharing the context. Through conflict, adjustment and compromise, 'new' selves – actually reconstructed selves – and situations may be formed. This is what we mean by socialization as an active process of world building rather than as a passive adaptation – after the manner of functionalism – to an institutionally defined role and pattern of relations.

METAPHORS

The meanings forming the teaching self are layered, and a goodly number of them, particularly those attached to the inner self, are tacit, unarticulated. In thinking about these characteristics of the meanings composing the teaching self and of the problem of how to access them, we have been drawn to the identification and analysis of teacher metaphors, specifically 'root' metaphors, that capture a teacher's 'core self-perception' (Ball and Goodson, 1985: 18), and that give coherence to self.

Recently interest has grown in the possibility of shedding light on teachers' self-understanding through the exploration of the metaphors and similes they employ (Hunt, 1987; Miller and Fredericks, 1988; Munby, 1986; Russell and Johnston, 1988;

6

Provenzo, McClosky, Kottkamp and Cohn, 1989), what Bandman earlier termed 'picture preferences' (1967: 112). Metaphors bear the images or conceptions teachers hold of themselves as teachers, their professional identity. In part this view is based upon a growing recognition that human thought is primarily metaphorical, as Lakoff and Johnson (1980) eloquently describe it, and a central means by which we come to terms with our experience:

> Just as in mutual understanding we constantly search out commonalities of experience when we speak with other people, so in self-understanding we are always searching for what unifies our own diverse experiences in order to give coherence to our lives. Just as we seek out metaphors to highlight and make coherent what we have in common with someone else, so we seek out *personal* metaphors to highlight and make coherent our own pasts, our present activities, and our dreams, hopes, and goals as well. A large part of self-understanding is the search for appropriate personal metaphors that make sense of our lives. Self-understanding requires unending negotiation and renegotiation of the meaning of your experiences to yourself. . . . It involves the constant construction of new coherences in your life, coherences that give new meaning to old experience. The process of self-understanding is the continual development of new life stories for yourself (pp. 232–3).

Like many of the metaphors we live by, the search for metaphors to give coherence and meaning to experience predominantly is a tacit one. The challenge faced is to 'make sense for oneself out of the experience and [the teaching] roles presented, and at times [to] find new meanings' (Provenzo, McClosky, Kottkamp and Cohn, 1989: 556). Hence, metaphors arise out of experience and give coherence to it (Lakoff and Johnson, 1980: 105) and therefore play a central role in self-formation as Blumer (1969) conceives of it. Furthermore, metaphors represent 'purposeful modes of expression whose truth-value functions, while not literal, do reflect accurately *how* people think about their lives' and the situations confronting them (Miller and Fredericks, 1988: 269). Thus, not only does the exploration of metaphors provide an avenue for understanding how others comprehend and construct their worlds, but, through the analysis of changes in metaphor, changes in self-understanding can be identified, both of which are essential to gaining a reasonably complete picture of the process of becoming a teacher as it takes place over time and in context. As Russell and Johnston (1988) put it, 'Shifts in the imagery that teachers use when interpreting classroom events suggest changes in their perspectives on teaching' (p. 13); and, we would add, when root metaphors are involved, indicate changes in their conceptions of self as teacher.

Additionally, we have been drawn to the analysis of metaphor because of what appears to be a growing confusion over the institutionalized teaching role.

> it would appear that the conception of teaching as a profession in its own right is unclear. This lack of clarity (meaning) in both the profession and the [educational] system may be a significant factor in the difficulty many teachers have in finding for themselves a clear role or a place in the system. The profession is unclear as to the authority, responsibility, and freedom teachers have when they teach, while the system is unclear as to what authority, responsibility, and freedom society has given it.
>
> (Provenzo, McClosky, Kottkamp and Cohn, 1989: 569)

Teachers, it seems, are increasingly finding little help as they seek to form appropriate roles and in this process the generation of metaphors plays an important part; they form the basis of the stories that are acted out and define the situational self when first becoming a teacher. *Emerging as a teacher is, therefore, a quest for compelling and fitting metaphors that represent who beginning teachers imagine themselves to be as teachers.* Hence, given the confusion over the teacher's role, we would expect to find many teachers holding to multiple metaphors; and we would expect to find beginning teachers possessing and being possessed by vague, and sometimes even contradictory teaching metaphors and attendant images as they seek to establish a coherent and integrated professional identity that is consistent with the inner self.

Finally, a word should be said about the relationship between metaphor and practice. Clearly, while metaphors inform practice, they do not determine it. Rather, in a manner roughly similar to that suggested by Elbaz (1983) in her discussion of the function of images in teacher thinking, they inspire rather than require conformity. But, perhaps even more importantly, and consistent

8

with a symbolic interactionist view of meaning-making as historically grounded, contextual, reflexive and purposeful, it is apparent that there are many factors outside the individual teacher that constrain practice and thereby produce conflict between the inner and the situational self. Thus caution must be exercised when seeking links between metaphor and practice for, as Madeleine Grumet puts it, 'A metaphor for educational experience will illuminate some aspects of educational practice and leave others in shadows' (Grumet, 1988: 80). In order to make any connections at all between metaphor and practice it was necessary to spend time not only talking about practice but also observing the teachers in context. This said, we recognize that, because metaphors inherently represent a simplification of experience (Dickmeyer, 1989), much is inevitably left 'in shadows'.

TEACHING SCHEMA

When thinking about the role of interpretation in meaning-making, we obtained some fruitful insights from schema theory. In particular, we have found in schema theory, somewhat loosely conceived, some important insights about how meaning is made and about the process by which meanings develop and change, or resist change. Let us be clear about this. We are quite aware that symbolic interactionism, in particular, and schema theory represent very different language and philosophical traditions; that they come at the problem of making meaning from different angles. Nevertheless, in our view the notion of schema, understood as 'an abstract knowledge structure' through which we organize our knowledge about any given subject (Livingston and Borko, 1989: 36), in combination with symbolic interactionism, allows a filling out of the process of self-formation and meaning-making that has significant implications for this study.

With his comparison of schema to theory, Rumelhart (1980) provides a useful point of departure for this portion of the discussion:

> Perhaps the central function of schemata is in the construction of an interpretation of an event, object, or situation – that is, in the process of comprehension. In all of this, it is useful to think of a schema as a kind of informal,

9

private, unarticulated theory about the nature of events, objects, or situations that we face. The total set of schemata we have available for interpreting our world in a sense constitutes our private theory of the nature of reality. The total set of schemata instantiated at a particular moment in time constitutes our internal model of the situation we face at that moment in time.

(Rumelhart, 1980: 37)

From this view point, beginning teachers bring with them to teaching a schema for teaching, embedded in the teaching self, which, like all schema, 'provides the skeleton [of meanings] around which the situation is interpreted' and made meaningful (Rumelhart, 1980: 37). This schema, operating as an 'implicit theory' of teaching (Clark, 1988), is formed over years of experience interacting with teachers in various capacities and perhaps of prior teaching. It reflects a model of what the individual believes that teaching is 'supposed' to be. It includes meanings about students and the student role, about parents and the nature of schooling, knowledge, and knowing.

Operationally, according to Rumelhart, the 'primary activity of a schema is the evaluation of its goodness of fit' (p. 39). The unarticulated question always facing a schema is, therefore, 'How well does the model account for the actual situation?' In writing the stories composing this volume we have paid careful attention to the question of fit, finding in how it is answered an important source of insight into teacher socialization and development. Briefly, Anderson (1977), drawing on Piaget, uses the concept of assimilation to describe how schema operate when there is a 'goodness of fit', and the concept of accommodation to describe when there is not.

Assimilation refers to the process whereby objects and interactions are made meaningful through application of a schema without necessitating a stretching or adjusting of the schema; the schema is fitting and the situation is thereby made sensible and more or less predictable. In contrast, accommodation refers to moments when schema necessarily must change in response to the inability to make a situation adequately and appropriately meaningful; that is, attending to a new situation necessitates a reorganization or a reconstruction of meanings in order to behave in ways that will achieve a desired end.

10

From our interest in teacher socialization and development the processes of assimilation and accommodation have proven to be analytically and theoretically very useful. If a sufficient number of meanings do not prove to be fitting, the teaching self is thrown into jeopardy and a second question presents itself: 'How well do I fit teaching?' At this point, the root metaphors that gave the teaching self coherence may crumble or call forth a variety of 'survival strategies' (Woods, 1977: 275) aimed at self-preservation. But assimilation and accommodation do not tell the whole story. For this book we observed beginning teachers who, like a few of those studied by Sikes and her colleagues (Sikes, Measor and Woods, 1985), resisted pressures to conform to an institutionalized teaching role and succeeded in establishing a productive and coherent teaching self and concomitant style. For these teachers to accommodate would not have been a virtue; instead they remade the situation.

When thinking about the teachers who failed to create a productive teaching self, Anderson's claim that 'The more fully developed a schema the less likely it will be to change' (p. 425), and two related claims, provided a set of very tentative hypotheses with which to begin sorting out what we thought transpired. The two additional claims are: that individuals will go to great lengths in order to maintain a strongly developed schema – and related conception of self as teacher – such that 'Apparent inconsistencies and counterexamples [may be] easily assimilated' (p. 425); and that 'People whose important beliefs are threatened will attempt to defend their positions, dismiss objections, ignore counter-examples, keep segregated logically incompatible schemata' (p. 429). Finally, it should be noted that there is another side to these claims that is of genuine importance to the book and in turn to teacher-education, as will be noted in the last chapter: when analysing the data we found that the teachers who had the most difficulty teaching had only weak or a deeply contradictory teaching schema and weak root teaching metaphors and attendant images of self as teacher. These persons encountered extreme difficulty when facing teaching situations that demanded decisive and consistent action. On occasion they actually became immobilized. Each of Anderson's claims plays a part in the case studies that follow.

At this point, we trust that it is now clear that our interest in the concept of schema represents more than just an intellectual

11

detour into abstractions. It has allowed us to sharpen our understanding of the processes by which conceptions of self change, an understanding central to comprehending the means by which beginning teachers come to terms with and attempt to recreate institutionalized teacher roles in their own image. But, more than this, for us the concept opened up fresh ways of thinking about and better understanding beginning teacher socialization and development.

CASE STUDIES

We began our data gathering utilizing a variety of case-study methods. As Yin (1984) suggests, case-study methodology is particularly valuable for investigating situations in which the researcher has little control over the events that occur in the real-life context. When properly used, case-study methodology preserves the integrity of informants' experiences and their meaning, and encourages sensitivity to changes in the context. It is a responsive methodology, avoiding rigid data-gathering strategies, just as it avoids interpretations made in advance of data gathering – strategies and interpretations evolve together in response to shifting researcher understandings. In other words, case-study methodology is not necessarily bound narrowly to preconceived courses of research action or understanding – a decided advantage when dealing, as were we, with fluid, kaleidoscopic teaching and classroom situations and when seeking to access and understand changes in teacher held meanings.

Case studies themselves have value to us as teachers of teachers. As descriptive narratives, as stories, well-written cases have a unique pedagogical power not unlike that enjoyed by other forms of narrative (Noddings, 1991). They present tales of human triumph and failure that, in the telling, hold the potential to enrich and enliven the reader's self-understanding. Thus, as Shulman asserts, 'Although principles are powerful, cases are memorable, and lodge in memory as the basis for later judgements' (1986: 32). Well-written cases – good stories – invite the readers to enter into conversation and to compare their own experience and understanding with that described in the case study. In this way, the reading of case studies can influence the basis upon which teachers – particularly beginning teachers – make decisions, an important value if one takes Shulman's perspective to heart. He

12

states: 'To educate a teacher is to influence the premises on which a teacher bases practical reasoning about teaching in specific situations' (1986: 32).

Case studies present yet another advantage. Good case studies are more than just good stories; and good stories compel the reader or listener to take note. Case-study narratives, compared to the reporting of other types of empirical research, have a unique ability to present the 'essence of schooling' and teaching, and as Ryan (1983) asserts:

That [essence] is rarely captured in educational research. Somehow, the reality slips through the net of our research paradigms. . . . Much of the wisdom about education has been captured in constructed narrative accounts based on some human experience – or more simply, in stories (p. ix).

It was for these reasons and on the basis of the methodological implications of our theoretical orientation, that we settled on a case-study approach. No other approach, we believed, would enable us to examine in as rich and complex ways the changes over time that occurred in the lives of beginning teachers and in their understanding of themselves as teachers. Moreover, no other method would produce data of sufficient richness to enable the kind of analysis we intended to conduct including giving careful attention to individual's teaching schemas and metaphors.

This said, we recognize there are difficulties with case-study methodology. One set of issues that requires mention has to do with establishing the validity of the interpretations made. The challenge is to 'capture and portray the world as it appears to the people in it' (Walker, 1986: 203). Those close to a situation, or the persons whose experience is being described, are clearly in the best position to judge whether or not the portrayal is authentic and accurate. Accordingly, each case was read and critiqued by the teacher whose story is presented and, based upon this critique, changes were made until they felt the stories were their own. The use of the teachers' actual names reflects their belief in the validity of the stories told. Perhaps it should be noted here that in contrast to our use of the teachers' names, all student names are fictitious.

The six case studies included in *Emerging as a Teacher* are of first-year teachers who had been our certification students[1] and who volunteered to participate in a year-long, bi-monthly seminar and support group within which problems and issues associated with the first year of teaching were discussed. The senior author served as seminar coordinator. Prior to the first seminar meeting it was explained to potential participants that they would be expected to participate in a series of interviews, allow periodic class observations, and keep a journal, and a curriculum 'log'. It was stated that the seminar's purpose was two-fold, to assist them in producing a text of the first year of teaching that could be studied for the purpose of better understanding their experience and for improving practice; and second, to provide data that would help us better understand the process of teacher induction and development. Throughout the study the first purpose held priority over the second when conflicts arose, as they did on occasion.

Before the first day of school in late August, formal interviews were conducted with all the teachers that focused on their teaching ideals, how and what they had planned for the first few weeks of class, and any concerns they might have had. In addition, background and family-related information was gathered and expanded upon in future interviews. This information, as Beynon notes, is crucial to understanding teacher thinking and development: 'classroom researchers [should] bear in mind that all teachers and pupils have lives that are largely spent outside classrooms and which strongly influence (even determine) [what they do]' (1985: 164). All interviews were transcribed for analysis and, starting in December, transcripts were given to the teachers to become part of the text they were creating. Subsequent interviews followed approximately every three weeks. Later interviews continued to explore the nature of the experience of the first year of teaching, problems, planning, and images and understandings of self-as-teacher. Observations took place at least every other week and resulted in extensive field notes that informed the interpretations made. During the observations and in the interviews careful attention was given to identifying important contextual factors that influenced the teachers' thinking.

As noted, in addition to these sources of data, the teachers kept journals and curriculum logs. The logs contained, for a single class period or a subject area in the elementary schools, very brief descriptions of the activities planned, and a sentence or two about their origin, and why they were selected for inclusion in the lesson. The logs provided a record of the curriculum and modest information about how the teachers' thinking about content changed over time. The journals, initially, focused on the 'best' and 'worst' events of the day but later, as the teachers became more comfortable with the process of writing and sharing of the journals, on more personal topics and interpretations.

Early in the year a problem surfaced with the journals that deserves mention: perhaps not trusting us, the teachers wrote the journals for us, and not for themselves. In so doing they inadvertently reduced the educational worth of the journals, a worth found, in Ira Progoff's words, in the discovery that:

> a connective thread has been forming beneath the surface of our lives, carrying the meaning that has been trying to establish itself in our existence. It is the inner continuity of our lives. As we recognize and identify with it, we see an inner myth that has been guiding our lives unknown to ourselves.
>
> (Progoff, 1975: 11)

By writing the journals for us, the 'connective threads' were hidden from view.

Happily, this problem with the journals and with our relationship with the teachers surfaced very early in the year in one of the seminar sessions. By the time of this meeting a sufficient level of trust had been established for the teachers to feel comfortable in confronting us on what we were doing with the journals and why we were doing it. They were pleased to hear that the journals were meant first and foremost for themselves, again forming a central part of the teaching text, and only secondarily for us. In fact, we told them that whatever they wished to write about teaching would be of interest to us, although, from time to time, we would appreciate their addressing a specific question or issue if they were willing. Journal entries improved immediately following this meeting, in length, in depth of analysis, and, we believe in openness and honesty. The initial focus on 'best' and 'worst' events quietly disappeared.

A second problem with journal writing also should be mentioned. Not all of the teachers continued throughout the year to keep up their writing. Indeed, two of the teachers found journal writing to be a source of increased anxiety and frustration and by mid year had stopped writing all together. The other teachers found in journal writing a useful means for thinking about and making sense of their experience and faithfully maintained them. Of these teachers, two produced remarkable documents not only because of their great length, but also because of the depth of analysis evident in them.

Our interpretations of the data emerged gradually over several months as we studied the data, participated in the seminar, and engaged with the teachers and each other in ongoing conversations about teaching and the beginning teachers' experience of teaching. Once pen was put to paper, we continued to explore the stories we were writing to determine if and in what ways they rang true or failed to do so. As noted, eventually, all the teachers read and critiqued their own stories which were revised until seen by the teacher as being accurate and authentic, a true representation of their experience and self-understanding.

BOOK ORGANIZATION

The book is divided into two parts each containing three case studies of first-year teachers. The first case in Part I is of Larry, an eighth- and ninth-grade (students age 13 to 15) science and math teacher; the second of Nancy, a seventh-grade (students age 12 to 13) language teacher, the third of Marilyn, a fifth-grade (students age 10 to 11) teacher. While the contexts within which they worked were very different, and certainly secondary and elementary schools differ in important ways, Larry, Nancy, and Marilyn shared a set of problems common to beginning teachers. Specifically, each had serious discipline and management problems, problems with consistency, and with providing a suitable and responsive curriculum for students. But, more important from the perspective of this study, each had a particularly difficult time negotiating a productive and fitting teaching role and this produced debilitating feelings of self-doubt and high vulnerability. In sum, these teachers, using Huberman's phrase, had 'painful beginnings' (1989: 42). In saying this, we wish to be very clear, 'painful beginnings' do not necessarily lead to tragic endings. As we have analysed the data, in particular seeking to identify their root teaching metaphors and changes in metaphor and the factors that influenced these changes, we found that these teachers, in contrast to those discussed in part II, entered teaching holding either weak, seriously undeveloped, or deeply contradictory conceptions of themselves as teachers. Part I concludes with a chapter that identifies and explores the common themes from the three cases in relationship to some of the available research on teacher socialization and development.

Part II also contains three case studies but, in contrast to the cases presented in part I, these beginning teachers began their first year of teaching with comparatively well-developed teaching schema and strongly held, but adaptable, conceptions of themselves as teachers as reflected in their root teaching metaphors. Again drawing on Huberman's terminology, these three teachers, by comparison, enjoyed 'easy beginnings' (1989: 42). As with our caution respecting painful beginnings, we should note that 'easy beginnings' do not necessarily lead to happy endings. The first case is of Barbara, a junior-high-school (students age 12 to 15) English teacher; the second of Heidi, a high-school (students age 15 to 18) foreign-language, English, and Debate teacher; and the third of Kay, a first-grade (students age 5 to 6) teacher. The problems encountered by the teachers discussed in parts I and II, and how the teachers understood them, are in some respects quite different, and present somewhat differing challenges to teacher educators, as will be noted. As with part I, part II concludes with a chapter within which themes are identified and discussed in relationship to the wider research literature.

Emerging as a Teacher concludes with a chapter within which Professor Bullough addresses the 'so what question'. So, what do the findings and interpretations presented have to say that is deserving of consideration by beginning teachers and teacher-educators?

Part I

2

WHO AM I? WHAT AM I DOING HERE?

LARRY

Larry, a married, 37-year-old father of two young children, and biology graduate, never planned to be a teacher. While working as a laboratory technician (lab tech) in a large government lab, and specializing in the study of viruses, he frequently engaged in discussions with a fellow technician about making a career change. In the laboratory Larry was, as he put it, 'consistently unhappy for a long time'. The work had become routine and boring and involved few opportunities to exercise initiative or autonomy. And too, it was lonely and he did not enjoy the people he was working with. He felt that if he was to make a career change, he would have to make it soon: 'If I was going to ever get out of being a lab tech, the time was running out. I'm 37 now [and] I'm not getting any younger.' Sharing similar feelings his colleague had decided to become a teacher; Larry too thought this worth exploring.

What was appealing to Larry about teaching was first and foremost that he thought it would allow him to continue to work in biology in intellectually challenging ways. 'I liked the subject of science,' he said, and 'enjoyed talking about it, intellectualizing it.' Further, he 'enjoyed the whole process of learning about science ... reading about [it, and] talking about [it]'. Then too, there was the problem of having already obtained a degree and not wanting to start all over again: 'I was thinking, what can I do with [my degree] besides be a lab tech?' He was clear about not wanting to pursue a doctorate, which would take a long period of time and perhaps not result in a desired career: 'A beginning professional scientist has a hard time finding work now.' With these thoughts in mind, and far from certain about his decision, Larry enrolled in a graduate teacher-education programme. The programme ran for an academic year of nine months. The first term of three months Larry spent studying curriculum and instruction and began working a few hours a week in the junior high school[1] within which he would practice teach the second and third terms. While practice teaching was a full-time assignment in the school, he was formally responsible for teaching three of seven class periods. A weekly problem-solving seminar ran concurrently with student teaching. Thus Larry found himself heavily involved in a junior high school not far from the one within which he eventually secured employment.

While in the programme Larry continuously wondered if he had made a wise decision to switch careers: 'It seems like you're constantly making that decision all the time'. By continuing to work nights in the laboratory throughout the year, although at reduced hours, Larry put off the decision and resigned only at the last possible moment. Testing the programme and wondering whether or not he wanted to become a teacher, Larry committed himself initially to complete only the first term's coursework and only later, after finding the programme of interest, did he make up his mind to practice teach.

COMING TO TERMS WITH TEACHING

During student teaching the move from a lab where reason and order reigned surpreme, to four classes of junior high biology, where chaos was forever lurking just around the corner, represented more than just a journey of a few miles; it represented movement between two radically different worlds. The former was predictable – perhaps too much so – obviously purposeful, adult-centred, and respectful of expertise. The latter was uncertain, often seemingly lacking in purpose, and driven by the hormones and passions of children to which he and other adults were to respond and thereby demonstrate the presence or absence of expertise. Moreover, in teaching, unlike laboratory work, personality mattered a great deal and successes and failures were immediate and ultimately more public. Despite these differences, Larry saw the world of teaching as a means of staying in science, which he loved, without being trapped in a laboratory, and of developing intellectually.

As a student teacher Larry entered this new world with very

22

limited knowledge about it. He had not been a student himself in many years and, given the young age of his own children and limited experience with other people's children, he had scant personal resources from which to build an image of students. Moreover, he possessed a limited knowledge of what teachers did: 'I had a very vague idea of what teachers do, then.' And so, it was from the vantage point of lab work that Larry built his conception of teaching and view of students which he carried with him into the classroom and through which he sought to make his experience sensible.

INITIAL TEACHING METAPHOR

Initially he thought of teachers as experts who possessed specialized knowledge to be passed along and down to students: teacher is subject-matter expert. In practice teaching, this view immediately produced problems. Consistently he taught over the students' heads; he was puzzled by their lack of interest in the content and frustrated by his inability to design engaging activities. While practice teaching his views of teaching began to change and flesh out:

> I . . . realized that there's a hell of a lot more to [teaching] than . . . subject matter. Subject matter is a very small part of . . . teaching. There's a tremendous amount more to it. [Realizing] that has been very difficult for me . . . and . . . it has been a great discovery for me: [I found out that] I'm a people person . . . I really enjoyed the contact with professional people who cared about what they were doing. . . . I really enjoyed the kids even though I couldn't always control them or impact their behavior the way I needed to. But, I discovered that I really liked them. I found them [to be] fascinating human beings.

Finding his expert-driven view of teaching unproductive, and lacking an alternative way of thinking about teaching and himself as teacher, the views of Larry's cooperating teachers[2] elevated in importance. Both cooperating teachers emphasized science as process, a view consistent with Larry's own interest in science, and he sought to copy how they worked in the classroom with reasonably good success. These teachers, Larry reported, were 'very creative at [using classroom] time [to] maximize student interest and [produce] student learning even in some of the lesser motivated kids.' 'Science . . . is doing things with your hands and your mind,' he said. And further,

> Now, I think what teachers do is [that] they try to arrange and design an experience for a child to maximize understanding [of the content]. . . . [so] they're doing something productive–they're thinking about what they're doing; they're learning from it. Then, you're setting up part of the environment so that they think about it some more and learn from that–in other words, inquiry.

In addition to leaving practice teaching thinking of teaching in terms of how to establish the conditions for inquiry, he left it hoping to emulate other values held by his cooperating teachers. Especially he hoped to be able to establish the caring and productive relationships with students he observed in his cooperating teachers' classes: '[Their relationships were] always positive and good . . . the communication was there'. Echoing this value, Larry commented, 'I'd like [the students to be] comfortable around me and trust me.' In addition, he wanted to emulate the cooperating teachers' flexibility, 'The ability to change one's plans at an instant when the need arose.' These were the qualities that represented the 'more' to teaching that Larry discovered through student teaching.

While recognizing these qualities and their worth, Larry did not have sufficient time in practice teaching or the additional experience necessary for them to be internalized nor to shape them into a coherent vision of self-as-teacher that could be used when thinking about the classroom and his work within it. Rather, he only tried on the role; he did not get the opportunity to wear it and see if it actually fit. Thus, he left practice teaching able to recognize the ability of others to structure classrooms for inquiry and wanting to be such a teacher himself, although he was uncertain if he could be such a teacher. Clearly he did not yet possess this ability and would have to develop it on the job and without assistance if he was to obtain it at all.

WORK CONTEXT

Larry completed practice teaching in the spring and immediately began seeking employment. The job market was extremely poor that year, and Larry did not secure a position until the middle of August, only two weeks before school was to begin, and even then, it was a job with some significant drawbacks, as he viewed it. But, in his new found resolve to become a teacher, he wanted the work (and needed it after having resigned from the laboratory) and was thrilled to get it. Just before school was to begin, however, Larry began to have grave doubts about whether or not he would be able to be the kind of teacher he envisioned: '[It] will not happen at [Jordan River Junior High School],' he feared, 'there are factors that [will] prevent me from doing [inquiry].' He was correct in his assessment.

Jordan River Junior High School, where Larry began teaching, was one of three schools (of a total of fifteen junior highs within the school district) which qualified as a Chapter One school (Chapter One is a special federally funded programme for economically disadvantaged students). The school qualified for (Chapter One status by virtue of its large student population that received free school lunch and the large number of families receiving Aid to Dependent Children, a form of welfare. The student population of 1100 was generally poor, highly mobile and, according to Larry, little interested in school. It was a 'tough' school within which Larry had a 'tough' schedule, teaching two regular periods of eighth-grade (students age 13 to 14) physical science, four periods of low-ability mathematics in a special, highly structured, individualized learning programme funded through Chapter One, and, for reasons of increasing his income during the first semester, one period of ISS (In School Suspension) within which he worked with varying numbers of students ejected from other classes for relatively serious misbehaviour. The Chapter One mathematics programme required no teacher planning whatsoever, nor did ISS. Larry's preparation period was filled by ISS.

TEACHING ROLE

The role thrust upon Larry in Jordan Junior High was entirely different from the one he sought to create while practice teaching, and had hoped to establish during his first year of teaching. This role significantly downplayed the value of subject matter and of process. Additionally, it brought him in contact with a particular type of 'fascinating human being' that proved troubling and foreign to his experience even during practice teaching, and especially as a young person growing up the privileged son of a physician. As mentioned, Larry had virtually no planning to do for either ISS or the basic math classes he taught. While this meant he conserved energy useful for other activities, in mathematics it also meant that he had no influence over the content or how it was taught. It also meant that, as he put it, he had 'a second boss . . . she's been running the show and has developed the entire program.' In this programme the content was prescribed, and intellectually stultifying, emphasizing memorization of facts above all else. Larry, to his chagrin, would spend his time disciplining, running from student to student helping with mundane problems, checking work, recording progress, and passing out tokens for work completed adequately. The tokens were used to buy time in an adjoining recreation room that contained a pool table, games, food machines, and a variety of other diversions from the academic work of schooling. In neither setting were the students in the least interested in learning the material; and yet Larry was supposed to keep them on task. This was not his idea of teaching.

The problem of finding ways for emphasizing process in teaching was even further complicated by Larry's teaching assignment in physical science and by the culture of the science department. While he had an extensive science background (and only a modest background in mathematics), his strength was in the biological not the physical sciences. He felt insecure teaching physical science and, because of his insecurity, found himself needing to stick closely to the textbook at the cost of process and his own intellectual interests and aspirations. Apologetically he remarked in interview: 'My planning has basically been revolving around the textbook.' Furthermore, the lack of materials in the school for laboratory work or demonstrations, elevated the textbook in importance while downplaying the value of learning science through process. Larry had hoped to plan laboratory sessions so that the students might have some experience with science as inquiry and at the beginning of the year he did so. But they were very few in number because he could not afford to pay for the necessary materials out of his own pocket, as, another teacher told him, he would have to do if he wanted to teach experientially. He discovered that in the science department all the available money was spent on textbooks rather than laboratory materials. Further, members of the science department told him matter-of-factly that 'it's not a reality to have a student-oriented classroom out here [in the school].'

DISCIPLINE PROBLEMS AND THE SEARCH FOR SELF

In each of his classes, excepting first period physical science, the 'fascinating human beings' he encountered included a number of seriously troubled students who seemed to enjoy challenging teachers' authority. Individually they remained fascinating, but collectively they were threatening. Based upon his practice teaching experience Larry had expected to be 'doing a lot of discipline. I'll be doing a lot of confronting and communicating, which is okay'. Like his cooperating teachers he had hoped to be able to discipline in a way that would represent a 'positive communication with [students]'. But he was simply unprepared for the students who greeted him. For a person struggling within a hostile environment to define himself as an inquiry teacher, one who would stimulate students to explore problems, and yet used to being respected, student challenges to his authority were sharp and painful blows to his already fragile sense of self. Each challenge increased Larry's vulnerability and his self doubts; and he wondered if it would ever be possible to establish caring relationships with such students. The first day of school foreshadowed things to come. Writing in his journal:

> The whole day [was] so traumatic! . . . I wasn't ready for eighth graders in general . . . Somehow the lack of contact [with students] over the summer had lulled me into forgetting how it's like to be around them. Third period remedial Math is the worst combination of defiant and mouthy boys . . . I've ever seen. Most of my other classes were more or less silently nervous. These guys took me to the cleaners immediately.

Facing such students, classroom control quickly became Larry's first priority. Within days of the beginning of school he was nearly overwhelmed, encountering situations that demanded immediate and consistent responses. But not being able to function as he had imagined, Larry was uncertain about how to respond. Lacking a teaching role model to guide him, he fell back on the only solution that presented itself, the institutionalized role of policeman, but with little success: 'I just don't have that hard edge yet that is needed in a class like that [to establish control], to come down immediately and kick ass!' He was of two minds: he flipped back and forth between wanting to be the caring inquiry teacher that his cooperating teachers represented and the tough authority figure – a policeman – that he feared and other teachers told him the situation demanded.

Like the students, Larry recognized his inconsistency. Writing in his journal: 'During my instructions for a lab there came a time [when] I should've retracted the [activity] and put them to work writing or [doing] other seatwork, but I didn't! Damn it, what's wrong with me?!' Two months into the school year and unable to resolve the dilemma, Larry found himself in a constant emotional turmoil: 'I experience . . . a constant conflict between being personal and positive, on the one hand, and being distant and consistent on the other.' This dichotomy – personal and positive/distant and consistent – is revealing. To be personal and positive toward students, in Larry's view, meant being inconsistent, to make exceptions and to be overly spontaneous and responsive to students, with dire consequences for classroom control. Larry saw no alternatives, no middle ground between extremes. Larry had never thought about the possibility of there being a middle position and, lacking one, he found himself, as he put it, on a 'kind of emotional roller coaster . . . one minute . . . angry and fed up, and a moment later . . . encouraged and positive'.

Larry desperately did not want to be a tough cop, but given his teaching situation he began to doubt there was a reasonable alternative. ISS, for example, not only meant that he did not have a planning period, it meant that he spent an hour each day with the worst-behaving students in the school. During one observation, for example, Larry momentarily stepped out in the hallway and turned around just in time to see two students spitting at one another across the classroom, seemingly oblivious to his presence. Immediately Larry sent the offending students to the vice-principal's office for disciplining. Similarly, the four remedial math classes he taught placed him in contact with significant numbers of misbehaving students, many of whom were unable intellectually to do the work of the regular classroom and were little interested in schooling. These students required constant and careful monitoring. Facing these students and in such large numbers Larry begrudgingly began to conclude that he could not hope to be an inquiry teacher:

It would be impossible for me to run a class like that. The kids just would not be able to handle [it]. A lot of them would be too irresponsible to [do] something on their own . . . doing hands on stuff; I don't think they can do it.

Larry certainly did not enter teaching to spend his time with these kinds of students or to do this kind of work and before the Christmas break he began to question, sometimes openly, the wisdom of the decision to switch careers. He was obviously very unhappy.

Not being able to be the kind of teacher he had fantasized about, and not being able to function adequately or with any degree of satisfaction as a policeman and not being able to see any alternatives, Larry was lost between conceptions of himself as teacher, and was at a loss as to what to do: 'I don't know what I'd like to be [as a teacher]. I think that is part of my problem . . . I don't know what I want to be.' His sense of being lost is graphically portrayed in a journal entry within which he was asked to identify a metaphor that captured his experience of teaching:

Have a hard time pinning down any one metaphor for this experience. I thought of a blind person or a young child or baby, who stumbles and falls, and bumps into walls, gets frustrated easily, and doesn't seem to really know what is going on or see the bigger picture. No matter how much I realize this lack of perspective, it doesn't come any faster or easier.

A month later the situation had not improved, and Larry, who as a lab technician had been used to functioning as an expert and knowing what to do, was nearly immobilized: I . . . feel like I'm . . . lost. I don't know what I'm doing a lot of the times . . . . That's so very frustrating . . . I really don't feel I've got a grasp on [teaching].

OTHER TEACHERS AND OFFERS OF HELP

Larry was not the only teacher having serious problems; he was one of two first-year teachers within Jordan River Junior High School. The other teacher, a young female English teacher, resigned after the first month of school. During that month Larry would see her walking around the hallways of the school and recognized in her face what he thought to be the same frustrations he was feeling. He wanted to reach out to her to offer comfort and to try and help, but, being overwhelmed by his own troubles, he could not. 'It hurts [so] much that you don't want to talk about it. [But what is worse], you don't have the ability to help yourself . . . . It's happening too fast.' Furthermore, not knowing anyone in the school, Larry 'felt alone' and did not know where to go for help even if he had been able, which he was not: '[Going for help] is a sign of weakness,' he said. Reflecting on the beginning of the year from the vantage point of late springtime, Larry concluded that being in the school was 'like combat . . . . They (the students) are firing at you . . . . The English teacher was the guy who got hit and you just keep moving . . . .[It's] every man for himself.'

Fortunately, for Larry, near the end of the first quarter, and after the resignation of the other first-year teacher, the principal sent an energetic, interested, experienced teacher, a person 'sensitive enough to know what's going on,' to check on Larry. The teacher immediately recognized that Larry was having serious problems and relayed this message to the principal who urged him to befriend Larry, which he did: He 'saw me falling apart and knew he needed to step in and reach out . . . . Since then [he has become] a good friend. While having a friend in the school did not result in a significant improvement in instruction, it did have the important effect of letting Larry know that he was not alone and that there was someone within the school who cared about him and to whom he could confide his troubles. Having a friend made it easier to cope. The principal also urged a teacher within the science department to assist Larry. This teacher, a veteran of many years' experience, offered a variety of suggestions about how to gain control and improve classroom climate and eventually came to function informally as Larry's mentor (his assigned mentor offered little if any assistance). This teacher, Larry said, threw him a 'lifesaver'. There was a third teacher who helped Larry get through his first and most difficult months of teaching, a friend who taught in a nearby school and who exemplified to Larry the kind of teacher he initially wanted to become, and in his brighter moments still hoped to become: 'He's very creative and a good problem solver.'

Without the encouragement of these teachers, Larry reported that he may very well have quit teaching. Primarily they served as sounding boards for Larry and offered him encouragement when he was most upset about teaching. Also, they offered him advice on how to cope with the situation within which he found himself; their aim, like his, was to help him survive the year. However, while greatly admiring these teachers and being appreciative of their efforts on his behalf, they, like his cooperating teachers, also proved to be sources of some difficulty. To his great disadvantage, Larry compared himself to them which magnified his self-doubts. He wondered if he would ever become an effective teacher and, as with his cooperating teachers, he longed to be just like his friend and thereby end his struggle with himself. Writing in his journal: 'I got great ideas [from him], but . . . came away frustrated by not being able to plan and think and *be* like him as a teacher'. And further: 'When I'm thinking about the experienced teachers in the school I know . . .I find myself shaking my head or talking to myself about how this is beyond me. [I do this] regularly at the end of the day as I'm leaving school.' Despite the assistance he received, Larry remained uncertain about who he was as teacher.

GETTING TOUGH WITH STUDENTS

As the months wore on and Larry continued to vacillate between conceptions of teaching with unhappy results, he began to accept what increasingly seemed to be inevitable: despite his feelings to the contrary, if he was to survive his first year of teaching he would have to be a policeman, for without control nothing of positive value was likely to take place. The ability to establish and maintain class control became the standard by which he judged his teaching competence; and without it he could not maintain any semblance of self-respect. In the quest for control, begrudgingly Larry gave up his desire to become an inquiry-oriented teacher and to establish caring relations with students. By mid-year the first issue to be considered when planning an activity was whether or not the students were likely to go off task. Student control, not learning, was the primary criterion for selection. This was evident in Larry's curriculum log where comments such as, 'Thought it might help with the noise level,' and 'need to settle them down,' found a prominent place alongside reasons for content selection having to do with student learning. Anything having to do with student interest, or fun, dropped out of his thinking about teaching. In desperation Larry almost ceased trying to engage the science students. In his journal he wrote: 'Demonstration in first [period] got some student interest. Almost didn't try it.'

Dominated by the concern for control and the need to police students, and frustrated about not being able to teach as he had hoped, Larry became increasingly irritable and negative toward students as the year dragged on, and as he continued to send comparatively large numbers of them to the office for disciplining following frequent and hostile confrontations. In the negative behaviour of the students he saw a major reason for his frustrations with teaching; and he came to view all students through lenses coloured by his images of the very worst students, particularly those in seventh-period physical science, but he felt badly about it. From his journal:

> Deep down, sometimes, I still can't accept that some of [the students] just have a meanness about them, or a dishonest and out-of-control nature . . . And yet this is the nature of the beast . . . I still grapple with this. A [teaching] day like today makes me feel incredibly inadequate and incompetent, no matter who I am or what kind of person I am . . . I feel at times that I've just 'written' these classes off as a lost cause . . . [and] this leads . . . to poor quality or too little planning. . . . I find myself feeling resolved to the idea that no amount of planning can 'protect' me from the experience of feeling ineffective educationally, or getting frustrated and hurt by [student] behaviour.

As Larry thought about his classes, one characteristic seemed to unite the students, their dislike for authority: 'They don't like it'. And, he took this dislike personally: 'It almost seems to be my role to be their target,' he lamented but, 'Somebody has got to do it.' It was, he said, 'the nature of the beast' to challenge authority, which he resented. And yet, he felt sorry for some of the students as individuals, seeing them as victims of difficult home situations and lack of parental support. He even felt badly for some of the Rockers,[3] his worst students, who tend to 'come from poorer home situations where there's one parent, no parent, and low income, welfare. . . . Some of them come from pretty shitty situations . . . [and] they bring that stuff to school!' Recognizing situations like this complicated Larry's efforts to accept a policeman's teaching role, even while increasingly he came to accept it as necessary in order to maintain 'crowd control'.

Larry also blamed himself for his teaching failures. Recalling his cooperating teachers who had succeeded with similar age students in establishing inquiry-oriented classrooms, he concluded that his lack of teaching skill prevented him from achieving his hoped-for classroom. Perhaps, he thought, the problem was not only the students' but also his: 'I'm incredibly skeptical that these kids can ever handle [inquiry, but may be] they just couldn't deal with it with me [as the teacher].' Thoughts like this one further undermined Larry's already sagging confidence.

BATTLE-WEARY

The more negative Larry became toward the students and toward himself as teacher, the poorer quality his planning, or so he reported. The physical-science curriculum, for example, came straight out of the textbook without embellishment and was, as Larry put it, 'academic crap . . . [that] the students don't relate to' but they lacked 'the self-control' necessary for other approaches; in effect, the students got just what they deserved. And, the more negative he became, the worse became his relationships with the students. While teaching he would be simmering internally over student misbehaviour and would suddenly explode at a student's acting out in ways that just moments before had gone unacknowledged. He would single one student out of a number of misbehaving students for ejection from class. Reflecting Larry's internal conflict, classes often seemed tense and uneasy and he was deeply troubled by how events were unfolding: to his chagrin, teaching had become a form of warfare. 'This will be a *very* long year if I can't change this [negative] feeling about the environment or [improve the] relationship between me and the students,' he mused. But he did not know what to do, despite occasional suggestions about ways of obtaining and maintaining classroom control from his teacher-friends in the school.

Five weeks after this journal entry and feeling battle weary, Larry was working very hard to follow the advice of his teacher-friends to distance himself mentally from his teaching problems in order to check his continued and deepening feelings of failure and frustration at not being able to teach. Feeling unable to alter the situation, he tried not to care.

I'm [working] mentally on not letting the kids and things

33

that happen at school get to me so much. I have to really try
at this. I have to try to create a mental set or frame of mind
that keeps me relatively unaffected .... It helps me get
through the days and feel not so stressed about this job ....
I've also been listening and thinking about other teachers'
suggestions [about how] to simplify [my work] and distance
myself from the students.

Inherently such actions ran counter to Larry's initial and incipient
teaching values, and certainly counter to his inner self. Indeed,
even the possibility of such actions would have astonished and
shocked him at the beginning of the year when he remarked that
the distinguishing characteristic of poor-quality teachers was that
they did not 'want to get involved with the kids'. Despite such
beliefs, in response to his teaching situation and failing to see a
middle position, Larry numbed as he tried not to let problems with
students or failures in teaching 'get to him'. To save a semblance
of self-respect and to preserve his relationship with his family
which had deteriorated under the stress and the time
requirements of teaching, he discounted his teaching ideals as
being unrealistic. After all, throughout the early part of the year he
had worked himself to near exhaustion by spending virtually every
evening and weekend trying to come up with a productive
curriculum and better ways of organizing the classroom. And for
what purpose? More failure and rejection? Feeling numbed and in
a siege mentality, for a time during the early spring Larry stopped
planning in advance and was planning the night before: 'I can't
worry about it, I can't sit around wrenching my hands so I put
[planning] off until the last minute and then [I] throw something
together.' This approach to planning, he said, 'sometimes . . .
works and sometimes . . . it doesn't. . . . [But] I don't have the
energy to worry about it.' And yet, while doing so, and perhaps as
a result of having given up his dreams, Larry felt 'empty' and
'depressed' about teaching.

Over the course of the year Larry's goals changed. Reflecting on
the year, near year's end, he concluded,

I always thought I would like to stress process types of
learning goals over content in my curriculum, such as *doing,
constructing,* problem solving [and so on]. Sort of
non-teacher-centered classroom activities. But that seems to
have been sacrificed . . . to discipline-management issues

that I'm incessantly concerned about, [and] to my inexperience and lack of ingenuity.

Desiring at one time to teach science as process and to establish caring relationships with the students, by late spring he sought something else: 'I'm hoping for a truce ... I've lowered my expectations'. Based upon our observations, near year's end, Larry seemed to have achieved the desired truce, at least with the students, if not with himself. To be sure, the students engaged in far less off-task behaviour and, on Larry's part, we noted far fewer dramatic swings in mood and behaviour. While classes only occasionally seemed to flow easily, they were rarely strained or tense as before. Some days Larry even appeared quite at ease and comfortable in the classroom. With the truce teaching did not become pleasureful, but it did become tolerable. There were some good days when formerly there had only seemed to be bad. But, despite the truce with the students – their acceptance of him as policeman – Larry continued to wage a scaled-down inner battle, a civil war, over who he would be as teacher. Although behaviourally less apparent, Larry continued searching for an alternative to being a policeman, a different kind of relationship with the students and a different kind of teaching role, to fill the emptiness he often felt.

SIGNS OF HOPE

At year's end Larry was still seeking to identify who he was as teacher but he had become reasonably comfortable playing a policeman role and reasonably good at playing the part: 'I've grown ... to accept [the role] – kind of.' As he became more comfortable with the role, he became less arbitrary and more consistent with the students, and for them more like a teacher. Larry too, began to feel like a teacher:

> I think I'm starting to feel like a teacher ... I'm more comfortable saying [that I'm a teacher]. ... For most of the year I haven't felt like a teacher. I felt like someone pretending to be [one], stumbling and fumbling with [the role].

In some respects policing became almost second nature to Larry. It was as though he had played the part so long that he began to be the part even while feeling uncomfortable with it:

After school in the hall there are kids around the corner [from my room] pitching pennies. I automatically walk down there and see what's going on. I've sort of taken on [that] role. . . . I'm walking down the hall [and] there's kids in the halls and there's a certain response [that follows from me]; there's a game that gets set up immediately: 'What are you doing here, [I say]? You better give me a good excuse.'

But, still, Larry wanted to be more than just a policeman. What he gained from being a policeman was a measure of class control; it was a role the students understood and to which they responded. Indeed, the students expected him to crack down on them when they misbehaved and respected him when he did, even though occasionally they complained about it. For Larry, however, it was not a pleasant role to fulfil, only a necessary one. He recalled his practice teaching, when the pleasure of teaching came from connecting with students individually and seeing them learn, which only became possible once he had the classes under control. Within tightly run classes, Larry could venture out into brief explorations of other types of relationships with individual students, but always within the context of policing. Within this context, he began to experiment slightly with the curriculum-seeking activities that would be more interesting to the students, after having for so long given up trying to locate such activities. At year's end, for example, to break the monotony of worksheets for himself and the students he planned an occasional and highly structured process-oriented activity: 'Last week I really caught myself getting worksheet crazy. I thought, "This is ridiculous. . . . God, this is getting a little old"'.

Occasionally, while seeking more enjoyable relationships with students, Larry let the policeman façade slip, only to be reminded by student misbehaviour that he had strayed too far from the part and needed to return to it, and crack down on them. For example, occasionally he would become too playful with students and would engage with them in a kind of teasing but friendly banter, which he enjoyed. Unfortunately, once begun, the banter frequently and quickly would get out of control.

One thing I find fun . . . I don't know what you call [it] . . . bantering [with the students]. You've got to think fast on your feet. [It's] spontaneous [but] it can get out of control. You've got to watch it because they don't have a sense of

when to quit and when to get back to work. . . . You have to
be careful with it . . . . Sometimes I am not very careful with
it. [I let it go too far] because it's something that feeds me
. . . [that] makes teaching fun.

Moments like this, when Larry allowed the policeman role to slide
somewhat into the background, and times when students seemed
to be working productively, kindled his hope that he could
eventually produce a role that would make teaching more
comfortable and enjoyable despite the teaching context. At year's
end he was uncertain, however, about what that role would be,
although clearly it would grow out of insights gained from
functioning as policeman and the view that the students 'just
[cannot] handle a lot of freedom.' Although the year had been in
many respects a miserable experience and he was 'tired . . . really
tired – burned out,' in retrospect, Larry felt reasonably good about
what he had accomplished, especially the fact that he had survived:

I've made it through the year . . . [And], I'm kind of feeling
somewhat functional. I get through the day, I do most of the
things that are expected of me from the administration and
from the kids. Most of the time the kids seem to do what I
want them to do and perceive it as reasonable.

IN SUMMARY

Larry entered student teaching with a very limited understanding
of teaching and of students and a weak sense of himself as a
teacher. Indeed, he found it difficult to imagine himself as a
teacher. What he sought initially in teaching was a job within which
he could continue his long and loving association with biological
science. He left practice teaching hoping to teach as had his
cooperating teachers for whom the teaching of science was a
matter of organizing classrooms to facilitate inquiry. Although far
from certain about how to obtain this end, Larry looked forward to
his first year of teaching as an opportunity to try to work out such
a role. Assuming a position within Jordan River Junior High, Larry
encountered a context and teaching assignment hostile to the
teaching role he was beginning to form upon completing student
teaching. Specifically, he was overwhelmed by the students so
many of whom, like the 'Rockers,' were uninterested in school and
resentful of authority. Feeling vulnerable, they seemed to him to

be 'beasts'. In response, and unhappily, Larry fell back on the only role that presented itself, 'teacher is policeman'. By springtime, Larry had obtained a 'truce' with the students but continued to be frustrated with teaching and fraught with self-doubts as he continued to struggle with the question of who he was as teacher. The year ended with his feeling somewhat comfortable with the policeman role and cautiously looking forward to a second year of teaching in the hope that he would be able to remedy many of the problems encountered during the first, so many of which were tied to his confusion about who he was as teacher.

3

STUDENTS LIKE GOOD TEACHERS

NANCY

Both of Nancy's parents had been teachers. At one time her mother was a highly committed and successful teacher but her interest had waned and, following a 'horrible experience', she left the profession. Her father thought of teaching as a 'nice secure profession . . . [an] O. K. job [that] would get you through life,' and for this reason, when Nancy was in college, encouraged her to consider teaching as a career. Although Nancy did not set out to become a teacher, as a college student she assumed that, if other employment opportunities did not open up, she could always fall back on teaching. With this thought in mind she entered and completed a teacher-certification programme that culminated in an extremely frustrating and difficult ten-week period of practice teaching in a large suburban high school where she felt ill at ease with the students and the school environment. Uncertain about whether or not to pursue a teaching career but lacking other options, Nancy sought employment and found it just prior to the school year at Markham Hall, a private, non-sectarian secondary school. She accepted the position because it was the practical thing to do.

As a single, 25 year-old, the position to teach at Markham Hall was not only her first teaching job but her first 'real' job as well. For a short time her positive feelings about Markham Hall softened her deep-seated self-doubts about starting a new position and her ambivalence toward being a teacher. Nancy anticipated that, unlike the school within which she taught as a student teacher, Markham Hall would be a comfortable place to work. However, despite her positive feelings toward Markham Hall, Nancy worried.

39

As a college student, when she had thought about teaching as a career, it was always in terms of history and social science, not Spanish, her minor area of study. Yet, the job she accepted was to teach Spanish to seventh- and eighth-graders, a responsibility that concerned her. But, an even greater source of concern when Nancy thought of teaching was that she was unable to picture herself as a teacher – even though she had grown up with teachers as parents.

Nancy had regarded herself as 'a good student' in school, although she acknowledged that it was not until she went to college that she 'started to be very good at learning'. However, she freely admitted to having difficulties in school: 'I had a hard time with the social scene.' This was because she felt 'more awkward than most' students and because she was 'shy . . . and wanted really badly to be popular.' There, also, she claimed that she was overly influenced by 'what other people thought of [her]'. This last matter was particularly important in the Markham Hall school environment; and she desperately wanted approval of both adults and teenagers. In addition, she said, 'I tend to . . . pick out certain people as my mirror and wait for them to tell me my image is beautiful' and, when praise was not forthcoming, 'It makes me very nervous and unhappy.'

INITIAL TEACHING METAPHOR

Nancy entered teaching being quite unsure of herself and of who she was as teacher. The few images she did possess of teachers were vague and uncertain ones mostly associated with the possession of certain desired personality traits. Recalling her own experience as a student, for example, Nancy remarked that 'The most effective [teachers] were the ones that were able to be most personable . . . . A teacher is a friend who knows what is relevant to students.' And:

> I was a shy kid. The most effective [teachers] for me were the ones that reached out to me and . . . made contact with me. I enjoyed their classes more . . . and it helped a lot; my attitude [toward school] changed [as did] how well I did in class.

Drawing primarily on her experience as a student, she thought of the ideal teacher, which she hoped to be, as friendly, warm, enthusiastic and especially humorous: 'The mental picture that comes to mind is [that] I walk into my class and there would be a lot of humor going on, I'd be laughing a lot. The kids would be laughing a lot.' As a consequence of these attributes, good teachers were liked and respected by their students, they were 'buddies': Teacher is buddy. To be liked by the students was proof of being a good teacher. In contrast, poor teachers where those who held 'negative attitudes [toward students which influenced] their whole approach to teaching' and were not liked by students.

THE TEACHING CONTEXT

The school year began with Nancy's being given five classes of first- and second-year Spanish to teach. Together, her assigned classes represented four different preparations and, because the school timetable was set up with large blocks of instructional time, she met alternatively with two classes on one day (White Day) and three classes on the other (Green Day). On White Days she did not begin teaching until after lunchtime, a situation that left her with large amounts of discretionary time; during the mornings she usually prepared lessons, read, duplicated instructional materials, graded, or worked alone in her classroom. Occasionally, more often at the beginning of the year, she spent time observing other teachers' classrooms.

Having completed her student teaching in a senior public high school, Nancy was well aware of the advantages that Markham Hall offered. There were three significant and obvious differences compared to the local public schools that had available teaching positions that year. First, the classes were small. None of the courses that she was assigned had more than eighteen students. Second, the students were generally very bright and mirrored, for the most part, financially comfortable suburban lifestyles and the concern of middle-class parents for the educational well-being of their offspring. Third, the school environment was personable, a reflection on the institution's small size – about 250 students – and the small classes, and was renowned for its supportive community spirit, evident in the behaviours of faculty and students alike. Indeed, the school administrators prided themselves on the closeness of the school community, and for providing very supportive teaching and learning environments. Together these elements were significant for Nancy and she thought they would help mitigate the 'feelings of despair' that she had experienced during practice teaching amid the tumult of a relatively large

41

senior high school with very large classes. Going into the academic year Nancy had felt 'intimidated by the big job ahead [of her].' She was also apprehensive about the dynamics of working at a 'sort of an exclusive [private] school.'

The first days of teaching

Nancy's first days in the classroom were characterized by a great deal of Spanish conversation as she dived headfirst into presenting the subject matter and objectives, and conducting lessons according to the principles of the 'immersion method of language acquisition', an approach advocated by her foreign language, teaching-methods professor. The basic premise and underlying philosophy of this approach suggest that students should be constantly exposed to listening to and participating in the foreign language they are learning. Nancy sought to make the classes fun and approached the students hoping to become 'buddies' with them, a decision she later was to regret: '[I] was lenient and [had the attitude] of "let's be buddies and have fun." I wouldn't do that again to start out the year.'

For the most part, the classes on the first day of school at Markham Hall went well, except for one eighth-grade class. From the onset the class was troublesome: 'They were rowdy from the very first day . . . . It seemed [as though] they were controlling the class more than me.' Nancy began to regret her decision to try to be buddies with the students: 'It backfired because they got the impression that they could play around.' After several weeks of teaching the situation had not changed. This was her 'worst class' and remained so, even at the end of the school year, although occasionally there were hopeful moments. One such moment occurred toward the end of the first month: 'Yesterday was the first day that I actually enjoyed [the] class. I usually feel so grumpy that . . . I dread it . . . and don't want to be there.'

By the second week of school a pattern of sometimes confrontive and disruptive interactions between teacher and students had been established in the eighth-grade class. In response, as Nancy admitted, she began to 'blame the students'. It was '*their* fault' that she had difficulties. Her struggle with this particular group of students coloured her views of teaching and influenced her perceptions of the other students and classes with whose progress and conduct, when compared to the eighth-grade class, she felt mildly satisfied. More importantly, as Nancy increasingly felt threatened, they eventually crushed any hope she had of filling out the vague images she possessed of herself as teacher into a satisfactory teaching role. When asked during her fifth week of teaching to describe herself as teacher, Nancy paused and remarked: 'That's difficult because I don't see myself really as a teacher.' And pausing again: 'I guess some days I do, and some days I don't [see myself as a teacher].'

Quest to connect with the students and to be liked

The root of Nancy's problems rested, in part, upon her desire to be a 'buddy' with the students. Instead of the difficulties that her actions caused, Nancy had fantasized quite a different scenario:

> I like the idea of . . . setting the wheels in motion and having the students do most of the talking . . . . As it turns out I do most of the talking. I don't have really strict rules except for the [difficult eighth-grade] class.

In reality, her rules for the eighth-grade class were not nearly as strict as those of some other teachers in the building but, more importantly, she could not consistently enforce those rules that she had. In fact, Nancy did not want to discipline the students. She mused: 'Do I have to discipline? I *do* need to have firm rules and be consistent about the consequences that follow. Is that discipline?' She did not want to discipline the students because she believed that to do so would jeopardize her relationship with them – leniency was a precondition for the students to like her and, above all else, she wanted to be liked: 'I'm worried . . . that they're not enjoying my personality.' And:

> I feel that I learned the most from the teachers that I liked the best . . . . I've always wanted everybody to like me. I have [an extremely] hard time if somebody is mad at me or feels bad about me; it really affects me.

Nancy's ideals were immediately frustrated by the actions of the eighth-grade class who seemed to reject her: 'I'm really bothered by the fact that they don't like me'. Being so vulnerable, and feeling rejected, Nancy found herself having difficulty acting naturally and comfortably with the students and thus, in turn, increased her feelings of vulnerability, a point that was intimated in a number of journal entries. For instance, at report-card time she wrote: 'Nervous kids scrambling for points. Nervous teacher trying to be fair . . . trying to be liked . . . [and] being forced into learning about human relations.' And, 'When students aren't being attentive, or may be even fascinated, I feel twinges of panic. "Oh, what am I doing wrong? Oh, this isn't the way it should be going."' Moreover, Nancy felt distanced from the students, a troubling situation, 'I feel separated from the kids,' she remarked several times throughout the year. Nancy was not only learning about teaching, she was also learning about students and how to interact with them, both within the context of struggling to establish her own identity in the classroom as teacher and to be liked by the students.

Conflict with Barry

There was no more graphic illustration of some of the insecurities that Nancy felt, as she struggled to establish herself in the classroom, than that found in her response to the vindictive outburst of an eighth-grade boy:

> When I was walking out of my classroom . . . a little eighth-grader . . . yelled at my back, 'I don't like you teacher.' I turned around and couldn't tell who it was. I didn't recognize any of the boys . . . . I had just turned around and he yelled 'Nobody likes you.' That was really hard to take.

At the time she did not respond to the boy's attack: 'I wish I had the strength to [talk back]. But I didn't. Damn it.' The hurt lingered and turned inward.

Eventually, Nancy came to suspect that Barry, her most troublesome student, was the culprit but there was nothing she could do about it. Well into the first term, and prior to the incident in the hallway, in a faculty meeting other teachers who taught Barry talked about observing improvements in his classroom behaviour. Nancy, however, had observed no improvement, although she had been working diligently in the attempt to improve their relationship. In her journal in late October, prior to a meeting with Barry she wrote: 'I had a dream about [Barry], the student I had such turmoil over last week. Dreamed we had formed a new understanding of each other and were friends.' Despite the dream, he remained her nemesis and she reasoned, as a result of what the teachers told her about him, 'I'm going to have [more] strict guidelines for him with specific consequences' of his actions. On one hand, knowing that other experienced teachers had difficulties with Barry was comforting; on the other, that his behaviour had not improved in *her* class was very discouraging. Following the faculty meeting Nancy applied her 'redefined rules' with Barry. The result: 'One of the best classes I've had so far,' an outcome that reinforced the value of rules, and sticking to them, and of asserting her authority in the classroom, which she found difficult to do. She had also forewarned Barry: 'He was better today ... [because] I let him know the conditions [and] he didn't cause me any trouble. He was argumentative at first but, at least, he raised his hand.' However, the more she applied the management techniques of others, the less she was like the friendly, warm, humorous, and likeable teacher she had fantasized being. Moreover, the problems with Barry continued, although they became somewhat less frequent.

Riding a roller-coaster and depending on student responses

Being so very dependent for her emotional well-being and sense of self on the students placed Nancy on an emotional roller-coaster. Small events had a profound effect on her, as is indicated by what transpired during one week in December.

> I felt discouraged Monday and Tuesday ... the feelings were strong. The tension was so great that I was questioning my being in the teaching profession. But Wednesday [through] Friday everything turned around.

This change in her thinking occurred because of a single class activity. 'I believe it started to turn around,' she said, 'with a game that I played with ... [the] kids on Wednesday called "Kiss the frog".' Each student was required to 'pay compliments' to others in the class, including Nancy. Of this, she said, 'I must admit that I enjoyed the receiving part the most.' Clearly, before the game she 'was feeling quite depressed – I felt my students didn't like me much or my way of teaching [and] I worry about that' – but, because of the accolades made during the game, her perceptions were reversed.

Moreover, following a confrontation and a subsequent

45

conference during which she ameliorated student ill will, Nancy would feel renewed, and the roller-coaster car she was riding would begin to climb. For example, she periodically ejected students from class for misbehaviour and then would meet with them to discuss what transpired, why it transpired, and what could be done to improve the situation.

> I talked to him afterwards. He was upset in the beginning, but after talking we left on good terms. I admitted [that I had been hard on him] and he gave suggestions as to how not to add to the disruptiveness in the class. What was it he said he would do? I can't remember . . . I'll have to ask him at the beginning of class next time which will be a nice reminder for him also.

Inevitably, each climb was followed by a crash, and Nancy began to have problems with migraine headaches and bouts with depression. Writing in her journal:

> I'm knocking myself out. I've got to have them doing more on their own. [I] talked too much today [and] have quite a headache . . . [I] cried too much last night . . . [and] talked to [my boyfriend] about the discouragement I feel . . . . Why the compressed head? Rough fucking day, man!

Clearly these and other similar feelings were also related to her perceptions of herself as teacher. Often she found it difficult to come to school, especially on Green Days, the day in which she taught the eighth-grade class.

Facing such days and these feelings, Nancy began to doubt her decision to become a teacher. After a particularly gruelling day in mid October, for instance, she remarked: 'On days like today I wonder if I should be in a career that requires so much social interaction.' These feelings were not isolated instances and they served to illuminate her recognition of her inadequacies in handling human relationships in the classroom setting. They continued throughout the year and often set her in a pessimistic frame of mind for thinking about teaching and students.

Seeking and not seeking support of peers and others

During the times when she felt down emotionally, Nancy generally relied on her own resources to pull herself up and out. She knew that in order for her to continue teaching she had to feel better about it:

> I don't know how to improve how I feel about teaching . . .
> but I do know that I've got to enjoy it to go on with it. I need
> to go ahead with activities that I enjoy . . . . One of the most
> worthwhile lifetime tasks – self-actualization – [is] finding
> your simplest self, [your] most straightforward self.

One way that Nancy tried to feel good about herself, for example, is illustrated by a journal entry late in the first term: 'I've been talking to myself positively about the [eighth-grade] class – although at times I feel like I'm lying and have to convince myself [that I'm not].' What did help, however, was the regular interaction with her peers in the beginning-teacher seminar and writing about her difficulties in her journal. For example, she frequently made statements such as, 'I'm feeling better after [getting] . . . my concerns down on paper,' or 'I'm glad I took time to write. I feel better now.'

In addition, on a few occasions Nancy made requests for assistance from other teachers in the building but with mixed results. About midway through the first term, for instance, she asked the history teacher to observe her teaching the eighth-grade class. During the class Nancy 'made a substantial judgement error' – by giving a student 'unequal treatment' – and 'wished [the other teacher] was not there to witness it.' She was very embarrassed, although afterwards reasoned that '[the teacher's] criticism was constructive and, after giving [the situation] more thought . . . [was] glad that [the teacher] had been there . . . to [help her] work through the mistake.' This situation was a good example of the way Nancy felt about soliciting the assistance of other teachers. Afterwards she was able to appreciate their input but, at the time, being observed was often painful and very uncomfortable.

On one occasion Juanita, the senior school Spanish teacher, taught the feared eighth-grade class with Nancy looking on. According to Nancy, Juanita 'found them quite enjoyable,' and was able to joke with them, and be playful, a response that left Nancy with further doubts about herself as she made comparisons of her reaction to and relationship with the students to Juanita's.

My first reaction was disappointment in myself because . . .

my history with them . . . has been so unpleasant. The second, more controlled, reaction was that I could flow with them more, not take things so seriously, and joke with them about themselves instead of feeling mad and angry with them.

This second reaction lead to a temporary change in Nancy's presence in the classroom, a situation that led to the first day that she reported enjoying the eighth-grade class – 'her one best day'. She went on to analyse the situation which was, she said, also related to her mood: 'One of the students had made the observation that I was very serious about Spanish and didn't smile much.' In the class that went well, Nancy relaxed and smiled, a welcomed change for the students. More good days followed.

Other Markham Hall faculty and visitors, such as pre-service teachers from the university, often commented to us about the 'warmth and support' available within the school community. This was particularly evident, they said, in the relationships between teachers and students in the extra-curricular activities of the school – activities which Nancy never got involved in. The small full-time faculty of about thirty-two regularly met together, both informally and formally, in the faculty lounge. It was not merely a lunch room, although lunch could be had there for those who did not eat in the cafeteria, but it was a place of interaction and discussion, designed, according to the principal, to 'encourage intellectual conversation'. Regularly we observed teachers quietly working or actively and excitedly engaging others in the room. During the early portion of the school year Nancy often used the faculty room to prepare classes and to eat her lunch. Gradually, as her problems increased, that changed. She began to isolate herself. She did not frequent the room as often as initially. Lunchtimes were often spent alone in her classroom.

The four foreign-language faculty members, including Nancy, shared a large and airy common office; in the room each teacher had a desk, chairs, and bookshelves, and the walls were decorated with posters and artwork. Initially, Nancy also used this space for much of her preparation, but that also changed. She grew to feel uncomfortable working in the foreign-language department office, partially because of student interruptions, lack of privacy, and because she began to 'feel uncomfortable with the other teachers' – they made her 'nervous'. In summing up her

48

relationships with the faculty at the end of the school year, she admitted, 'I felt isolated.' In reality, she isolated herself.

Towards the end of the academic year Nancy felt a little better about her relationships and standing within the school. She recognized faculty in the hall as being people she could call 'friends' and felt thankful that she had not been in school with a very large faculty – as occurs in most public high schools. Yet, despite the friendliness in the halls they were not people that she could freely go to for help, especially once her difficulties became public knowledge.

Nancy did not make optimum use of the support offered by faculty and the resources of the small school and, perhaps understandably, gained most solace from her boyfriend. He was an artist and, apart from his own experience as a student, he had limited understanding of schools. He was very willing to listen but, as the year progressed, he tired, so she said, of listening to her complaints and problems. Even when she did spend time with him she was preoccupied with school. 'I'm not there . . . ' she often said, referring to time spent with her boyfriend, 'He'll be talking to me . . . and I don't hear . . . . It happens a lot.' Other lesser and infrequent sources of support continued to be her parents; she even had her mother come and observe her teach. Her father, in particular, 'gave [her] a lot of advice about what to do,' especially in the early months of teaching but, by and large, these levels of support provided little concrete assistance for the daily operation of her classroom.

Relationship with the principal

Over the course of the first few months Nancy began to feel very insecure in the presence of the principal, a factor which probably negatively influenced her willingness to talk with her peers: 'I don't think she likes me . . . [or] . . . thinks that I am a good teacher,' she lamented after a few months of teaching. 'I worry . . . what [the principal] thinks of me'.

In part, the origin of Nancy's insecurity about the principal's view of her was found in a classroom observation during the early weeks of teaching: 'She observed me . . . and I think she would say that I needed some more organization but that I had some creative activities as well'. What Nancy's comment did *not* express was the fact that the principal *never* said anything of substance about the visit to Nancy's classroom. She clearly did not heap Nancy with praise and this caused some uncertainty in Nancy's perception of their relationship and of her own abilities. In addition, and increasingly so throughout the year, the office of the principal was the recipient of many of the unruly boys in her classroom, especially Barry, whom she ejected from class. Nancy's struggles behind the closed doors of her classroom became public knowledge.

Christmas break: a new beginning

By mid year Nancy was still fighting for her very existence in the classroom, and doubts about continuing in the profession lingered, paralleling her decreasing commitment to her job at Markham Hall. The toil of continually battling with the eighth-grade students, especially Barry, took its toll: 'The problems [associated with the eighth-grade class] have become all consuming.' During this time another class was also very enervating and, for a short period, she had similar responses to them: 'We went through a period just before Christmas that was horrible'.

Nancy was dissatisfied with the job of teaching. It prevented her from enjoying more freedom in her life; teaching obstructed her engagement in the recreational pursuits that she enjoyed, particularly snow skiing and simply being out of doors. As the winter drew on, and the snow got deeper in the mountains, she increasingly resented the long hours spent on teaching. Lesson preparation was never completed and there was always grading to be done; situations that her boyfriend never quite understood. Besides, the approaching holiday season brought excitable students and more pressing demands on her time: 'There were . . . lots . . . of problems right before Christmas . . . . It was so messy and chaotic, I didn't want to deal with it.'

After the mid-year break in which she enjoyed skiing and doing things that were not related to teaching, there was a turnaround in the way in which Nancy felt about teaching. The changed state of affairs was partially rooted in the benefits that the 'peaceful holiday' provided. '[During] the break was the only time that I've been calm in the morning for a long time,' she claimed. She was 'utterly relieved' not to awake 'worrying about [what] might go wrong.' The holiday season, 'with lots of socializing,' provided

Nancy with a respite that seemed to help her through the remainder of the year. She gained perspective on her work, and as a result, having been with friends and engaged in activities she enjoyed, she returned to teaching initially less vulnerable to student criticism, and less interested in being a 'buddy,' although she hoped to be responsive to the students and provide a 'relevant' curriculum for them. Nevertheless, she would be more like other teachers in the school, and she would discipline the students.

Despite her resolve, however, she continued to struggle throughout the year seeking to find and to establish herself with the students as teacher. For example, she reported:

> I find myself alternating between two different attitudes [about] running my classes. Half of the time I [think] . . . the most important thing is having a good time in class and learn as we go – get through whatever we can with enjoyment. My other attitude is more of a disciplinarian – where I demand a quiet room, strict adherence to rules and we get . . . through more material.

She was very apprehensive about the first day back following the vacation and was 'nearly as nervous as the first day [that she] started school' but, feeling refreshed, she was, 'better able to deal with . . . confrontations.' She found she had more energy to put into teaching after having been worn down, and she determined that she would assert herself more in the classroom. A period of curricular experimentation and experimentation with a variety of classroom-management strategies followed. One of the most dramatic changes that accompanied this invigoration, for example, was Nancy's new-found determination to make more substantial long-range plans. She decided to set aside much of the immersion approach to language teaching that seemed to encourage off-task behaviour that was so threatening. Using herself as the referent and taking the State Curriculum Guides for the Spanish curriculum as an overlay, then thinking carefully about how *she* learned, she designed her lessons, all within a framework of the approved textbook format and content. She explained her organization: 'It follows the way that I learned and the way that most languages are taught [by emphasizing a lot more grammar which, as already mentioned, did not pique her interest in teaching] and I'm throwing in some other stuff like readings and lectures.' She had also consciously decided that, when she 'came back from the break, [she would] go faster in grammar.' This translated into 'doing a lot more book work and workbook exercises . . . than had been done before.' In a sense, Nancy's solution to her problems in the classroom was to substitute the authority of the textbook for her own lack of authority. Trying to be a buddy had discouraged students from respecting her. Despite the changes that induced less disruption in the classroom through less spoken Spanish, the most obvious result of changed practices, Nancy felt a little guilty: 'I feel I'm cheating them when I think about all the English I speak.'

Whereas the focus on workbook exercises and book work represented 'the pattern of January', by February more changes would come: 'We switched . . . and we're spending a lot more time reading [a Spanish] newspaper.' This new situation came about because she was able to order class sets of a Spanish newspaper, which came once a week, signifying a recent awakening to the availability of alternative curricular aids and texts.

This change, Nancy explained, was because her 'goals changed from month to month' as she grappled with the process of teaching and her views of herself as teacher. Moreover, it signalled a slight turn to her desire for a warm, personable, and humorous classroom. Another change came about because of her continuing responsiveness to students, and her feeling somewhat less vulnerable in the classroom. Weeks of following Nancy's new programme of relying on the textbooks had produced some negative effects: 'Scott entered the class, plopped down in his seat . . . and said, "Why is this class so boring?"' Normally she would have discounted his remark: 'Some days that may have pissed me off and I probably would have ignored it . . . but . . . I decided to address it [by] telling him he may have a valid point.' Instead of being crushed by the student's remarks, Nancy identified and listed some 'changes that [she] wanted to work on and keep fresh in mind' as she prepared. The changes included working on 'the discipline system', methods for controlling discussion ('open discussion until it gets out of control'), fewer book exercises and more activities for grammar, and more discussions ('conferencias').

By March, yet another round of changes followed as a result of a traumatic event that took place in the eighth-grade class. Throughout the year Nancy had been thwarted in her attempts to 'take action in [her] eighth-grade class'. This was because 'every time [she] took action,' as she said in early February, 'something unpleasant happened.' On several occasions her actions led to unpleasant talks with parents or feelings of anger at them when they completely bypassed her and went directly to the principal with complaints: 'I hate it when parents don't deal with me directly.' Such situations only heightened her feelings of anxiety and insecurity and she 'got on the defensive' about her practices when confronted by the principal or others.

The events associated with the last week in February were climactic and profound in their effect. The Wednesday was the day before her birthday and proved to be notorious:

> Got a nasty note on my door today. What a way to be greeted .... 'Fuck this class and Miss P. is a ... bitch.' ... I decided to ignore it .... It ... hurts ...I have no way of knowing who did it.

The next day, being her birthday, she 'decided to have a good day at the expense of everything else.' Up until the last period, the eighth-grade class, the 'day went well'. But, even as she heard the eighth-graders at their lockers in the hall outside the room, her stomach 'tightened' in 'knots' and she had 'an awful feeling'. For this day she had, yet another, 'new discipline method' to unfold on the class; this one used 'assertive discipline' techniques. This new plan was another attempt 'to improve their learning' and, as she explained, '[it] came out of a frustration at not seeing much progress from them.' Despite this and other 'new plans' the eighth-graders' behaviour had, compared to her other classes, improved imperceptibly. This particular class period proved to be little different from the myriad of others which had witnessed the students' disruptive and confrontive actions. It was as though they had returned to their December behaviour and Nancy's feelings of vulnerability returned with a vengeance. In desperation and frustration she burst into tears. The outpouring proved beneficial, although she was at first most embarrassed. She expressed many of her 'feelings about them and about teaching'. The students, like her, were surprised. Later, they were very subdued. On subsequent days even Barry – whom she suspected of writing the note on the door – was subdued and surprisingly pleasant: 'I don't feel they dislike me as much as before. Barry ... actually said, "Hello!" to me in the hall a couple of times. I was shocked . . . . This *is* a drastic change'.

While the eighth grade-class remained her nemesis there was a distinct change in her thinking about them. She felt that it had been 'most useful' for her to 'share her emotions' and let them know that she 'was a real person'. Soon afterwards Barry was considered for expulsion from the school. It was suspected that he wrote the note to Nancy that was left on the door and for that, and other long-standing behaviours, his continuation at the school was questioned. Central to some of the contentions about his obnoxious actions were Nancy's responses to him. On a number of occasions she had spent time with him in the principal's office trying to solicit improved behaviours. One of the side effects of the final discussions – and the ones that had gone before – about Barry's continuation in the school was that she sensed a validation of herself. She was not the only one who had difficulty with the boy, although, to be sure, her experiences were the most traumatic. Eventually, he was withdrawn by his father, a situation in which Nancy felt simultaneously 'bad' for the boy and 'relieved' and elated that she no longer had to contend with him. With Barry gone the class improved noticeably and she had fewer tension headaches which had returned.

In response to her discussion with the eighth-grade class she again made some changes. She increased the number of 'content-centred discussions' and group investigations and ventured into a broad range of topics including politics, especially about issues surrounding the countries of Central and Latin America. She introduced role playing, drama activities, and even tried meditation exercises, all in an endeavor to make the classes 'more interesting and relevant'. That this new phase was less stressful to Nancy was especially obvious because fewer of her journal entries focused on negative experiences. As a general observation she said that her lessons were now 'less scattered and . . . more cohesive'.

Another factor that helped Nancy during this period was a consistency in her time spent working at school; she completed school work at school. For the first time during the year she managed to arrange and keep to a regular routine. Normally she arrived most mornings around 8 o'clock. She found that by staying at school until about 5 o'clock in the afternoon she could often get her preparation completed. This contrasted greatly with her actions earlier in the year. Now, when she went home, 'the nights were so much more pleasant and so much longer ... [and] much more relaxed.'

Looking toward the future after spring break

Nancy entered the spring break feeling that her classes were, for the most part, going reasonably well. There were, she reported, fewer disruptions, a cause for great relief. But she was tired of teaching and the old feelings of resistance to working at the school resurfaced after the week-long vacation: 'I didn't want to go back . . . .I felt depressed and overwhelmed by the amount of work in store for me.' She was tired of disciplining students and of having to assert herself in the classroom, and of seeking their approval. Her relationships with the students were far from personally satisfying; and too little about teaching was pleasurable. More than anything, she longed for the end of the year which she joyously greeted: 'Hijole! ... It was a tough year!'

Nancy did not renew her contract at Markham Hall for the following year. Initially she expressed doubt as to whether the school would renew it, given her difficulties, but she may have thought that way because of her feelings of insecurity. She ended up leaving the state with her boyfriend and did not seriously seek a teaching position. She is now working for a small corporation and in her spare time has taught gymnastics – one of her 'loves' – and is teaching English as a second language to adult Hispanic immigrants, something that she has found success and reward in.

With distance between her and the first year of teaching at Markham Hall, Nancy has been able to make some observations about her performance. She saw herself as swelling the ranks of 'those who go through ... teacher training, ... teach, and then drop [out].' In some ways it felt 'like a failure' to her. But, she said, 'other times I think it's actually a success to have freed myself from seeing [teaching] as an obligation.' The idea of teaching being an obligation of Nancy's is important in light of her father's vision for her. Her response: 'Sometimes I feel that it's his voice that's holding me back from [doing] what I really want to do.'

IN SUMMARY

One of the difficulties in understanding Nancy's first year was the frequent shift in her thinking about herself as a teacher and working in classrooms. Her initial metaphor for teaching never represented her experience at Markham Hall and, as the year progressed, seemed further from her reach. To be a 'friend that knows what is best for students' did not result from the kinds of interactions that emerged from her teaching or from her dealings with students who did not quickly warm to her as she had hoped. Further, she was not able to negotiate productive relationships with them and her mood swings were evidence of the despair that she regularly felt about encountering sometimes very difficult, arrogant, privileged and challenging students. While her upbeat moods coincided with the more satisfying of teaching days, the more frequent downward mood swings only precipitated more disruptions in the classroom.

Nancy entered the first year of teaching with, essentially, conservative viewpoints about teaching which were initially enlightened by her enthusiasm for the 'immersion' approach to foreign-language teaching. The attempt to teach using principles which emphasized conversation was valiant, although there seemed to be an inherent mismatch between the method and Nancy's personality and she gradually employed the traditional grammar-based methods, by which she herself had learned the language as a student.

Nancy never clearly articulated a meaningful vision of herself as teacher. She vacillated in her approaches to discipline and instruction. As her instruction became, incrementally, more reliant on textbooks and resembled traditional methods, her thinking in other areas also became more conservative. Further, while she tried to implement the sugestions of others, she did so with little confidence or success. As a result, she was very uncertain about some of her new-found practices, especially those of disciplining and managing students; and she did not feel altogether comfortable with them or with her role in the classroom.

After the mid-year break Nancy slowly climbed out of the depths of discouragement, loneliness, and confusion about students, curriculum, and instruction that she had earlier felt. After listening to students' complaints about her classes, repeatedly modifying the curriculum and her instruction, crying in front of the eighth-grade class and, especially following the eventual removal of Barry from the school, the process accelerated only later to fade. Despite the tendency towards being more conservative, during the first half of the second semester Nancy approached teaching with a new enthusiasm. For that brief period, Nancy was more settled in her role as teacher, having identified a few effective strategies, and despite not being totally at ease, her classes occasionally approached the ideals represented by her original metaphor for teaching. Yet, despite the positive changes, for most of the year she had not met her own, perhaps unrealistic, expectations.

Following spring break many of Nancy's doubts returned. When the school doors finally closed at the end of the academic year, Nancy's commitment to the school and to teaching was low. She was especially disappointed by her inability to establish engaging relationships with the students. Not only did teaching tire her, but in class she lacked animation. The year had not been easy. She had been severely tested and in her own eyes had not passed the test. 'Teaching,' she concluded, 'in traditional classrooms may not be for me.'

4

RESCUING AND BEING RESCUED

MARILYN

Marilyn, a 45-year-old mother of two grown boys, wife of a
high-school counsellor, and recent graduate of the elementary
education programme always wanted to be a teacher: 'I've always
wanted to teach since I was in kindergarten. That's the truth.
That's all I ever wanted to do.' As Marilyn started school she
entered a new world that was very different from that of her home
and family: 'I was raised in a household where there wasn't much
affection shown to us kids from my parents. There wasn't affection
between my parents. They had a lousy marriage.' For Marilyn,
kindergarten became a refuge from the pain she felt at home, and
school became a haven where she was loved and cared for. Marilyn
explained:

> [School was] where I got my strokes. That's where somebody
> said, 'Nice job, Marilyn.' Nobody ever said that at home. So,
> that's a lot of why I want to [be a teacher]. Plus, now that I'm
> older and I've lived as long as I have and I know what my
> childhood meant . . . . I want to give what I can to kids who
> may be growing up in a house like I did.

After graduating from high school, Marilyn entered a large,
mid-western university and majored[1] in elementary education in
pursuit of her ambition to be a teacher. A year and a half later, she
quit school because of low grades and a desire to return home to
her family. While at home, Marilyn attended a local college for one
semester and then quit. Shortly thereafter, Marilyn married and
followed her army-officer husband across the country living in
three different locations. After her husband left the army, Marilyn

and her family settled down in a new location where Marilyn began working as a secretary in an inner-city elementary school, a job she held for six years. She liked being around teachers and being friends with them, and she liked the interaction with students because it gave her an opportunity to influence their lives positively. Marilyn enjoyed being associated with schools and teachers and, with a little encouragement from friends and family, returned to college to finish her degree in elementary education.

Marilyn completed her education by practice teaching a second-grade class (age 7 to 8) in a middle-class suburban school. From the beginning of practice teaching, Marilyn liked teaching, and described it as 'wonderful' and 'fulfilling'. Although she and her cooperating teacher differed in temperament and philosophy, Marilyn learned from her how to develop textbook-centred curriculum and how to use direct instruction methods. Having student taught in the spring and with a cooperating teacher who had a strong classroom-management system in place, Marilyn learned very little about classroom management. However, she anxiously looked forward to having a classroom of her own and felt confident that she could be an effective teacher.

Even before practice teaching had ended, Marilyn began telephoning school administrators seeking to locate possible teaching positions. It was a tight year in the job market and no firm leads turned up until late in July when Marilyn discovered that a principal she knew had a fifth-grade opening and was willing to interview her for the position. Marilyn was nervous and hesitant about the interview because she wanted to teach only in the lower grades. Despite her desire to teach younger children, when offered the position, she accepted it. Two weeks after the interview, and a week and a half before the start of school, Marilyn signed a contract to teach fifth-grade at Midvalley Elementary School.

WORK CONTEXT

Immediately after Marilyn was hired, she began learning all she could about the school. She discovered she was not the only new teacher in the building; there were two university intern teachers. Along with the interns,[2] Marilyn would be mentored by the school's "teacher facilitator", Dianne. One of the interns, Sam, was also a fifth-grade teacher. Joining Marilyn and Sam on the fifth-grade team was Barbara, the team leader, who had nineteen years of teaching experience and was considered an outstanding and supportive teacher.

Marilyn had thirty-two students in her classroom, part of a fifth-grade that was characterized as being composed of 'some of the toughest kids [ever in the school] ... everybody is making negative remarks [about them] ... [I'm told that] we're really in for it.' Marilyn seemed almost to welcome the large size and 'tough class' reputation of the students. She thought she might be able to make a positive difference in the lives of such students. Additionally, it gave her a reason to expect less of her students academically and, consequently, less would be expected of her. How could she be expected to be a 'perfect' teacher if she had to teach a lot of 'tough' students? As the year progressed, the 'tough' class situation proved to be a blessing and a curse for Marilyn.

EARLY METAPHORS

Marilyn's childhood experience produced a life-long ambition to become a teacher, yet those memories were surprisingly vague, as Marilyn confessed:

> I can't tell you anything that went on in any of my classrooms [as a child]. Nothing specific ... but I can tell you that I liked my teachers and in my mind I can see myself talking to them and they were always gentle. They were always positive.

School was a place were Marilyn had always felt cared for, and secure. Based upon these memories, Marilyn developed her conceptions of school, teaching, and self as teacher. From these experiences and feelings, two metaphors formed: 'teacher is haven-maker' and 'teacher is rescuer'.

As a 'haven-maker', Marilyn sought to create for herself and her students a refuge in the classroom, a place of security and love, like the one she had experienced long ago as an insecure child. But this was no ordinary haven, for Marilyn to feel secure it had to be highly structured. Although Marilyn fantasized herself as being a creative and spontaneous teacher, once in the classroom she 'decided to [adopt a highly] structured curriculum in order to reduce her anxieties about being a first-year teacher'. For Marilyn to feel secure in the classroom, the classroom environment needed to be predictable, and she needed to feel a strong sense of control. She sought to accomplish this aim through heavy reliance on textbooks. The teacher's edition of the textbook provided a daily road map of topics, assignments, and learning activities which she would follow. 'I love structure and the textbook gives me structure, I know what's happening today and tomorrow . . . . I go to the books and open them up and plan'.

Alongside her need for structure, Marilyn also sought, as an expression of her love for children, to be responsive to students' needs and interests. As she eventually discovered, this aspect of her 'haven-maker' metaphor proved to be contradictory and a source of continuing difficulty.

Marilyn had a second metaphor, 'teacher is rescuer'. This metaphor reflected her desire to give students the warmth, love, and positive self-esteem that she received as a child from teachers. When compared to the need to 'save children', academic learning played a secondary role. Such things as reading, writing, and arithmetic fit in somewhere between the primary focus to enhance students' self-concepts, make learning fun, and create a classroom where students felt loved and, especially, secure. Marilyn stated:

> At the risk of having students drop out of school when they reached junior and senior high school, I feel it is necessary to create an environment where the students feel needed and supported. It's a classroom where students develop positive attitudes towards themselves and school.

In order to become a 'rescuer' of children, Marilyn believed that as a teacher she would need to provide 'soothing and aiding and mothering' to her students. Moreover, she conceptualized teaching very broadly to include: '[her students'] problems at home and their problems with their friends . . . and, my problems at home'.

Finally, interwoven into the 'haven' and 'rescuer' metaphors was Marilyn's need to feel loved and wanted. Marilyn yearned to recapture the love and security in the classroom she felt as a child in school. In this way, being a teacher would be personally thera-peutic, and healing. Indeed, Marilyn came to envision teaching as a personal refuge from a world characterized by suffering and pain, a place where she could find happiness:

> To me [teaching] is not like a job. It's like if I had a place to choose . . . this is where I would be. [The classroom] is like

61

being in the best place I can be [because] I'm very happy here all day long.

PLANNING

Marilyn had little over a week to plan the first week's schedule and formulate the entire year's curriculum before school began. Marilyn started planning with what she knew best and, drawing on her experiences as a secretary, she organized the physical elements of the classroom, taking care of books, moving desks, and locating supplies. Yet, underneath her busy activity, she worried: 'I was really panicked about planning. It was like not knowing where to start'. Luckily, Sam and Dianne had got together and worked out a tentative schedule for the first week that included topics and activities broken up into fifteen- or thirty-minute segments. Sam offered the entire plan to Marilyn who took it and 'copied it word for word', except in a few places where she substituted other materials and ideas. For example, she inserted many of the school district's self-esteem programme activities in time slots where she did not like what Sam had planned. She explained that the first week would not contain 'a lot of academic work' so that relationships could be established in a non-threatening environment. The week would emphasize activities like puzzles and creative writing that would help the students and the teacher get to know one another.

The second week would begin the 'serious' learning including topics and activities of reading, math, social studies, and science – taken from the texts. The textbooks and Sam's first week's plans helped to ease Marilyn's concerns and provided her with a structure necessary to begin creating a 'haven'.

EARLY CONCERNS

Although planning the curriculum was difficult, Marilyn's greater concern was classroom management: 'planning management . . . makes me a nervous wreck'. Not having had experience as a classroom manager during practice teaching, Marilyn could not imagine herself as a manager. What images of classroom management she did possess came from her experiences as a school secretary. Marilyn was aware, for example, that students could easily become unruly and facing frequent misbehaviour, teachers can become complacent or abusive:

I saw some things that went on [in that school] that were
inconceivable to me ... like when I saw a child get out of
control or ... [saw] a teacher drag a student down the
hall ... that's what my fear is in an upper grade classroom.

Lacking positive images and ideas for classroom management and
desperately wanting help, Marilyn was open to virtually any
suggestion. She adopted Midvalley's school-wide discipline
strategy called the Point Out System: '[Their discipline programme]
is something I had never heard of. It's called the "Point Out
System". When this school opened four years ago the Principal put
it into effect.' The Point Out System was a modification of assertive
discipline with the addition of a 'time-out' desk. The plan was
simple: if a student was disruptive, the teacher would point to a
desk at the back of the room where the student was to go and work
quietly. If there were further student violations, then the teacher
would point to the door – point the child out – and the student
would go to another teacher's room and sit in the back of that
room. Although she now had a system to follow, Marilyn still was
unable to see herself as a classroom manager. Feeling insecure,
during the week prior to school, she role-played using the Point
Out System.

SCHOOL BEGINS: THE RESCUER AND HAVEN-MAKER
EMERGE

Marilyn planned the first day of school carefully, and after it was
over she was not disappointed with the results: 'It was everything I
hoped it would be, and more.' She explained: 'I love the
fifth-graders [partially because] I can talk to them about more
sophisticated ideas'. As Marilyn spoke about the day, the 'teacher
is rescuer' metaphor was evident:

Being a teacher is like the lady in the Nutcracker who has the
large dress and gathers the [children around her]. I feel that
way. It's a gathering of them close to you.

During the first days of school Marilyn was happy as she began
playing out her 'rescuer' metaphor, loving and caring for students,
and began making her classroom 'haven' – a highly structured and
predictable learning environment. Marilyn thrived on structure:
'Fridays are really [routinized]. They're wonderful. I have a

structure and I bend it and mold it around that makes it easier to plan.' It was on Fridays that she planned for the entire next week: '[Using the textbook] I sit down on Friday and [plan] what page we are on next in the English book and what social studies page we are on and what we are going to do.'

Each day was routinely scheduled with reading, language arts and math in the morning. The afternoon included spelling, science, health, and art. Each subject was highly routinized, emphasizing direct, whole-group instruction and textbook activities. For instance, reading instruction came right out of a Science Research Associates, Inc. programme, a scripted curriculum of stories, questions, and workbooks. Even art was highly structured: 'sometimes the art lessons require the use of dittoed sheets and standard images. I dittoed [duplicated] a 4 page art project.' Social studies involved the students' reading the textbooks, answering questions at the end of chapter, and participating in discussions. Marilyn's discussions were also routinized, being guided by questions taken from the teacher's manual. Standing in front of the class with the manual cradled in her arms, Marilyn read the questions from the manual and then called on students to answer them. At times, the discussion strayed from the list of questions, but soon Marilyn would pull the discussion back on track by referring to the next question in the teacher's manual.

CONFLICTS EMERGE

Within the first few weeks of school, conflicts between her two metaphors became apparent. Her need for structure and her desire to respond to students' interests were at odds. She lamented:

> I looked at the books and realized what we're supposed to cover. That was what was on my mind. I must push, push, push. Of course, I realized that nobody would enjoy going to school if that's all they did all day long.

Despite Marilyn's frustrations with textbooks, she was not willing to risk the insecurity created by abandoning them. Her inner need for security took precedence over her professional need to make the curriculum engaging. For instance, Marilyn wanted to teach more science with hands-on activities. The tools were available to do so: she had available in the school a science lab full of items to use, booklets for each child, and teacher's manuals. She stated: 'I feel [science] is important but I'm not doing it very much this year.' This was because once, in an attempt to make the curriculum more interesting, she taught a science lesson using a 'lab' approach and 'the students [got] out of control – so noisy and inattentive. I couldn't take it . . . my anxieties shot up . . . and I couldn't teach that way'. She concluded that she dare not stray from the textbook: 'I'm not comfortable using things like that'.

Within this highly structured program, and when Marilyn felt in control, she found small ways of expressing the vision of herself as 'rescuer'. She used tests and grades as vehicles to 'save' the students from hurt and pain. For example, through making *ad hoc* adjustments in individual student's grades she thought she could fight discouragement and low self-esteem, and yet maintain a highly structured curriculum. She described grading a boy's social studies assignment this way:

> We did reports on the states [and] the kid who is going to drop out of school the soonest, if we're not real careful, [handed in] a rough draft of the report. But it wasn't supposed to be a rough draft; the words were misspelled and he didn't include everything in it. But, I gave him a 'C' on it. I didn't give him a 'D' or 'F' because it would have damaged his self-esteem.

In the name of rescuing students, Marilyn could justify the inconsistencies which her grading produced.

> I'll give one kid a . . . 'C' in something and another kid a 'C' and they won't exactly have the same type of grade in reality. But . . . it's okay to give the two people the same grade even if both of them didn't do exactly the same kind of work.

Marilyn also used tests as a means for building student self-esteem and confidence.

> [I] make the tests easy. I want high grades. I want them to feel good . . . So far, I've made the quizzes I've given simple. I want them to have successes . . . I've looked at some of the chapter tests from books that are already made up. I think I'm not going to test them on all that. If I ask them to memorize it or whatever, I know that they'll fail it.

During the first few weeks of school, using the structured lesson plans borrowed from Sam and Dianne, and relying on the textbooks, Marilyn worked hard to establish a structured and secure environment in which to work. However, her need to establish a secure and predictable 'haven' for herself and her students conflicted with her need to be responsive to the students and to 'rescue' them through love and warmth. The conflicts produced by her metaphors made Marilyn feel uneasy and anxious about teaching and sent a mixed message to the students which further complicated her problems with classroom management.

TENSIONS INCREASE

Marilyn was unable to establish a consistent classroom-management system. She lamented:

> I have not been consistent in my discipline. Sometimes I let some talking out go on and won't say anything or won't point anybody out. I know I have to be consistent with everyone and not be unfair to anybody else.

She was uncertain about who she was as a classroom-manager. She confessed: 'Everybody says be real firm the very first day. I thought I was ... so I find out the third week I was not firm enough because now they're just getting more and more out of hand.'

By the middle of October, and in the midst of the rising anxiety levels and classroom noise levels, Marilyn discovered, albeit serendipitously, that school policy included a referral system designed to deal quickly with disruptive students. Marilyn learned about the policy while observing one of Dianne's lessons: 'John talked back to [Dianne] ... and she told him about referrals ... and that was the first time I'd [had heard about them]. He talked back to me today, so I wrote a referral.' The referral system provided Marilyn with an anchor in her foggy framework of management strategies. A referral was warranted if a student violated just one of the school rules and the consequences were established as a matter of school policy. A recurring referral meant being sent immediately to the principal's office where a variety of actions might be taken.

However, knowing about referrals and the Point Out System did not help Marilyn develop a conception of herself as classroom manager nor did it help her develop consistent patterns for dealing with student misbehaviour. Marilyn struggled to define herself as classroom manager and to understand the relationship between being a disciplinarian and that of being a 'rescuer' and 'haven-maker'. She realized that being a disciplinarian was not an element of either metaphor and was incongruent with both conceptions of herself as teacher. Indeed, providing order in the classroom and having students follow her commands would, in her mind, create unhappy, disaffected students. Under such conditions, Marilyn's need to provide a 'haven' would be compromised. Furthermore, she wondered how she could be an authoritative teacher and still be caring and comforting to her students, the 'rescuer'.

Unable to find an acceptable definition of herself as a classroom manager, Marilyn continued to struggle, and her anxieties about teaching and feelings of incompetence skyrocketed: 'I'm grouchy [and] I'm the one that is getting myself all worked up. Then I take it out on the students. That's not how teaching is supposed to be.'

Her classroom was often out of control. For example, she tried getting students to quiet down by counting to five. If they were not settled when she reached five, punishments were to follow. So, she counted, and counted, and counted, in frustration. And, the students talked and talked and talked. Marilyn described the 'counting to five' ritual performed throughout the day this way:

> We go four and three-quarters. We get to four and nine-tenths, sometimes [the students say] 'She said four and nine-tenths. The next one is five. Be quiet you guys.' One of the kids will do that, [say] 'Quiet everybody!' . . . then I just wait. Then they'll quiet down.

The tension and disorder continued. And, through it all, Marilyn ploughed ahead and taught her lessons out of the textbook and over the chatter, all the while yearning for the security of a 'haven'.

Amid the turmoil of her own classroom, Marilyn searched for ideas about how to become a classroom manager. She sought help from Barbara, the fifth-grade teacher and leader across the hall, and received some disturbing advice. Barbara was firm and direct. She told Marilyn that management strategies without consequences were inappropriate and harmful to the classroom environment, and that she should develop and enforce a sound set of consequences for disruptive behaviour. Marilyn was devastated: 'I didn't have any consequences [other than issuing referrals]. I was a nervous wreck . . . I shouldn't be teaching. I'm going to fail. I don't have consequences!'

Barbara's remarks only increased Marilyn's feelings of vulnerability. After seeking aid and comfort from Barbara, Marilyn found herself feeling even more alone in the classroom and ineffective as a teacher; the stark reality of not having a conception of herself as classroom manager and the consequences of such a void were terrifying. The few remaining remnants of the 'haven' were crushed; and she felt nothing like a 'rescuer'. Marilyn wondered, what to do? Who should she be as a classroom manager? And how did being a disciplinarian fit in with being a 'rescuer'? How could she create a 'haven' – a place of comfort and warmth – amid the responsibilities of enforcing rules and consequences? And so, Marilyn wondered: should she ignore Barbara's advice or ignore student misbehaviour? Feeling at a loss she began to question whether or not she should leave teaching. Leaving teaching meant leaving more than a job, however, it meant abandoning a lifetime ambition. Unable to leave teaching, and unable to establish herself as a classroom manager, a 'rescuer', and a 'haven-maker', Marilyn continued to be inconsistent in managing student behaviour, and put up with, and ignored, her noisy, bored, and distracted students.

By the end of November Marilyn looked worn out. The strain of dealing with the uncomfortable noise level and her constant reminders to students to be quiet took their toll. Each day was a battle to gain control. With increasing anxiety, Marilyn lamented:

> I see everything as a gigantic mountain . . . that I have to go over. I don't see things in little steps . . . [rather], it's just everything is out there – ready to get me.

Marilyn was miserable. Moreover, life outside the classroom provided little rest and relaxation from the pressures of work. In fact, the weekends and holidays seemed only to intensify her feelings of anxiety. The fear of failure, the feelings of incompetence, the feelings of being overwhelmed, and the sense that things were out of control in the classroom, played on her mind. However, oddly, returning to the classroom and her students each Monday morning somehow softened many of her anxieties. Seeing the children and, remembering the importance of positive and loving relationships like those she experienced long ago in a kindergarten class, revived in her some of the images of her fantasized teacher 'rescuing' role. She commented in her journal:

I must write. I was worried about myself when I came to school this morning. Over the long Thanksgiving weekend (in late November) I was rather down on my self concerning my teaching capabilities. Up until the moment I went outside to greet my students . . . I was feeling inadequate. However, as soon as I saw my students, my feelings of inadequacy vanished! I have experienced this before – maybe three or four times this year.

However, by Friday the joy had faded and, feeling battle-weary and fatigued, the weekends offered only grief and increased anxiety.

The classroom was far from enjoyable, comfortable, secure, and predictable – it was a miserable place to be. Her inconsistent management of the classroom, above all else, was the magnifying glass that illuminated her unsettled conception of herself as teacher. She searched among her metaphors of 'rescuer' and 'haven-maker' for images of herself as disciplinarian. She came up with only contradictions. How could there be security and comfort amid the turmoil of disciplining the students she loved and worried about? How could students feel loved and needed when she constantly yelled? And, she furthered wondered: how could a fun and exciting curriculum exist when 'getting through' the textbook curriculum was the aim? Marilyn's need to fill in her definition of herself as a classroom manager was destroying her ability to function as a teacher. Moreover, Marilyn's desire to establish a 'haven' was in jeopardy, for how could she be a saviour of children when she needed to be saved herself?

IN NEED OF RESCUING

Needing to resolve her glaring management problems and relieve her growing anxiety, Marilyn looked to be rescued. She was not shy about asking for help: 'I'm not afraid to ask for help . . . I'm not embarrassed to say that something is wrong.' Similarly, as when a child in the classroom, Marilyn searched for strength from the teachers.

Within the school Marilyn found the help she needed. For example, Dianne was responsive and made herself available several times a week to observe Marilyn and teach lessons for her. Marilyn explained: 'I [go] to Dianne constantly, [and] ask her to come to [my] classroom and help. To teach this lesson or whatever. To give me some ideas and help me.' Having Dianne teach in Marilyn's class served several purposes. It gave Marilyn more time to plan. On one occasion, Marilyn remarked: 'Dianne taught different lessons . . . that freed me to work on report cards.' And, although, Dianne may have only substituted for one or two forty-five minute lessons a week, it was enough to help Marilyn lower her anxiety by not having to face the noise and disruptions of the classroom. Additionally, Marilyn was able to observe an experienced and excellent teacher who modelled effective practices. Marilyn commented on the value of those observations in her journal: 'I know I need to change most of my strategies for dealing with discipline. I know because of what I learn when I observe Dianne'.

However, Dianne's influence began to go beyond merely teaching classes and modelling effective practice; Marilyn became dependent on her. Dianne helped with curriculum planning, sometimes, on a moment's notice. Marilyn reported: '[The teacher interns and I] meet on Fridays for an hour. She gives us some great ideas to do. Her number one thing is self-esteem, and of course, learning. . . . I pull some of her ideas out.' In effect, Dianne became Marilyn's rescuer, functioning like a therapist, and assisting in every way to build Marilyn's self-esteem. Unlike Barbara's advice about consequences that had devastated Marilyn and highlighted her management inconsistencies, Dianne admonished: 'Don't worry! It's okay [because] you don't have to have a consequence for what happens when you get to five . . . I'll bet you they'll quiet down before you ever get there.' Marilyn's took Dianne to mean, 'Oh, just relax. It's not a big deal.'

Dianne's encouragement and Marilyn's interpretation of it obscured Marilyn's problems in coming to terms with classroom management. Implementing her suggestions had no effect on student behaviour. However, Dianne's comforting did have the effect of lowering Marilyn's anxiety, even if temporarily, as Marilyn gratefully observed:

> Two weeks ago I was concerned about discipline. I thought they were getting out of line too much. I thought I wasn't having enough control. Then I talked with Dianne and she just made me realize that I can relax a little bit.

In response, Marilyn began more and more to ignore student misbehaviour: 'I'm remaining calmer and ignoring a lot of [bad] behavior.'

Dianne was not Marilyn's only rescuer. She was also cared for by the principal who volunteered to teach a lower-level math group composed of twenty fifth-graders which included seven very disruptive children. The principal responded with the assurance that at least two teachers would be available to help Marilyn with the class which, oddly, at first, Dianne took every day, but Thursday. However, other obligations soon took Dianne out of the math class and Marilyn was left with the dreadful prospect of teaching it alone. Almost immediately, the principal responded by assigning Brenda, a resource teacher for the upper grades, the task of teaching the math class.

Brenda came into the class and took charge immediately. Marilyn's responsibility was to take care of the related administrative duties and to offer one-on-one attention to students. Marilyn was relieved of the burden of teaching and was given the opportunity to work individually with students and thereby establish closer relationships with them, a central component of being a rescuer herself. Having Brenda in the classroom every day provided Marilyn with another opportunity to observe and work closely with an outstanding teacher who was effective with disruptive students. Marilyn explained one day after the math group left the room: 'I need the help. I really have learned a lot about discipline and running a class from having [Brenda] in here.'

Despite the rescuing attempts of Dianne, Brenda, Barbara, and the principal, at mid year Marilyn's management inconsistency persisted. Although she was, at times, aware of her inconsistency, she seemed helpless to resolve the problem. And, despite the support that other teachers gave her, she continued to be fraught with self-doubts. As fall turned into winter, and still seeking help, Marilyn enrolled, along with several other Midvalley teachers, in a management class offered by the school district entitled, 'Elementary Solution Book Training'. She explained: 'These classes cover behavior management techniques which are appropriate for elementary age students. After three classes I have learned many things I can do to improve the learning atmosphere in my classroom.' The classroom-management course came at a time of great need, offered her emotional support and gave her suggestions about implementing various methods. Additionally, Marilyn found some relief, and felt less isolated, as she listened to other teachers complain about their problems in class.

With instruction on the use of assertive discipline and a better understanding of the Point Out System, Marilyn believed that she had found a structured approach for management. However, the knowledge she gained in the class did not help her resolve the conflicts between images of herself as teacher. She continued to search for understanding about the relationships between being a classroom manager and also being a 'rescuer' and 'haven-maker'. How could she build student self-esteem while she was now, more than ever, punishing them for misbehaviour? How could the classroom become a 'haven' – comfortable, secure, and enjoyable – while she was becoming increasingly strict toward the students?

Answers to these questions did not come easily. Struggling with them was fatiguing, and made her tense and on edge. At times she was very depressed about teaching and insecure about her teaching potential. The weekends remained long and painful although seeing the students on Mondays, when they gathered around her prior to the start of the school day, brought momentary relief. In consequence of her deepening depression and growing anxiety, she sought help from a professional therapist.

CONFLICTS CONTINUE

February found Marilyn adrift. Solutions to her management problems remained elusive and she continued either to ignore them or to relax more when problems occurred. She continued to deal inconsistently with students, and thereby negated the value of the district management class. Amid the confusion, in late March an incident occurred that was particularly revealing, and that had an appreciable effect on Marilyn's anxiety which was proving to be immobilizing. She reported:

It was a Friday afternoon planning time. I walked out into the hall and the Principal was coming down the hall to give me something. She said, 'How are you?' I said, 'To tell you the truth I'm really getting burned out.' She said, 'Everybody [feels like] that about this time of the year'. ... I told my therapist that I had been more relaxed since that happened. She [said] ... I was giving myself permission to be announced as 'o.k.' To be there and to be burned out if I wanted to be burned out. I didn't have to try to hide it. So,

72

that was the beginning. Ever since then I've just become more and more relaxed.

The incident revealed how dependent Marilyn was on others for her sense of self and for her feelings of self-worth. But, more than anything, the principal's remarks justified Marilyn and gave her permission to be inconsistent without having to resolve the tensions she was feeling. In effect, the principal and the therapist redefined for her the nature of her problems with management, and thereby reduced the expectations she had for herself. Marilyn felt relieved, and less anxious, as a result.

YEAR'S END

As March turned into April tensions between Marilyn's teaching metaphors, 'teacher is haven-maker' and 'teacher is rescuer', remained. She continued to use the textbook for structure and guidance yet, in doing so, she undermined her desire to be responsive to students' interests. With six weeks of school remaining, a new dimension was added to the conflict, time was running out and she had covered only half of the textbook material. In an attempt to deal with the situation within the limited time constraints, Marilyn began 'picking and choosing' lessons from the texts. Inadvertently, feeling pressured to 'cover the textbooks' but being unable to cover all the content, Marilyn found herself less bound to them. She selected from the texts several activities of interest to the students while skipping some topics and activities that were less engaging. While she continued to emphasize duplicated sheets and workbooks, to read out of the textbook, and ask student questions from the teacher edition, other types of activities began to creep into the curriculum such as fun puzzles and end of the year projects.

Despite this subtle shift, Marilyn ended the year much as she began it with both metaphors intact and their contradictions unresolved. Furthermore, by the end of the school year, Marilyn's image of herself as a classroom manager remained unclear, and her problems with classroom management, although slightly less severe, endured. In May, she lamented: 'My discipline is lacking, somewhat. Today, for instance, the kids were pretty noisy'. However, despite her inability to define herself as a classroom manager and to be consistent in handling misbehaviour, Marilyn, at times, did demonstrate improved management skills especially through the use of assertive discipline and the Point Out System: 'I'm giving more [referrals] to them. The first half of the year I hardly gave any'. Also her transitions between activities became more directed and purposeful. And she became less willing to ignore misbehaviour and more willing to address it aggressively. Often, at year's end, raising her arm to signal 'quiet' resulted in a greater reduction in the classroom noise level. Overall, the students offered less resistance to her. Yet she was unsure as to why they did. For example, she stated: 'I don't think I'm getting tougher. I really don't. [But] they know when I put my arm up . . . what it means.'

Although encouraged by her momentary displays of management skill, Marilyn remained tentative and insecure. Every day was a battle with the students for control of the classroom. She ended the school year worrying and wondering about how to establish a 'haven-like' classroom, and to rescue and express her love for her students, while needing to discipline them forcefully.

IN SUMMARY

Marilyn wanted to be a teacher from the time she entered kindergarten and discovered in the classroom a world of affection and stability she had not known in her family. Marilyn's conceptions of teaching, school, and of herself as teacher derived from her family and school experiences, including when she was a secretary in an elementary school. From these experiences, two metaphors formed: 'teacher is haven-maker' and 'teacher is rescuer'. As a 'haven-maker', Marilyn sought a classroom environment that was secure and predictable, a place where she and her students would feel loved and cared for. She sought to accomplish this aim through heavy reliance on the textbook. However, Marilyn's 'rescuer' metaphor demanded that she be responsive to students' needs and interests. From the beginning of the school year, both metaphors were at odds with each other. Feeling insecure, Marilyn structured each school day and each subject around the adopted textbooks with the result that the students quickly became bored and uninterested, restless and disruptive. Within this highly structured programme, Marilyn found ways of expressing her 'rescuer' metaphor in a variety of ways, including giving students higher grades than they otherwise deserved which she felt would help build self-esteem. In the name of rescuing students, Marilyn could justify inconsistencies in grading and dealing with student misbehaviour.

However, the conflicts produced by competing metaphors made Marilyn feel uneasy, anxious about teaching, and unsure of herself as a teacher. Uncertain about who she was as teacher, and lacking requisite knowledge and skills that might have aided her in her struggle for professional identity, Marilyn was unable to define herself as a classroom manager. She was adrift in an ocean of student misbehaviour which she eventually tried to ignore, following repeated failed attempts to gain control. By the end of each week of school, Marilyn was extremely fatigued and mentally exhausted by the battle with the students. Weekends offered little relief and by Sunday evening the thought of facing another week packed with student misbehaviour was depressing and nearly overwhelming. Happily, the smiles on her students' faces early Monday morning would dispel much of her anxiety which would, however, return by week's end.

Eventually, Marilyn sought to be rescued. She returned to a professional therapist, attended a classroom-management workshop, learned more about her own school's discipline system, and sought help from her colleagues at school who responded favourably. By year's end Marilyn had improved in her ability to manage the classroom, but she did not come to terms with her conflicting conceptions of herself as teacher. She did, however, feel cared for and loved by Dianne, Brenda, the principal and the members of her team. With this knowledge, and recognizing that her classes were better at the end of the year than they were at the beginning, she found reason to be optimistic about the future and about herself as teacher. She held tightly to the memory of what had gone well, especially of her good relationships with some students, and found confidence in the care and concern shown by others. After all, that others within the school had worked so hard to assist her and had gone to such lengths to build her self-esteem, most assuredly meant that she could become a good teacher: 'I knew I could be a good teacher . . . [I knew] because I've had so much help.'

5

SURVIVING AND LEARNING
TO TEACH

INTRODUCTION

Ryan (1986) suggests that, when becoming a teacher, teachers go through four loose but distinguishable stages, the first three of which are of interest to us here: the fantasy, survival, and mastery stages. While the cases presented suggest that the boundaries separating the stages, especially the survival and mastery stages, are blurred, and their relationship is not obviously sequential, they none the less are useful for speaking about these teachers' experience. The fantasy stage, most noticeable in Marilyn's experience, begins when a person 'starts to think seriously about becoming a teacher' (p. 10). During the fantasy stage, which often lasts only through the first few days of teaching, the beginning teacher is euphoric as she begins to test her teaching schema and establishes seemingly self-confirming relationships with students. The survival stage of learning to teach begins with the discovery of inadequacy of various kinds which crushes the fantasy and ushers in a fight for one's professional survival. For most beginning teachers it is the struggle to establish and maintain classroom control that destroys the fantasy:

> At some time during their first year, teachers often experience 'critical incidents' to do with discipline. Frequently these incidents take the form of a direct challenge to their authority, and thereby their professional identity. If teachers keep control and resolve the situation, it seems that their identity as a competent teacher is strengthened – both in the eyes of pupils with whom they are

likely to have 'easier' relationships; and of other staff who begin to respect them as fellow professionals.

(Sikes, *et al.*, 1985: 29)

The survival stage, which encompasses the 'reality shock' discussed by Veenman (1984), may be short or long in duration and of greater or lesser intensity. The challenge encountered by the beginning teacher is to negotiate a place in the school and a set of relationships that provide a satisfactory level of security and belonging, respect and self-esteem, and a sense of personal competence. Without these needs being fulfilled, as Gehrke (1981) implies, it is unlikely that a satisfactory transition into teaching can take place. Ironically, some of the means beginning teachers employ to fulfil these needs may in fact work against their ultimately being successful at role negotiation, as shortly will be noted. The mastery stage of learning to teach, which is somewhat inappropriately labelled, is the 'craft stage, where the new teacher begins to learn the craft of teaching in a step-by-step fashion' (p. 14). It is at this point that the beginning teacher, feeling reasonably confident and secure in the classroom, starts to focus more or less systematically on the improvement of teaching which results in an increased level of influence over the teaching situation.

For the three teachers, the survival stage was both long, lasting until year's end for Larry and Nancy, and of great, although eventually lessening, intensity. Indeed, not one of these teachers, in contrast to those discussed in part II, achieved the mastery stage; instead they continued to react to their situations and not control them. For each, and again in contrast to the teachers in part II, the central challenge was associated with gaining and maintaining classroom control and proved to be nearly overwhelming, driving them to consider seriously whether or not they should remain in teaching. Nancy did not return. In this chapter we seek to understand what happened to these teachers and why they spent most of the school year struggling to survive.

CONTROL PROBLEMS

As noted in the case studies, for each of the teachers discipline and management problems began early and intensified throughout the first several weeks of school. Within the first few days of school Larry, for example, felt that he had been 'taken to the cleaners' by the students who openly defied his efforts to control them. Similarly, shortly after school began Marilyn and Nancy, especially within her eighth-grade second year Spanish class, found themselves in a struggle with the students over who would control the classroom. None of the teachers knew quite what to do to gain control and each engaged in a kind of desperate experimentation, seeking virtually any strategy that promised relief. At one point, for example, Larry gave tokens and rewards to his seventh-period class, despite the offence such actions presented to his inner self, after concluding he could no longer continue to expel them from class. Responding to the suggestions of the teacher facilitator and the team leader, Marilyn used the Point Out System and counted to five as means of trying to gain control, neither of which 'worked' effectively. Finally, she tried assertive discipline. While seeking to be a 'buddy' to her students, Nancy did not know what to do to gain control of her classes, especially the eighth-grade class: buddies did not discipline buddies. Following the Christmas break, and with new-found energy and determination, Nancy experimented with a variety of discipline strategies with some success. It was not until late in the school year, and following a tearful outburst and the suspension from school of Barry, one of the ringleaders of the students causing her grief, that Nancy felt she enjoyed a reasonable level of control over her classes.

THE PROBLEM CONSIDERED

It is tempting to dismiss the difficulties the three teachers had with establishing classroom control as simply a reflection of their lack of teaching skill; they were poorly 'trained'. While lack of skill and of knowledge of available techniques obviously did have something to do with the severity of their control problems, the issue goes much deeper than this. Given our interest in teacher socialization and development, the issue needs to be considered in terms of the interaction of the teachers in context and in relationship to the meanings associated with this interaction. We begin, then, with a general point applicable in varying degrees to any type of professional socialization (Soder, 1988), but of particular relevance to teacher socialization: all professionals learn their jobs while performing them; beginning teachers, as Wildman and his colleagues remind us, learn to teach while teaching.

> Although no one would disagree that beginning teachers must teach, we often ignore the fact that beginners have much to learn about teaching and little knowledge related to this new role. Moreover, they must learn it quickly if they are to survive. (Wildman, Niles, Magliaro and McLaughlin, 1989: 471–72).

As learners about teaching, beginning teachers face a daunting problem: while teaching, they must demonstrate skills and abilities they do not yet possess:

> The paradox of learning a really new competence is this: that a student cannot at first understand what he needs to learn, can only learn it by educating himself through self-discovery, and can only educate himself by beginning to do what he does not yet understand. (Schon, 1987: 85).

In the face of this paradox – really more a problem than a paradox – beginning teachers are highly vulnerable to criticism and to feelings of failure; and even the best educated and most able and emotionally secure of beginning teachers face moments of frustration and self-doubt, feeling perhaps a bit like Nancy when she commented in January, 'I feel like I'm letting everyone down.' Moreover, the work of teaching itself, which Clark describes as 'complex, uncertain, and peppered with dilemmas' (1988: 9), sharpens and deepens the paradox as at every turn the beginning teacher is reminded in various and powerful ways by students, other teachers, and by small private and personal disappointments, of what she cannot do or does not understand.

The specific school context into which the beginning teacher enters to start teaching either helps or hinders resolution of the paradox. Some contexts increase the teacher's vulnerability and the difficulty of learning to teach and forging a satisfactory teaching role and self-understanding. Larry's situation serves as a prime example. Not only was he assigned to teach out of his subject areas, he was assigned to teach perhaps the worse performing and behaving students in the school, students that even experienced teachers had some difficulty controlling and sought to avoid. Moreover, he did not have an assigned mentor, nor was he given any assistance early in the year with curriculum planning or with planning for discipline and management. In effect, during the first several weeks of school, Larry was virtually on his own. Under similar conditions the other first-year teacher in the school left teaching crushed emotionally. It was only after this teacher's resignation that the principal sent another teacher to check and see how Larry was doing and modest assistance followed. And further, within the teacher culture of the school, the teaching role he was implicitly expected to embrace and to which in large measure he eventually accommodated, 'teacher is policeman', was deeply disturbing.

In contrast to Larry's situation, both Marilyn and Nancy entered schools characterized by warm and caring faculty relations and supportive administrators. And yet they responded very differently to these contexts: Marilyn took advantage of the opportunities for professional development offered her; Nancy did not, for the most part. Thus, context must be considered in relationship to the person. Although initially fearful of having to teach fifth instead of second grade, Marilyn expressed her feelings of vulnerability rather openly and sought assistance wherever she could obtain it. She made good use of the school resources and came to rely on other teachers within the building not only for ideas but for actual assistance within the classroom with the students. It is our view that without this high level of support Marilyn probably would not have finished the school year.

Nancy entered a private school to teach Spanish, her minor area of study. Compared to her public school counterparts, like Larry, she had a very light teaching load, perhaps involving a third fewer student contact hours and 40 per cent fewer students. In addition, she had her own classroom, while Larry travelled between two rooms on opposite ends of the building, and an office which she shared with two other foreign-language teachers. She had ample opportunity to prepare lessons, to observe other teachers in the classroom, and to have other teachers visit her classroom to observe her teach and give feedback on her performance. Despite these opportunities, as Nancy sought to find herself as teacher and establish satisfactory and self-confirming relations with the students, she remained, for the most part, to herself and on the fringes of the faculty. For instance, she only rarely visited her office preferring, instead, to stay alone in her classroom. Moreover, even when she experienced her worst days with the students, Nancy only occasionally requested assistance, preferring to share her frustrations with her increasingly uninterested boyfriend and occasionally her parents. Like some of the teachers in Nias' study (1989), she protected herself, and gained a small measure of self-respect, by relying on out-of-school referents, which only increased her sense of disengagement. More will be said shortly about the influence of coping strategies of this kind on beginning teachers.

A RETURN TO SELF-CONCEPTIONS

The teaching schema, brought to the classroom by beginners, and the conceptions of self-as-teacher and attendant images around which they revolve as reflected in their metaphors, either enable or limit resolution of the paradox just as more generally they have a profound effect on teacher development. The meanings that beginning teachers bring with them provide the initial content for, as well as the backdrop against which, the internal conversation discussed by Blumer takes place. Through this conversation the context is interpreted and made more or less sensible and, through trial and error means, meanings are tested and adjusted, just as sometimes adjustments in the context are sought in order to achieve a productive course of action. It is this process that Schon characterizes as 'reflection-in-action' (1983; 1987). In effect, and again following Blumer (1969), the schema and the meanings that compose the teaching self frame how the situation or context is understood and what is seen as problematical. Moreover, the schema frames how problems are understood and how they are addressed by establishing what solutions or courses of action are seen as possible and desirable.

From this viewpoint, a central aspect of teacher socialization and development is the evolution of teachers' thinking about problems (Livingston and Borko, 1989). Echoing the premises of symbolic interactionism, Schon (1983) further develops this point when he states that:

In real world practice, problems do not present themselves to the practitioner as givens. They must be constructed from the materials or problematic situations that are puzzling, troubling and uncertain ... When we set the problem we select what we will treat as the 'things' of the situation, we set the boundaries of our attention to it, and we impose upon it

81

a coherence which allows us to say what is wrong and in what directions the situation needs to be changed. Problem setting is a process in which, interactively, we name the things to which we will attend and frame the context in which we will attend to them. (p. 40)

Learning how to set and frame problems productively is central to the successful resolution of the paradox faced by beginning teachers. And in this process it makes a great deal of difference if the beginning teacher enters the teaching context with a relatively complete teaching schema, *and* that the meanings associated with it, particularly those attached to self-as-teacher, are not only reasonably well developed and coherent but also fitting to the situation. In effect, and despite the overall uncertainty and insecurity felt when first confronting and grappling with the paradox of learning to teach, a comparatively well-developed teaching schema (well-developed for beginners, we should add) offers the beginning teacher a relatively firm, but inevitably partial, base upon which to build richer, fuller, and more powerful and productive meanings useful for framing and responding to problems and thereby shaping the situation. Moreover, coherence and fit enable the beginning teacher to function in the classroom with at least some degree of consistency and predictability which is especially important to obtaining and maintaining an acceptable degree of classroom control.

Beginning teachers whose teaching schemas are poorly developed and whose conceptions of themselves as teachers are weak, confused, or contradictory, like Larry, Nancy, and Marilyn, or, on the other extreme, very well developed but rigid and poorly fitting, face a potentially devastating challenge. While becoming a teacher always involves a measure of un-learning, for the later individuals, who are of only passing interest here, the challenge is to remake their conceptions of themselves as teachers completely or to find or create a situation within which their conceptions are fitting, if they wish to remain in teaching. For the former, the paradox is complicated by the necessity of, in a sense, discovering who they are while on the job and in relationship to establishing other meanings essential to possessing a productive teaching schema.

Understanding the effects of poorly developed, weak, confused, or contradictory teaching schemas and especially conceptions of self as teacher in beginning teachers' attempts to forge a productive teaching role, will help explain the different reactions of the three teachers to their respective teaching contexts and bring us closer to an explanation for their prolonged sojourn in the survival stage of learning to teach. Three questions focus the discussion that follows: How did these teachers frame problems, and what resolutions were seen as possible and reasonable? And, given their weak, confused, or contradictory teaching self-concepts, how did they obtain a measure of satisfaction, security, respect, self-esteem and competence?

METAPHORS AND PROBLEM FRAMING

Larry

Larry had only a weak and very partial conception of himself as an inquiry teacher. He did not have the skills to play out this teaching metaphor whereby he might have been able to alter the situation to make it more conducive to inquiry, but rather looked toward the first weeks of teaching as an opportunity to begin to develop the necessary skills and understandings. Without a strong sense of himself as teacher and without a useful conception of 'student', Larry was extremely vulnerable to pressures to conform to the dominant-teacher role within the school. It was, more than anything else, his vulnerability to the students and his need to obtain control over them that prompted his begrudging acceptance of this conception of teaching and of himself as teacher. By adopting the policeman metaphor Larry imposed a coherence of meanings upon himself and his teacher story as well as the context. Yet, in doing so, he was far from comfortable with the outcome. His inner self conflicted with his teaching self. Shortly after the Christmas break he lamented: 'I am doing what I don't believe'. Despite the tension Larry felt, this new conception, which came with the force of the entire institution behind it and especially of student expectations, was found to be compelling. Through the coherence it gave to his experience and its fit with the institution, Larry found it easier to engage in consistent, albeit sometimes unpleasant, action, which, he assumed, was essential to obtaining classroom control, the primary goal. Although at year's end Larry was not fully comfortable with this metaphor, he had become reasonably good at playing the part and was becoming more comfortable with it. He remained, however, uncertain whether or not he eventually would become the part or even if he could continue to play it since it made him miserable.

At the beginning of the year, given his weak and incomplete metaphor and limited ability to perform the tasks associated with it, Larry was virtually unable to frame several of the most basic teaching problems in productive ways. He was adrift. Besides being unable to conceptualize a discipline plan, he was unable to think through the kinds of activities and how they should be organized to appropriately engage the students in inquiry, for example. Moreover, he was uncertain about the kind of relationship he should have with the students, and especially troubled over how to exercise authority in the classroom while simultaneously allowing the students to explore topics as inquiry demands. Lacking coherence and the consistency that it allows, and recognizing his vulnerability, the students took control of the classroom until Larry settled into being a policeman, a conception of teaching perhaps consistent with an upper-middle-class view of the needs of lower- and working-class youngsters. For the sake of achieving control, he would be an authoritarian figure in the classroom which, in a manner consistent with the work of Elbaz (1983), involved a set of images that grew out of the principles and rules that Larry found himself instituting in order to survive in the classroom. This shift, as Veenman notes, is a common one for beginning teachers whose ideals are seriously threatened:

> The more discrepancies the young teachers experienced between school reality and their teaching training ideals, the more their attitudes changed in a conservative direction, and the more they were inclined to use authoritarian behaviour.
> (Veenman, 1984: 146)

Through the policeman metaphor Larry was enabled to frame problems, but in the framing many of the solutions provided were somewhat disquieting, although institutionally fitting. Student misbehaviour was a threat to his authority and the solution was to clamp down on the students and demonstrate his power over them. The aim of teaching was essentially that of establishing and maintaining classroom control, the measure against which he judged his competence: with a high degree of control he felt a measure of competence. Without control, he felt a failure. To maintain control Larry stuck closely to the textbook and took few instructional risks, thus further undermining the possibility of exploring inquiry. Furthermore, as he functioned as policeman, he found it increasingly difficult to establish playful relationships with students, as indicated by his avoidance of 'banter', which he enjoyed, but feared would encourage off-task behaviour. However, at least, as he established a reasonable level of control, he was able to think of the students in ways other than as 'beasts', although in a sense, and implicitly, he made them potential criminals in need of careful guarding.

Nancy

The youngest of the three teachers, Nancy brought with her to teaching a cacophony of implicit metaphors, hovering around a loose conception of herself as a 'buddy' to students, a metaphor that seemed to invite student misbehaviour. As the child of two junior-high-school teachers, it was somewhat surprising to find that she had such a weak and confused teaching schema and related conception of herself as a teacher. But neither of her parents were enthusiastic about teaching. Moreover, Nancy had not intended to follow in their footsteps, although, as she discovered after having decided not to return to the classroom, her father, perhaps unwittingly, had been nudging her in a variety of subtle ways toward teaching, perhaps thinking it an appropriate occupation for a female. Thus, while she simply seemed to fall into teaching without having given it much thought, it may be more accurate to say that she was pushed, albeit very slowly, almost imperceptibly in this direction. In any case, to be a teacher was not her dream; it was a job like any other job and she needed to work to support herself. To be sure, she hoped to be an effective teacher but was not as highly committed to it as were Larry and Marilyn. Moreover, teaching was Nancy's first 'adult' job, and her struggle to come to terms with being a teacher was complicated by the difficulty of coming to terms with being an adult in authority who desperately wanted to be liked and confirmed by the students with whom she tried to identify. Also, Nancy began teaching in a private school within which she felt ill at ease and out of place, perhaps reflecting differences in social-class backgrounds between herself and the students and other teachers. Feeling out of place in the school certainly did not help her feel more committed to teaching or connected to it.

Lacking any clear sense of herself as teacher, and being highly dependent on the students for her feelings of self-worth and of belonging, for most of the year Nancy found it virtually impossible to frame problems in productive ways. Problems were taken as personal attacks; the students did not like her and, by inference, she was a poor teacher. Moreover, despite the opportunities available within the school for obtaining assistance, in her insecurity Nancy was unable to go for help, a feeling Larry shared with her especially early in the year. To go for help was to admit failure but, paradoxically, not to go for help was to assure failure! Nancy was unable to produce a coherent conception of herself as teacher and seemed to drift through much of the year, vacillating in response to events and reacting to the situations within which she found herself, but not controlling them. In her uncertain state, and needing to maintain a reasonable level of self-esteem, Nancy at first framed the discipline and management problems she encountered much as did Larry before he settled on being a policeman: the problem was with the students, and she had the worst ones in the school. In fairness, it should be noted that Barry was a problem for other teachers in the school, and that an individual student can make life in the classroom miserable for even experienced teachers. Furthermore, Nancy framed the problem of curriculum planning, again much like Larry and Marilyn, as a textbook problem; for the most part, like them, and especially following her rejection of the immersion method of teaching a foreign language, she sought to get through the texts as a means of protecting herself and of controlling the classroom by limiting student activity.

Marilyn

Marilyn's conception of herself as teacher was deeply contradictory. Recalling her experience as a child 'rescued' from a miserable home life by teachers, Marilyn sought to rescue her own students, to take care of them and protect them from failure in order to build their self-esteem: 'teacher is rescuer'. By building their self-esteem Marilyn's fragile feelings of self-worth were strengthened.

Alongside her rescuer metaphor, was that of 'teacher is haven producer'. Marilyn's particular conception of a haven, once again heavily overlaid by her own childhood experience, was a place within which she could feel comfortable and secure, it was a predictable classroom, which necessitated that she engage in virtually no instructional risks; the curriculum was totally dominated by textbooks and worksheets. Apparently, she assumed that what had made her feel comfortable as a child and as an adult, the haven, would have a similar effect on her fifth-grade students. Quite early in the year, Marilyn confronted the contradiction: to rescue students meant being responsive to their needs and this meant more than being kind and friendly, it required a more open and flexible curriculum and some variation in instruction from the direct strategies she relied upon. However, as the year progressed Marilyn was unable to produce a coherence between metaphors, and her concept of herself as rescuer was seriously undermined and weakened by the quest to produce a predictable, secure haven.

Student misbehaviour helped prevent Marilyn from achieving a coherence of metaphors. The more frequently the students misbehaved, and the more difficulty Marilyn found in gaining and maintaining control, the more she felt threatened and insecure. The more threatened she felt, despite her tender feelings toward many of the students, the more tightly she held to the textbooks and worksheets as avenues for gaining security and control. She maintained a semblance of the rescuer image through *ad hoc* means, by making private deals with some students and making exceptions and adjustments in grading, for instance. In effect, Marilyn engaged in a great deal of inconsistent behaviour but behind the scenes and in private where the effects on whole class behaviour would be minimized.

As means for framing problems, Marilyn's metaphors produced some fascinating outcomes. As a rescuer, she also expected to be rescued by other teachers and did not hesitate to go for help. Indeed, she was relieved and delighted to turn her math classes over to the teacher facilitator for teaching and grateful to have the additional time for planning. Also, as a rescuer, she thought of the aims of teaching entirely in interpersonal terms, establishing warm and caring relationships with the students. She gave very little thought to academic subjects which may have been yet another reason for her sticking so closely to a textbook curriculum. Similarly, when seen through the rescuer lens, student misbehaviour was understood as essentially a rejection of the relationship Marilyn sought to create and that she thought was for the students' good; thus, she experienced personal rejection and hurt at each outburst, a slap to the face and to her self-confidence.

As noted, throughout most of their first year of teaching, the three teachers were extremely insecure, and fraught with self-doubts. With weak or contradictory conceptions of themselves as teachers, their feelings of self-worth tended to be fragile, hinging on the outcomes of otherwise small and inconsequential events. As we observed, little successes or kindnesses were often blown way out of proportion, while little failures loomed large and possessed devastatingly destructive power. This tendency added to the difficulty of adequately framing problems. For significant portions of the year, especially during the first several months of teaching, each of the three teachers, but most notably Larry and Nancy, rode, with but short respites, a slowly revolving spiral downward toward deepening frustration: their confused or vague conceptions of themselves as teachers made it difficult to frame problems productively; their inability to frame problems productively and respond to them made it more difficult to develop a coherent sense of self as teacher, and so on around, and around, and down. It was while on this spiral that Larry, in desperation, embraced the policeman metaphor as a way of arresting his slide downward and potentially out of teaching; similarly, it was when on this spiral that Marilyn sought rescue from other teachers within the building; and it was after returning to it after a respite, that Nancy burst out in tears in class and appealed to her students' humanity for a little help and kindness, to which they responded positively, to her great relief and amazement.

COPING AND MAINTAINING SELF-ESTEEM

While on this spiral and in the face of their extreme vulnerability, each of the three teachers developed a variety of ways of coping by way of staying on the job and of maintaining a measure of respect and self-esteem by way of preserving their inner selves. They engaged in some of the common coping mechanisms employed by persons working in contexts within which they receive few psychic rewards and too little job satisfaction. Thus far we have only hinted at these; now we will speak to them directly. But, before doing so, it should be noted that coping mechanisms represent a way of framing problems that assures that they are not resolved – the situation is unchanged – but rather are managed (Pollard, 1982; Knowles, 1989), sometimes to the detriment of self and of the students. Woods underscores the problem: survival strategies 'do not necesssarily facilitate teaching. They often take the place of it, and even assume its guise. Success ensures the establishment of a strategy, but many outlive their usefulness and turn into problems themselves' (1977: 290).

Sikes and her colleagues make a useful distinction for thinking about the strategies these teachers employed. They observe that there are two types of strategies, 'private' and 'public'.

> Private strategies are employed by individual teachers to gain their own ends or cope with whatever is in front of them (1985: 72).

> By public strategies we mean those that involve a group of teachers acting together to gain their aims (1985: 95).

Public strategies have the most potential for altering those work conditions that contributed to these teachers' prolonged stay in the survival stage of learning to teach. And yet, given their uncertainty about themselves as teachers and their vulnerability, even if available, it is unlikely they could have been employed. Instead, these teachers relied upon private strategies.

Several different and useful descriptions of the coping strategies teachers use are available (Bullough, 1989a; Lacey, 1977; Nias, 1989; Woods, 1977), but here we will draw upon the work of Rosenholtz (1989). Rosenholtz (1989) notes one strategy that was especially evident: struggling teachers engage in a great deal of 'negative teacher talk ... which [paradoxically reinforces] their beliefs that teaching success or failure is attributable primarily to outside sources over which they have little control. In other words, they unwittingly convey to each other that, confronted by such overwhelming odds, no one can reasonably expect to succeed' (p. 426) and so, it is acceptable to fail. For Larry this strategy was most evident during his discussions of the student 'beasts' who resented his authority. After all, what possibly could be done with beasts like the Rockers? The best that could be hoped for was that they would be under control, and he was making headway in this area. It was also evident following the semester break, when he attributed an improvement in student behaviour to the work of the students' previous teachers to socialize them and not to any changes he made. On her part, feeling rejected by the students, Nancy also blamed her problems with control on the students, complaining that simply nothing could be done with some of them and there was no use in trying. Frequently Marilyn mentioned that she, along with the other teachers in the school, was grappling with the 'worst fifth-grade class ever'. Given such students, severe problems were an inevitable and normal part of teaching; she would simply have to accept them. To be sure, especially in Larry's case, some of the students were very difficult to work with, but this is beside the point. This strategy and the manner problems are framed by it most assuredly guarantee that little professional development will take place inasmuch as the focus of attention is outside the teacher.

Larry's and Nancy's generally unsuccessful attempts to distance themselves from the students and not to care about them are closely related strategies as is, to a lesser extent, Marilyn's concerted effort to ignore problems. Blaming students and devaluing them is very much a part of distancing from them; in effect, the students are not of sufficient worth to be cared about and to be affected by. The aim of distancing was to try to obtain protection from the negative messages sent by the students to the teachers about their performance in the classroom and about them as people. Ignoring problems, in the hope that they will somehow go away, also represents a devaluing of the students and a distancing from them. Implicitly the message to the students being ignored is that they are not of sufficient worth to deserve the teacher's attention and, in any case, it would do little good to attend to them because they would not or could not change.

Rosenholtz (1989) further elaborates on the effects of this particular strategy:

as Denscombe (1985) observed in his authoritative review of research findings, teachers who perceived students as lazy, noisy, and troublesome often ceased to struggle to get them to work because control problems were so great. Indulging normally unacceptable forms of behavior, they came to regard classroom disruption as a normal state of affairs and withdrew from confrontation with students rather than engage in embarrassing and self-defeating efforts to assert control. By sidestepping the need to confront and fail, quite ironically, indulgence and withdrawal can be counted among the many strategies teachers used to preserve and protect their self-esteem.

(Rosenholtz, 1989: 436)

An additional and extremely powerful strategy which the teachers used has already been hinted at:

when their instructional success is in doubt [teachers often] substitute definitions alternative to student learning as their measures of professional fulfillment.

(Rosenholtz, 1989: 427)

All three teachers measured their instructional success primarily by their ability to achieve and maintain classroom control above all else. In addition, Nancy measured her success by how well the students liked her. And, in a similar vein, Marilyn was especially concerned about establishing warm and caring relationships with the students she hoped to 'rescue'. 'Warm fuzzies' counted a great deal in her quest for self-esteem and feelings of success. Finally, it should be noted that each had an additional aim: survival of the year. Simply getting through the year was perhaps above all else the measure of success and to this end they used a wide variety of private coping strategies in addition to those mentioned.

TEACHER DEVELOPMENT

Personal insecurity and vulnerability, confused or contradictory conceptions of self-as-teacher, their approaches to coping with the challenges of teaching, and in Larry's case, the difficulty of his teaching assignment, were all factors that, interacting with one another, contributed to these teachers' prolonged stay in the survival stage of learning to teach. Although delighted at having survived the year, both Larry and Nancy generally ended it on a less than positive note. Larry was pleased with some of his accomplishments, however. He recognized he had made genuine progress in a number of areas, especially in obtaining classroom control, and was guardedly optimistic that he would be able eventually to negotiate a satisfying and productive role in the school, but he remained somewhat uncertain about what that role would be, especially given his lingering uneasiness about being a policeman and the violence that metaphor caused to his inner self.

91

On her part, Nancy was pleased she no longer felt so nervous when teaching and was 'not worried so much that [class] wouldn't go well or that we wouldn't have enough [content] to fill up an entire . . . period. That's probably the most dramatic change I've felt, that I can make use of an hour and one half on "one topic".' Perhaps the most important discovery for Nancy, however, was that she did not want or need to be a teacher. This discovery was emotionally liberating and represented her break from the career stereotype embedded in her and her father's expectations that reproduced the cultural view that teaching is women's work (Oram, 1989).

As we have considered Nancy and Larry's quest for productive teaching metaphors, we have noted a number of significant differences besides those related to gender. Of these, perhaps the most important one was their different levels of commitment to becoming a teacher, understood as being willing to give loyalty and energy to teaching (Nias, 1989: 31). While somewhat intangible, it may be that that commitment to becoming a teacher is one of the most critical variables in the success or failure of the quest: Larry was committed; Nancy, like the 'disillusioned' teacher-education students discussed by Cole (1985), was much less so. Perhaps born out of necessity, it is likely that it is this commitment that keeps many struggling beginning teachers coming back to school following frequent failure and keeps them more or less engaged in the quest. But commitment alone is obviously not a sufficient reason to continue the struggle to become a teacher. Commitment must be complemented by a satisfying level of pleasure gained from the work to which one is committed, which leads to another important difference between Larry and Nancy. Despite his struggle with the students, Larry genuinely enjoyed them while Nancy, ultimately, did not. She could never establish the kind of relationships with the students that she found necessary to enjoy teaching. Teachers, she intuitively discovered, are not buddies to students; the metaphor could never be fitting.

In contrast to Larry and Nancy, Marilyn ended the year feeling very upbeat about herself and about teaching, even though the contradictions in her metaphors endured. In trying to understand Marilyn's experience it is useful to return to Anderson's secondary hypotheses about schema and their operation noted in chapter 1. Anderson (1977) asserts that in order to maintain a strongly developed schema 'Apparent inconsistencies and counterexamples [may be] easily assimilated. . .' (p. 425); and that, 'People whose important beliefs are threatened will attempt to defend their positions, dismiss objections, ignore counterexamples, keep segregated logically incompatible schemata' (p. 429). We believe that Marilyn's experience is consistent with Anderson's hypotheses. Her conception of herself as a rescuer was deeply embedded in her experience; it was central to her inner self, and resistant to change. Indeed, to change it would likely have threatened much more than her teaching schema, the foundation of her being. While in Marilyn's classroom, we witnessed few examples of what might be called rescuing behaviour; nevertheless, to her what she did and how she did it all aimed at building the self-esteem of young people to the degree that she seemed virtually unaware of the apparently deadening effects on the students of the routine of reading textbooks and answering the questions at the end of the chapters and of filling out worksheets. In chapter 9 we explore in some detail the factors that encouraged the changes in metaphor in the three teacher cases presented in part II, factors of sufficient power to prompt a change that eventually lead to a growing self-awareness on the part of each teacher. What might encourage Marilyn to confront the contradictions in her thinking is uncertain. What is clear, however, is that Marilyn was surrounded by well-meaning and supportive teachers who were heavily invested in her success to the point that they were willing to take over the mathematics programme that she was struggling with, for example. On one hand these teachers rescued her and enabled her to complete the year with feelings of success and of belonging. On the other, it may be the case that they did too much or gave her the wrong kind of assistance in their generous effort to assist Marilyn with her struggle to overcome her feelings of anxiety, in that they may have prevented her from having the experience necessary for achieving the coherence of metaphors that will be needed for her to face and find herself as teacher. Larry obviously needed much greater assistance than that which he received, but Marilyn makes us wonder – and with this peculiarly troubling question, and a related question, we conclude our discussion – can a beginning teacher, like Marilyn, be given too much assistance, to the extent that it interferes with her development? And, what kind and how much assistance is most beneficial for professional development, given the paradox of learning to teach? While no pat answer can be given to either

question, both should be kept in mind particularly as teacher-educators and experienced teachers assigned to be mentors seek to assist neophytes in their quest to come to terms with their teaching selves in context.

Part II

6

TEACHER IS NURTURER

BARBARA

Barbara, a divorced, 34-year old mother of five, decided to become a teacher for pragmatic reasons. Being a mother had been her first career and was central to her self-understanding. She now needed a steady income, insurance, and a job that would fit the schedules of her young, active children. Teaching fitted the bill. But the decision was not only a pragmatic one. As a young, honours graduate in English, she recalled:

> [I] wasn't interested in teaching at all. But, over the time [of being married] I really discovered how much more I liked kids than I thought I did. I did like kids, but I was also very curious about the things that I could teach them . . . . I liked talking to them.

After entering her teacher education programme and beginning to work with young people, she discovered, happily, that she had found her career niche: 'When I got in there, it was just like: Boom! This is so wonderful! . . . I have a knack for it. Wow! Look at this!' Later, she explained more fully what this niche was:

> I was really lucky, that what I wanted to be was consistent with where I had to be, that is, a parent. I decided that's what really makes me happy. Giving love, nourishing, caring – giving love to other people is what ultimately makes me happy. It's a really selfish thing [to] have a child love me. Have a child care for me. Care for a child. Having that reciprocal relationship, even if it's only for one hour a day, makes me happy. I'd go home [from practice teaching] and I was happy.

Barbara was hired as a first-year teacher at Rifler Junior High School. Built in 1984, Rifler was a lower-middle- and middle-class school where, for the most part, schooling was taken seriously by parents and students alike. Approximately 20 per cent of Barbara's 170 students represented one or another ethnic minority group, particularly Southeast Asian and Pacific Islander. In Rifler, she taught six periods of English: two seventh-grade 'regular', two ninth-grade 'remedial', and two ninth-grade 'regular'. She had one planning period.

INITIAL TEACHING METAPHOR

Barbara thought of teaching as an extension of parenting, a view strengthened by practice teaching in an English programme for troubled students, students with drug and drug-related problems. These students responded favourably, but not without difficulty, to her desire to protect and care for them and to teach them something about English. Throughout the early months of her first year of teaching this view endured unchanged, and served as the centre of her self-understanding. In December, for example, she remarked that being a teacher was like 'being a parent for 300 extra [children]'. In effect, she overlaid the parent role on the teacher role; to teach was to parent, and to parent was to nurture: Teacher is nurturer.

INITIAL CONCERNS

Before school began Barbara worried most about whether or not she would be able to connect with the students in caring ways. Would they allow her to be nurturing, she wondered? Put differently, would they be children who responded affectionately to parenting? She wondered: would she be able to establish a curriculum that encouraged the development of caring relationships? Realizing she would face a classroom full of children who were strangers, she fretted over how to plan without knowing the students. Her teaching schema was but partial. 'The student element is missing,' she lamented. However, she felt confident in her knowledge of English and in this knowledge trusted that, once she got to know the students, she would be able to provide a suitable programme for them, one that would help create the desired classroom climate: 'I can only go so far with [the] material

I've got.... I'm going to get their feedback, and then [I'll] go with what they say... I've got to be able to [respond to them].' Ultimately, for Barbara, success would not only come through designing a programme responsive to student interests and concerns, but through one that would reach out into the broader world of ideas. But what were their interests, and what concerned them?

To answer these questions she drew intuitively on her experience as a mother and understanding of mothering, assuming that young people of a given age share similar experiences. She turned to her children for insights: '[I use] my son (who was an eighth grader), [I use] my kids.' By thinking about her children and their experience she identified a set of issues as being important to junior-high-school-age students. For example, she wanted her curriculum to present:

> things that deal with anorexia. Things that deal with bulimia; ... nobody deals with those issues. Seventh graders deal with those issues. There's not a short story in [the text] about divorce. There's not a short story in there about a kid in crisis.

As a guide for planning she also thought about what she was like as a junior-high-school-age student but this proved to be of limited use despite her remembering 'vividly what it was like to be a student. I remember what appealed to me.' Her intention was to:

> make this [English] literature ... meaningful to these kids, it's got to pick up something in their lives. There's got to be something, somewhere, that's going to reflect ... their lives. It's got to [connect to] what they've experienced.'

Based upon these recollections, knowledge gained as a parent, and hints gleaned from student teaching, she made her initial planning decisions. Using this knowledge as a filter of sorts, and secure with the nurturer metaphor, Barbara rejected outright the established English curriculum which she thought to be little connected with teenager's interests or needs. The curriculum would have to be adjusted to her values; she would not adjust to it. She settled on a thematic organization of the content, within which she included, where appropriate, those topics and content suggestions contained in the state and district curriculum guides. For example, early in the first term she organized a 'Coming of

Age' unit which included the novel *Dandelion Wine* and other material, suggestions presented in the guides, selected readings from the class anthology, and activities from, as she put it, 'her head'.

Barbara went to great lengths to include in her planning a variety of ways for encouraging student sharing. Each class, she decided, would begin with the students writing in journals. These she would read but not evaluate. As she had hoped the journals proved to be extremely important sources of information about individual students. Of one student she said:

> [This girl] put herself out on a piece of paper. What shouted through that paragraph was real low esteem. Not hate, not belligerence. But she said, 'I only sleep with guys when I really like them.' So, I've got to watch this child, I've really got to watch her .... She's a good writer. There's a lot of potential there.

Other students' writings were more mundane, but none the less of some instructional importance. One student wrote, for example:

> Eng[lish] is boring. I hate gramar (sic) and all that other crap we have to do. I think english (sic) is for the birds. I'm so tired today I'm going to fall asleep in one of my classes.

WORK CONTEXT AND PRESSURES

The context within which the beginning teachers work may or may not be fitting to their understanding of teaching and self as teacher; indeed, as noted previously, it may be hostile. Thus, as Blumer reminds us, attention needs to be given to the situation within which beginning teachers work and to the meanings others hold in that situation as they have a bearing on self and self-formation.

The tasks of teaching

Planning and organizing a programme for the first time is incredibly time consuming and, paradoxically, an enervating yet exhilarating experience. This was the case for Barbara; teaching consumed much of her life. Eventually, however, beginning with activities that intuitively seemed appropriate, she produced a fitting curriculum, although occasionally she had difficulty with activities that fell flat and with anticipating timing: 'Sometimes I think I'm going to get through [an assignment] and I don't. I go back and we're going to do it together. Well, that takes two days rather than one day.' These were not, however, the only difficulties she faced that demanded attention and drained her energy as she struggled with the 'paradox' of learning to teach. Paperwork was a problem.

> I've got to have them write journals; so, that's about [200] journals to read every weekend. That's a lot to read. That really cuts into whatever time that I have . . . [but] I've got to do [it] in order to be the kind of teacher I have to be.

And grading:

> Yesterday I was really strung out with kids because I'd spent several hours getting midterms ready so they would know a week ahead of time what everybody was behind in. And I had a couple of girls who – I had graded their papers but hadn't recorded them, and they just came unglued and were extremely belligerent . . . . During the next period, I just [lost it] and said, 'Okay, you bunch of ungrateful [brats]. You do that to me again and I'll never do midterms for you again . . . !' [Suddenly they became] so polite . . . so perfect . . . they knew I was strung out . . . .

Student pressures

Controlling the territory

As a nurturer, Barbara thought of her classroom as a home, as a place in which she was in charge, as her 'turf, as in my territory'. She jealously protected her territory and resented intruders such as the teacher who 'just cruises in and . . . calls a student out of . . . class'. While in her territory the students were expected to respect her wishes and to behave as she demanded. Not to do so was a serious offence. Nevertheless, discipline was occasionally a grave concern as when, for instance, she had to 'kick out of class' one of her remedial students who 'started swinging'. While generally speaking, the students were well behaved they nevertheless powerfully influenced what Barbara did in the classroom, how she felt about teaching and herself as teacher.

101

To obtain the desired behaviour and student attitudes, in addition to producing a responsive curriculum, Barbara paid careful attention and put a lot of energy into building caring relationships. She treated students in positive, warm, personal, affectionate, and honest ways; to do so was natural and proper to her. In turn she hoped to receive affection from the students; a major source of self-confirmation and job satisfaction. On any given day the observer of Barbara's classes would see her hug students; greet a shy student affectionately as he entered the room with the phrase, 'Come in, hon' (meaning 'honey'); have the class members stand up and 'shake [themselves] out' because they'd been sitting and working so long; stare at a misbehaving student with an icy and penetrating gaze until he got on task, and once he did, give him a quick and reassuring smile; as well as playfully tease or occasionally nag a student about an assignment poorly done, about not getting to work, or about forgetting to bring paper and pencil to class.

The hugging, and other physical expressions of love, that played such an important part in how she expressed herself to students, arose, Barbara said, because that was how she was raised; it was second nature to her: 'I was raised in a very physical environment by my parents. Hugging. Touching. Holding. [And,] that's what I do. These children,' she said, 'need someone to touch them.'

From the early days of the school year Barbara set the tone of her classes. One could not help but be impressed by her power in the classroom especially during 'show time', as she called it, when she explained with great great animation and dramatic, sweeping gestures, the meaning she found in a passage just read. Her energy virtually filled the room seeking engagements with students.

Student subculture groups

As powerful as Barbara was, however, the students also had considerable power; some days there seemed to be a tug of war taking place over who would control the 'territory'. While seeming to be always on the winning side, Barbara did not dare loosen her grip and this limited her expressions of nurturing and occasionally resulted in challenges to the metaphor itself. The influence of the students was subtle, an influence not really exerted by expressions of gross misbehaviour, but rather by behaving in small, unobtrusive, almost innocuous ways that made it difficult for Barbara to establish the caring classroom relations she sought. For example, in class meetings she discovered early in the year that some students would only very reluctantly join 'in the circle', while among those within 'the circle' some students would not sit next to others. While there was nothing initially surprising about this discovery she soon found that the behaviour was connected to group codes that she knew nothing about.

At the beginning of the school year she recognized that the students were very cliquish, hanging around in groups at lunch and in the hallways. But these cliques had no meaning for her; they were not part of her experience as either a parent or student. By the beginning of her second month of teaching, however, the groupings began to be meaningful as she identified and articulated some of the values students associated with them. Musical tastes and style, she observed, were the focal points of belonging. But, beyond this, she realized that affiliation with some groups meant that some students had classroom agendas at odds with her own. Accordingly, 'Wavers',[1] 'Rockers', 'Skaters', and 'Hardcores' (see Bullough, Knowles, and Crow, 1989; Kotarba and Wells, 1987), each represented a challenge to Barbara's aim to establish a family atmosphere in her classroom with herself as mother. Recognition of these groups brought with it a filling out of that part of Barbara's teaching schema linked to students which initially had caused her concern.

Barbara recognized in the groupings a potential challenge to her authority within the classroom and to her conception of herself as teacher, and a potential threat to student learning. Nevertheless, always the nurturer, she spoke of individual group members affectionately, almost endearingly:

Now . . . they come in and they're so tough. They say words that I didn't learn until I was in my 30s. They're so tough, and they're so strong. You look them straight in the eye and they're just as belligerent and as hard as they can be. But, yesterday at lunch I came out of my door – I was behind some of them – and I looked at their little backs and the backs of their necks, and [it struck me], they're just kids . . . . You look at their hands, look at the backs of their necks, they're little kids . . . . Some of them are tough, but they're still tender. I have little girls that come up and talk to me about the books

103

that they've read. The books that they . . . read . . . are children's books. That's why I picked *Dandelion Wine* for them to read. That's just the way they are; [and,] they're wonderful, they're marvelous.

Like the parent of the Prodigal Son, Barbara had a particular soft spot for individuals on the extreme fringes who needed to be cared for most. She saw such students as being trapped by their group affiliations. This was a particular problem with the ninth-grade students who had already more or less settled into group membership. These students, she said, 'respond according to [their] category – that's what's expected of them; they won't break out . . . even if their personal feelings come into play . . . . There's no crossing those lines.' In contrast, many of the seventh-grade students, particularly girls, she said, 'haven't figured it out yet.' Barbara thought that group affiliation made 'a lot of difference in their attitude towards each other . . . 'No, I won't work with this person because I'm a Rocker, and she's country (meaning a Cowgirl).' For example, in a class meeting she found that the 'Rockers wouldn't sit next to Wavers.' Situations like this bothered her, complicating her effort to create the kind of caring classroom learning environment she sought. She determined to challenge the groupings in order to encourage boundary crossing.

Barbara began to 'take [student] categories into consideration' when planning. Although she may not have liked them she accepted the categories, just as she accepted the students who bore them. For example, speaking a month into the school year of Annie, a Rocker, she said:

> She won't move out of that [group]. I'm not expecting her to . . . . Now, that may be a chicken way to do it, but I don't want to lose her . . . . Maybe later in the year I could ask her to do something [that would] . . . challenge her to move out of [her group] . . . [but now] I want them to have the security of their group. I don't want them to lose that security right now. I don't feel like it's appropriate . . . . They've got to feel secure with themselves.

Later in the year and looking ahead, Barbara thought she might be able to challenge the groups, but first she needed to build more trusting relationships with the students. Ultimately, however, for the students' good she wanted to weaken not only the boundaries separating them but also the categories themselves because, she said,

> I feel like [their categories] weigh them down . . . . They have so many expectations that society [puts] on them, then to take on the load of a category! If a [musical] group came out with a song or a tape – this is just a frivolous example – [and] if they didn't like [the group] personally, they're still expected to like it, to rave about it, and put down $25.00 when these groups come to town . . . . Some of them have to break the law in order to fulfill these expectations. [They] steal – steal money to get the ticket to go to the [performance].

While saying the 'categories weigh them down', Barbara also realized that students needed to belong somewhere, that is what she meant when she said they needed security: 'I think they have to feel comfortable; they have to fill some category'. This said, it troubled her that so many of the available groups were destructive and worried about the students' futures: 'I can see these guys when they're thirty years old and . . . trying to work out some of the things they did when they were in junior high '

Recognition of the groups added support to Barbara's initial decision to build a curriculum around student concerns and interests, a curriculum that would enable students to explore values. But she needed to do more than this and began thinking about ways of including in her curriculum increased opportunities for students to cross groupings in relative security; while she could not push them across, she thought she might be able to seduce or trick them into crossing. One of the surprising aspects of the groups in her school was that they appeared to cut across ethnic lines, suggesting that the boundaries could be breached (see Grant and Sleeter, 1988).

Barbara's curriculum included many examples of activities planned explicitly to soften the barriers between groups, even if only momentarily. For example, in the first week of November as part of a mystery unit, she created an elaborate 'who dunnit' game within which every student had a part. What distinguished this game from other games was that the parts were interdependent, students needed to work together to discover the murderer. If they did not, the mystery could not be solved. There was great excitement in class on the day the game was introduced and the excitement continued until the mystery was solved. During this time the students in Barbara's classes appeared to forget who belonged to what group and instead focused together on the task at hand.

As a nurturer Barbara took it for granted that students were children who needed to be cared for, protected, and sometimes punished. 'Reaching my kids and being there for my kids – my students,' is what she said she valued most: 'Anything else, I'm sorry, is totally secondary.' Reaching them meant, at times, having to accept aspects of their behaviour, like group affiliation, that she would rather have changed. But, in practice, connecting to students was but part of caring for them. Caring also meant that, as a parent-teacher, she necessarily would confront unacceptable behaviour and force the students, if need be and for their own good, to work in ways they resisted, even though to do so would be difficult, time consuming, and require a great deal of energy. Her view was that parents sometimes had to be tough for their children's sakes.

CHALLENGES TO NURTURING

As the year progressed Barbara began to know a great deal about her students' personal lives which was useful for thinking about planning and was a source of personal and professional satisfaction. But this knowledge came at a price: 'It's a big high, but [sometimes] it's a real dragging down low.' As she progressively got more involved in the lives of her students, as they opened up and connected to her as the trusted and trusting parent, teaching became progressively more complicated; it became, as she put it, like a:

> five-ring circus rather than a three-ring circus ... I'm concerned about [making my] curriculum relevant; I'm concerned about their personal lives; I'm concerned about their interactions with other students; I'm concerned about their physical environment; and I'm concerned about their future.

As she looked out on her classes she did not see merely students, she saw young people living lives that affected their performance in school and made her job more difficult:

106

I could see that she was tired. [I asked her how she was and] she said, 'I was up until 4: 00 a.m. because I had to go bail my mom out of jail'. I said, 'Bail your mom out of jail?' 'Yes. I got really, really, tired. First, I had to go to the bank and then I had to go to the jail'. Then I thought, 'Yes, and I have to worry about whether these kids are tardy!'

Much of what she learned about the students proved troubling. For example, she wrote in her journal: 'A lot of sadness in life – these kids are sad: depression, abuse, rampant promiscuity – that sounds harsh but they are making choices and they are just babies! . . . I hope I can do them justice.' The more personal information about the students she gained, the more she worked to make her curriculum responsive; simultaneously the further she was drawn into their lives and problems, the more strained her energies became. She worried, constantly, about her students:

Sometimes I just look out the window and stare. I dressed up today [for school] thinking that I would have a hard time, but after a night's sleep things seem to be better. They still haven't found Donna, but they think she is a runaway rather than a [victim of] kidnapping. Oh, gee, (crying) it comes flooding back.

As a nurturer committed to caring and loving children, some of the knowledge she gained demanded action; something had to be done and she had to do it: 'Tammy's been raped [by her step-brother], but it's going to stop! She told me about it today. [With the counselor, I contacted] protective services . . .' In responding to such situations, Barbara was inevitably forced headlong into the limitations of her influence, which she initially did not want to accept.

By November, Barbara looked very tired and yet continued to get even further involved in her students' lives and problems. Many of them willingly sought her out for counsel and advice. Indeed, before and after class and before and after school students were frequently clustered tightly around her desk seeking attention. At the same time she increasingly became concerned about her own five young children and her ability to parent them adequately in the face of growing student and teaching demands. While she tried diligently to avoid bringing student problems home with her, she simply could not leave all of them at the door.

After all, in her students' faces, she saw the faces of her children. Guilt followed the discovery that she was unable to respond to all that was required of her, but with renewed determination she did not withdraw from any of her commitments to either her students or her own children; she kept giving and continued to rely, and gratefully so, on her parents and sister to help cover some of the responsibilities that she could not fulfil, such as picking up her young son from school and watching him while she was at work. In a determined voice she said, as though trying to convince herself of the rightness of the decision:

> Sometimes I think it would be nice to be able to detach [from the students] but I can't function that way. I think, may be . . . I've come to the point where I accept this is the way I function. This is the way I'm always going to function. Be happy with it. Be happy. [I] may not make any Einstein's, [I] may not inspire the children, but I'm going to be happy with what I'm doing.

Despite this determination and the pleasure she felt when her efforts to help a child were fruitful, in her rare private moments she wondered whether or not she could continue to be the teacher-nurturer she wanted to be. Perhaps the price was simply too high:

> My own life, is there one? – and now there is a door decorating contest. Time, time, time – what's become of me? Am I who I wanted to be? Just a hazy shade of winter – I'm tired. [Are] my babies taken care of while I care for these souls, [these] little children?

FACING AN INSISTENT DILEMMA

Moments like these, moments of questioning her sense of self as teacher-nurturer or teacher-parent were generally short-lived, but they became increasingly frequent. When they appeared Barbara doggedly ploughed through them; 'gritting her teeth' she refused, at least early on, to compromise any of her values despite the apparent and growing personal costs. Her solution was to keep moving, believing that if she stopped to consider her situation, the problems would 'multiply . . . like two pieces of paper on your desk overnight. They'll have little babies and you'll have 29 papers the next day [to work on].' What she did was to make cuts intuitively in the energy and time she put into other types of activities. Very early in the school year she gave up any semblance of a social life outside the family, for example, only to realize it after it was gone: 'I'm not doing anything outside my family at all. I do my school and I do my family. That's all I do.' And later, she stopped putting in the time necessary to maintain a high level of performance in her continuing university coursework. She realized she simply could not do the work adequately and, as a result, she put minimal effort into her university final examinations. As a nurturer she expected to sacrifice her own interests for those of children, who always came first. But this decision, reflecting a significant sacrifice, was haunting and hurtful and produced in the English honours graduate, now teacher-nurturer, feelings of shame for having performed inadequately at the university – a foreign and distasteful experience: 'I felt very ashamed. I felt very ashamed that I hadn't taken care of what I needed to take care of.'

Barbara came face to face with a fundamental and particularly female dilemma: while nurturing was at the centre of her self-understanding and was the source of her greatest pleasures as a parent and as a teacher, the personal costs of maintaining this understanding of teaching were beginning to be too high. She could not continue as she had been; there was nothing left for her to sacrifice but her family and her health. Facing growing physical and mental exhaustion, coupled with concern about the welfare of her own children, Barbara gradually accepted that there were limits to how far she could or should sacrifice for the students. There was simply no end to the needs of the young people and no possible way for one person to respond to them all. Indeed, Barbara had become so involved that she thought it right and proper to take shopping, with the mother's permission, one of her female students who had problems with personal hygiene. Something had to give! Writing in her journal shortly before Christmas:

> How am I going to do everything? I am so tired, so tired. I don't know what I am going to do about Christmas. I wish there was someplace I could go, just to find peace, just a little while, just to find a break.

But, there was no such place, and no peace. Classes awaited and her own children needed her:

> Last night I came home and I had to take Thomas to the eye
> doctor because he needed a new contact lens. I had come
> home and it was a pretty rough day [teaching]. I'd done
> grammar all day . . . . Up and down, moving all the time: I
> came home; I had to . . . [go] to the eye doctor; go out and
> pick up some books for my classes (forty-two copies of a
> novel); then come and fix dinner; [and] help Katie with
> reading. If you catalog it [all], it doesn't sound like that
> much [to do] but it was just exhausting . . . . I started to cry
> last night . . . I cannot physically do it all.

Finally, fearing that her own children might be suffering because of
her dedication to nurturing other people's children, and finding
in her own children's well being the source of her greatest
pleasure, Barbara began to draw a line indicating how far she
would get involved in the lives and problems of her students and
how much she would do to satisfy their never-ending needs. In
giving so fully of herself she discovered that she had been
sacrificing her own children and the quality of the time she spent
with them. For one thing, when home she was bone tired. Her
children, she said, had to come first; she could not compromise
family life as she had compromised her own interests. Her family,
she concluded, had to come first: 'It's [my] family . . . [that] is
most important.' But, recognizing that she would have to pull back
somewhat in order to take better care of herself for her children's
sake, and then pulling back, are two quite different matters.

BETRAYED BY STUDENTS

While struggling with what to do, with where and how to say 'no',
two major situations eased the burden of resolving the dilemma.
First, she discovered that a few students, the children she had loved
so fully and served to near exhaustion, 'betrayed' her trust by lying
about the problems they were having at home as a way of
manipulating Barbara and tapping her sympathies. Hurt turned to
anger: 'I've found out I've been taken advantage of by the biggest
bullshitters in the world!' Nevertheless she maintained a
significant but now more guarded involvement following this
discovery:

> I let [teaching be a big job]. There are other people who
> don't and that's fine. That's the way they operate. I can't

operate that way. Just by the nature of the way I am, if a kid comes in with a long face, I've got to find out why . . . and sometimes they are incredible problems . . . they really are.

Second, Barbara found that during school hours and in the school parking lot someone had slashed one of her car's tyres. Although she could not bring herself to believe that any of her students had such negative feelings toward her and that they would do such a thing, she nevertheless wondered. And, in the wondering, she inevitably began asking painful questions about the nature of her relationship to the students and about the wisdom of becoming so involved in their lives and caring so deeply about them. Indeed, being less involved, less connected to the students, might have some virtue: students would perhaps have fewer strong feelings toward her; and then, too, their actions toward her would have less negative or positive impact on how she felt about herself as teacher. One implication, then, was that they might show her less affection, and this was a painful thought.

GROWING CONFIDENCE AND IMPROVING
TEACHING SKILLS

Additionally, she was also helped to draw the line by her discovery that she could succeed without continuing to put so much time into teaching. Through teaching, some aspects of teaching became less time consuming, allowing energy to be shifted elsewhere: to maintaining her relationships with the students and to her family, in particular, although not to developing a social life. For instance, she became a more efficient and confident planner and made much better use of her planning period. But even with improving skill, she still found it necessary to back off somewhat from her commitments and pull back her comforting hand; vowing after a long, depressing, and bitterly cold winter that, in order to protect her family and to strengthen family relations, she would bring no 'more than half an hour's school work home every night.' To do this meant that at times she would have to 'wing it', as she put it, not plan with such great care and in such detail as she had previously: 'Sometimes I make up things as I go along,' she admitted. In part she was able to do this without undue concern because she felt secure in her relationships with the students and in part because of her extensive content area background: 'I'm comfortable with everything I'm teaching . . . . There's a well [of information] there: I can keep drawing from that well.' But, more than anything, she did it because she saw no other alternative; she did it for the sake of her own children and her relationship with them.

PARENTAL PRESSURES

A devastating event, about mid-year, also helped ease the difficulty Barbara had drawing the line between an acceptable and unacceptable level of involvement in the lives of her student-children. For the most part Barbara was left alone by parents and found other teachers to be friendly and supportive, although, given her heavy family responsibilities, she found little time to be involved in faculty social activities, having, for instance, to miss the first faculty party in order to attend back-to-school night for her young son. This suddenly, albeit momentarily, changed. As part of a 'Friendship and Love' unit, Barbara decided to have her seventh-grade classes study *Romeo and Juliet*. For the first few days of the unit all went well. Indeed, the students enjoyed the play and Barbara's animated discussion of it; they liked 'showtime'. Suddenly, however, a number of parents complained to the principal and the school-district English specialist, both of whom quickly contacted Barbara for an explanation. Shakespeare, the principal was told by a few parents, was 'too difficult for the students' and, more to the point, 'What were they doing studying love and friendship?' In addition, the head of the English Department became involved because *Romeo and Juliet* was not on the approved reading list for the seventh grade. Barbara had committed curricular heresy!

Both the principal and the district curriculum specialist were satisfied with Barbara's explanation – that *Romeo and Juliet* provided a rich and interesting way of exploring human relationships and that the students were not only engaged in the content but were completing the assignments satisfactorily; they could, in short, do the work. The department head was not pleased but did not press the issue further. With the principal's support, Barbara began meeting with individual parents to explain that there was nothing to be feared and that the difficulty with her assignments was much exaggerated. Over a period of two or three weeks the storm passed but in its wake stood a shaken and somewhat irritated Barbara who, after a relatively successful period characterized by having established caring and productive relationships with the majority of her students, confronted a new set of limitations to being a teacher-nurturer.

The meetings with the parents were forceful reminders that she was not, after all, the mother of all these students. Others too had an interest in their education, an interest that placed limitations on what she could and could not do in the classroom, no matter how well intentioned, creative, or hard working she might be. Her territory, after all, was surrounded by their territory, and she could do nothing about it. By spring the sketchy line drawn in winter was pencilled in clearly.

A CHANGING TEACHER-SELF

The difficulty with parents over the teaching of *Romeo and Juliet* was but one of several factors that prompted Barbara to engage in some serious soul searching as the year began to wind down. But in the face of these difficulties she continued to believe that her nurturer teacher vision had served her and her students rather well. For the most part classes were characterized by caring, warmth, and open and honest exchanges just as she had hoped they would be before school began. She genuinely enjoyed the students, even loved them: 'They're marvelous kids, they're marvelous. All of them are!' In return they responded to her love:

> These kids feed me. They don't know that they do. But they come in and they're tumbling. They're rolling around just like little puppies. They look at me and we start. There's love there, there's happiness.

She found great pleasure in her students' little successes and even greater pleasure when one of them facing a crisis came through intact:

> They found my student! ... She'd run away and was living with this guy on the corner [who is] kind of a neighborhood creep .... [She's] going to live with her father and stepmother [out of state.] She'll get away from him.

But, in spite of all of this, Barbara began to feel ever so slightly unhappy with teaching. It was not that teaching was bad or unpleasant but, rather, that there was something missing; something somehow triggered by the *Romeo and Juliet* incident. That teaching had become less than fully satisfying was initially a surprising discovery that raised questions about Barbara's fundamental teaching values.

Barbara had a difficult time articulating what was bothering her. After all, she had succeeded for the most part in establishing precisely the kinds of bonds with students she had desired, although now she was determined to become somewhat less involved in their lives. She was not unhappy, just not quite happy with teaching. As she struggled to give words to feelings, she thought back to the time when she was a full-time mother at home and discovered a remarkable parallel:

> When I was home with my family, I was very up-to-date with what was going on [with everyone] but as far as my intellectual ability, I think I was pretty much stagnant . . . . I have to be continually challenged intellectually.

To be an effective nurturer, she remembered, requires that the nurturer be richly alive and developing personally, after all a nurturer must have something worth giving and getting. Barbara was beginning to feel stagnant in teaching, which too often seemed 'boring', and this worried her.

Reframing the teaching problem as she did, suggested possible solutions: the aim was not to escape her classroom home, but rather to intellectualize it for both her sake and that of the children. Nurturing was more than a matter of helping young people feel good about themselves and of protecting them. Caring meant challenging them to be better than they were and this meant challenging them intellectually. Moreover, it also meant that at times she could not and should not protect them, despite her desire to 'heal wounds'. For their own good they would have to grapple with 'adversity'; after all, some wounds were necessary in order for learning to take place. To be sure, Barbara had sought before to engage the students intellectually but she saw far too few instances of her challenging bearing fruit; the students were happy and busy and that, for them, was enough:

> This sounds awfully unparental, but they've got to respond to nurturing, you know. You've got to see some sprouting going on. Rather than just nice green healthy plants that just . . .

114

stay nice green healthy plants it would be nice to see some flowering!

The ultimate and most exquisite bloom would be if her students came to share her love of English, a source of great personal pleasure for Barbara. Speaking in the spring-time:

> My greatest disappointment is that I haven't convinced – and I know you'll laugh at this – every one of my students what a wonderful subject English is, and that they're not all immediately converted to the thrills [and] chills . . . that English can and does provide . . . .

For Barbara, then, a full relationship with the students by spring-time came to include sharing matters of the intellect; and the rarity of such moments was disappointing. Just as she was 'fed' emotionally by the students in response to her feeding them, she wanted to be fed intellectually. She wondered, however, if this was a reasonable expectation; after all, her students were young children who were very much dependent on adults. With this thought in mind, and recalling her practice teaching experience with high-school sophomores (ages 15 to 16), Barbara contemplated requesting a transfer to a high school where she thought she could realize her expanded vision of teacher-nurturer. In the meantime, however, she began to consider ways of making her classroom more challenging and in ways different from those she had thus far attempted. And so, through soul-searching, Barbara rediscovered the honours English graduate, recalled an emptiness experienced while mothering at home, and with this discovery her conception of herself as teacher shifted. To be sure, she still thought of herself first and foremost as a teacher-nurturer, but her conception of nurturing changed in subtle but significant ways, reflecting a change in her own needs and expectations for teaching.

THE PAIN OF SEPARATION

At year's end, Barbara had for the most part settled into a comfortable and productive teaching role but as the last day of school approached she found herself experiencing some surprising emotions that, while not affecting her understanding of herself as teacher, did affect her relationships with the students.

These bear mention because they illustrate yet another dimension of the teaching role Barbara had assumed. Like other teachers and the administrators, Barbara cracked down the last few weeks of school in anticipation of increasing student misbehaviour. This was a crazy time during which the students were doing 'really crazy things. . .' In response Barbara found herself feeling 'less tolerant [of students]. I'll kick kids out of class. I'll send them down to the [vice principal's office]. I won't dink around with anybody.' While Barbara had been tough with students before, these actions seemed oddly out of character. As she contemplated them, Barbara realized they were not motivated only by the desire to maintain a productive classroom learning environment; other feelings were evident.

A student's remarks, one of the students she had mothered and with whom she felt an especially strong attachment, helped her gain insight into what she was doing and why. The student was obviously concerned about Barbara, wondering if there was something the matter.

> Tammy, the little girl that was raped at the beginning [of the year] . . . came in and said, 'You've been kind of cranky the last two weeks.' She perched on the edge of my desk and I looked at her face. I thought, 'I'm never going to see you again, Sweetheart. I've lived with you. I've lived longer with you during this year than I have with my own children. I know every detail of your life. I know you inside and out. Then, I'm going to say 'goodbye' to you.'

Similar feelings arose within her when looking at other students:

> I was talking to my students last night. I looked at [them]. I've been looking at [them] lately and I think, 'I'm never going to see these kids again. I've been busting my [rear end] to connect with them, and I'm never going to see them again' . . . . This is going to rip me apart.

Intuitively, and in anticipation of the last day of school, Barbara the nurturer had been pulling back yet further from the students as a way of softening the 'pain of separation' and they noticed it, as did she once it was called to her attention.

> I think part of this pulling back [of being cranky], this discipline stuff, this heavy hand [I've been using in class], is

116

to harden myself against [the] pain of separation .... I need
to distance myself from my students. I've got to be able to
handle [the separation].

Having become so deeply involved in the lives of her students,
Barbara was concerned about the emotional effects of separation
particularly as they might spill out into her home life where, she
said, her children would 'need [her] straight off the bat I
can't be down wallowing in my own pain [once summer vacation
begins].' Barbara greeted the last days of school with ambivalence:
she needed a rest and time to spend with her children; but she did
not want to say goodbye to her students whom she had grown to
love deeply.

IN SUMMARY

Barbara's central teaching metaphor was 'teaching is nurturing'.
She carried this self-conception, which grew out of years of
experience of being at home mothering her own children, into the
classroom. Thus, she entered teaching, as she put it, 'expecting to
heal wounds', seeking to protect and care for adolescents. This
metaphor gave coherence to her inevitably partial and incomplete
teaching schema through which she made the teaching situation
meaningful. Through her teacher-nurturer eyes students became
children; the classroom became 'home', her 'territory'; and
personal satisfaction came from connecting with 'children', and
'feeding' and 'being fed' by them. These were strong meanings as
is indicated by the ease with which early in the year Barbara
rejected the school's curriculum as disconnected from children
and by the great effort she put into getting to know the students
intimately in order to serve their needs better.

For the most part Barbara's understanding of self as teacher
proved to be mostly fitting to the situation; the students responded
positively to Barbara and to her efforts on their behalf. However,
while Barbara was able to give coherence to the situation through
this understanding of her responsibilities in the classroom, and
the students were, she thought, responding appropriately and
well, by spring-time she found teaching to be not wholly personally
satisfying. Some aspects of her teaching self became problematic
and conflicted with her inner self. Despite her best efforts, she
could not, for example, adequately respond to all the demands of

117

the students and, even if she could, to do so jeopardized her relationships with her own children; ultimately, parenting at school came into conflict with parenting at home. This tension, coupled with paperwork and the numerous other demands of teaching that drained her energy, along with disappointment in the response of some students and parents to her and a growing feeling that she was becoming intellectually stagnant, forced Barbara to redefine the boundaries of the nurturing role she was implementing, and thus she reconstructed some of the meanings associated with her teaching self.

7

FROM EXPERT TO CARING ADULT

HEIDI

Heidi, a 26-year-old, recently married graduate in Spanish and English, came from a long line of teachers including her father and several aunts, uncles, and cousins. Her mother worked as a school secretary. Despite this, however, she claimed she never intended to be a teacher. 'I always swore I wouldn't be a teacher because everyone in my family is. It's something I just didn't want to do because they all did it.' It was her love of Spanish and her superior language abilities, developed while living in Argentina for eighteen months on a teaching assignment for her church, that ultimately led to the decision to become a teacher. Although discouraged from teaching by her family, and especially by her father who regretted his own decision to become a teacher due to lack of 'financial rewards and a lot of [administrative] hassles', Heidi concluded that no other career would enable her to work with the Spanish language in as interesting ways.

INITIAL TEACHING METAPHOR

Given her reasons for becoming a teacher it was not surprising to find that Heidi began the school year thinking of herself first and foremost as a subject-matter specialist: teacher is subject-matter expert. 'Competence' and love of subject-matter were key values evident in our interview with her prior to the beginning of the school year. This is not to say that Heidi's only goal was to teach students Spanish; other teacher responsibilities also seemed significant. She thought that teachers, when teaching, taught more than just content, they also taught responsibility and good work habits, for example.

WORK CONTEXT

South Nile High School, where Heidi began teaching, was a lower-middle- and middle-class suburban school with an enrolment of 1800, which also drew students from a large working-class area traditionally occupied by employees of the mining industry. The collapse of the industry in the 1980s crushed the expectations of many of the children of these workers who had taken for granted that they would be able to follow the path of their fathers into the workforce. Academically, it was an undistinguished school, neither outstanding, nor particularly weak. Heidi was assigned to teach one section each of advanced debate and beginning debate, sophomore English, and three sections of beginning Spanish. She had four preparations with one planning period.

Without question, had it been a year with abundant employment opportunities Heidi would not have accepted the position at South Nile, but she did. She was especially reluctant to teach debate which she was certified to teach only by virtue of possessing an English subject-area minor. She had been a high-school and freshman debater but had no experience whatsoever teaching it. Obtaining the position at the high school, however, was contingent on taking over the debate programme and so, out of desperation, Heidi accepted the assignment.

GETTING READY FOR TEACHING

The summer before Heidi's first year of teaching was spent attending university graduate courses; and she had comparatively little time to get ready for school. The task of getting prepared was complicated by her lack of background in debate, and very limited teaching background in English. Because of possessing very different backgrounds in each area, she approached planning in each area differently before and during the school year, trusting that, over time, she would be able to remedy whatever deficiencies arose.

In the process of planning in all three areas Heidi imagined what her students would be like, an image – the student portion of her teaching schema – based upon 'the kids I student taught'. She further fleshed out the image by recalling herself as a public-school student, although she had been academically clearly a much better student than most of those she was destined to teach and was more engaged in school, having been a student-body officer her senior year with the result that she felt much more positively toward school: 'I loved high school. Well, just today I sat down and thought, "If someone asks me to do this [activity] would I want to do it?" . . . I tried to draw myself back a little, [as] if I were an adolescent.' And later, 'I can still see myself there in the classroom as a student.' And, too, she called upon her younger brother for advice. Even while doing this, Heidi realized hers was a partial student image, a hypothesis really, and that, generally speaking, she would have to trust that the materials she had been given were appropriate – at least some other teachers had found them so. Given the uncertainty of this image, Heidi worried about how well she would get along with the students, perhaps recalling some conflicts with students over her grading practices that arose during practice teaching, and about how appropriate her curriculum would be.

Heidi had a solid academic background in English but had never taught the subject; she practice taught sophomores in Spanish. Before school began her aim was to get an outline of units for the term, and the first unit planned in some detail before school began. She started by reviewing the district programme in English: 'The district has some real intense guidelines . . . but I'm not sure how to work with [them yet].' The guidelines included topics to be taught and suggestions for student readings. Functioning, as she described it, like a 'puzzle solver', and with the guideline in mind, Heidi sat down at a large table covered with all the materials she had accumulated as a teacher-education student in methods courses, materials borrowed from friends both English teachers and teacher-education students, and some 'things an English teacher gave me at [the school]'. She then began sorting and sifting, trying to decide on unit topics and within topics suitable activities and a pattern of activities, the 'puzzle picture'.

As noted, planning the curriculum for debate was a worry. She inherited a fairly successful programme given up by the previous teacher because he was simply worn out by all the work. Six years were all that he could stand. In debate there were no district guidelines, no adopted textbooks, and really only a programme based on personality and a calendar of upcoming tournaments.

121

Heidi was very concerned: 'I have nothing,' she said. As a student, she had liked debate but had not thought of it in several years: 'I know how to debate, but I don't know how to teach anyone how to do it. So, that's what I'm wrestling with right now'. After talking with the former debate teacher, she decided she had no choice but to rely heavily on the more advanced students to help her with the less advanced, and that she would simply have to develop a programme while teaching it, keeping in mind that much of what she would do would be in response to the demands of tournament preparation. One result of this decision was that for most of the first two months of the school year, Heidi was only a day or two ahead in her planning, and this was stressful.

For a person whose initial conception of herself as teacher was tied to subject-matter expertise, this was a troubling situation. As Heidi put it:

> Those [debate] kids are smart. They know more than I do right now. . . . What I'm afraid of is [that] I have to sort of pretend like I know more than I really do. I'm afraid that they're going to lose confidence in me and not respect me as the person that's really in charge. For some reason it's important to me to be in charge . . . [to be a person] they can work . . . with, and that can kind of help . . . . I'm afraid that I'm going to lose . . . my credibility.

Heidi entered a foreign-language department with a programme already in place. Before school began she met with one of the Spanish teachers who gave her all the available programme materials, including a checklist of topics to be taught, along with an orientation, for which Heidi was grateful. Ironically, Spanish, the area within which she needed least help, was the one within which she was offered the most assistance. In deciding how to use the school programme Heidi relied upon her five months of practice teaching with similar-ability students and her own vast experience with the language and in South American cultures. She planned out the first week with some care, but was little concerned about it: 'I could go in and teach Spanish without much preparation.'

In addition, Heidi planned for discipline and management, basing her initial decisions primarily upon her practice-teaching experience. 'I think I was a little tough when I was student teaching. I expected a little too much. It was a tough situation. I've decided to just have a few common rules'. She intended for these to remain the same throughout the year; she was determined to stick to them. One set of rules had to do with how she would treat disruptions in class:

> I've decided as a teacher how many disruptions I'll allow a student to make in a class before I . . . turn them [over] to the principal, or vice-principal, or before I . . . notify parents . . . . I'll allow one disruption, and then the next one they're at the office . . . . [The administration] will support that.

THE FIRST WEEK OF SCHOOL

In anticipation of the first day of teaching, Heidi was 'pretty hyper'. The tension she felt on the first day of school was heightened by her being unaware of an assembly planned for first period that 'messed up the day's schedule'. Following the assembly in each class she made introductions and then shared a 'disclosure statement' which contained her academic and behavioural expectations. There was little formal teaching.

Actual teaching began on the second day of school. Each English class began with the students writing for approximately ten minutes in a journal on an assigned topic. Following writing, during the first weeks of class, Heidi had the students engage in a variety of activities, most frequently reading a short selection from an assigned novel for the purposes of discussion or for answering questions on a work sheet or written on the board.

On the second day she started the beginning Spanish classes by teaching the students how to answer the roll in Spanish, taught them how to ask 'What is your name?' and to respond 'My name is . . . .' The third day of beginning Spanish started with a review of the previous day's work, then she introduced the students to the use of Spanish gestures. From the curriculum log:

> I want the students to learn [Spanish gestures] and use them with each other. (I told them I unfortunately didn't know any of the 'crude' gestures used in Spanish). I did the gestures and had them write on a sheet of paper what they thought it might mean. I then did them again and asked for their responses. Sometimes they were right, other gestures were too difficult to figure out. The students then did them with me. We had a riot! They left class laughing and feeling like they could communicate, somewhat.

The next day she again reviewed what had been taught and then had the students role-play situations within which they could use what they had learned. The study of numbers, days, months, and time, followed.

In advanced (Varsity) debate Heidi presented the topic that would be the focus for the year's competitions (Varsity debaters represent the school in competition with other schools) and began making assignments to class members for gathering and organizing evidence. In the beginning debate class she gave an orientation to debating and made assignments to prepare outlines of speeches which would be given. Happily, only a week into the term, she found a speech textbook 'which contained a good chapter on debate' that she was able to use to teach fundamentals to the novices while waiting for the Varsity debaters to begin organizing and writing up evidence for the beginners' use.

Friday of the first week of school found Heidi feeling very confident about her work and good about herself as teacher. But she also felt tired, very tired: 'My feet and legs were cramping and throbbing most of the day. My voice was gone and I was dead tired.'

THE FOLLOWING WEEKS OF SCHOOL

The second week of school also went well. In particular Heidi began to feel she was connecting with the students in productive ways. She was, for example, very pleased at the growing honesty and openness expressed by the sophomore English students in their journal writing as they got to know and respect her:

> The things they write are just fantastic. I'm . . . really impressed with what they've been able to do. [I enjoy] watching them improve just in a few weeks. [They are] more open . . . . They trust me, I guess, [which] makes me feel like I'm somewhat significant . . . .

Also, the students were responding appropriately and well to her teaching: '[In] both my Spanish classes we're having a lot of fun. The kids are laughing. They're with me. I look out there and I can tell they're with me and they're excited [about the class].'

While much was going very well, little problems began cropping up. For example, on Tuesday of the second week she discovered that she had:

screwed up the computerized roll sheet all day. I marked the wrong week (why did they give me a new computer sheet with last week's dates on it?) Then, I got the right week but marked [it incorrectly]. They brought my rolls back during 7th period to fix them – in the middle of class!

There were other problems as well, each associated with not quite knowing what was going on in the school; she felt disoriented: 'I don't know what's going on in this school,' she lamented. Being consumed with her work, she did not attend carefully to administrative details which proved to be a source of frustration. For example, shortly before the first faculty meeting, she realized she did not know where the meeting was to be held. Other problems arose from not being properly informed. For instance, she was not told how seriously the administration viewed prompt attendance at faculty meetings. Because of needing to listen to a student speech after school she was late for a subsequent meeting and was reprimanded for it.

While troubling, these problems paled in comparison with the growing frustration she was feeling with other aspects of teaching. During the first several days of the year Heidi was so busy planning her curriculum that she had not anticipated accurately the amount of time needed to keep up with paperwork, especially grading. She found herself dragging home each evening an ever increasing pile of work to be corrected, only to be too tired to complete it: 'I'm taking home the same box of papers that I take home almost every night,' she complained. In addition to grading papers, at midterm there were 'grade/failing' notices that needed to be completed and sent home. And, too, simply finding the time to organize her roll book proved to be difficult. Indeed, she was into the fourth week of teaching before she found time to fill in the gradebook:

> The kids aren't asking for papers but last night I kind of set it all out on the counter and just thought, 'I've got to grade these.' So, I wrote all their names down in the grade book. I haven't even really done an official grade book yet. I was just ashamed [of] myself . . . I'm concerned about [how] I'm going to do that . . . . because I've got kids who I need to send failing notices on.

Furthermore, despite working very hard, Heidi found that she could rarely be more than a day or two ahead in planning for the classes. Given her lack of background in debate and in the teaching of English, and four different preparations, perhaps this was to be expected. And then, to compound her problems, the first debate tournament was scheduled for the first week of November with several others following each weekend thereafter! Feeling stressed, Heidi found herself putting only minimal planning time into Spanish, trusting that her excellent content-area background would get her through the lesson in reasonably good shape. In debate she resolved that she would simply have to run the classes as workshops where the students 'won't be as dependent on me giving them instruction'. In English, she found herself working very hard to gather materials from other teachers who were generally very helpful.

> Two of them are preparing a packet [of materials] for me [on *To Kill a Mockingbird*]. [Having these materials for teaching is] going to save me. That's going to help. But, there are days when I'm not sure I can get the reading done and keep up. I'm assigning them ten pages to read tonight and I hope I can get the ten pages done! This is a book I've not read!

Occasionally, Heidi did not decide what the activities for the day would be until the English students were writing in their journals at the beginning of the period. For a person needing and wanting to plan far ahead, this situation was extremely troubling:

> If I got sick tonight, I don't know what I'd have a substitute do tomorrow in some of my classes. [My planning] is day by day . . . . I hope my kids can't tell I'm winging it!

STUDENT PRESSURES

Fortunately, Heidi had few discipline problems during this period of time. She was relatively consistent in her enforcement of rules, although at times she found it to be, as she said two months into the year, 'really hard'. She did not like being 'tough', as she put it:

> My policy was that you [turn in the assignment] the day it's due. The next day you get half credit. After that you don't get any credit. I had some kids give some really good speeches a day late. To think that I have to give them half credit has been really hard for me . . . . [But] I knew I needed to do it.

In addition to her consistency in enforcement, the routines Heidi established in English for beginning class helped eliminate off-task behaviour in that setting, as did the pressure of tournament preparation in the debate classes. Although there were few routines established in Spanish the pace was usually brisk and minimized student misbehaviour. And too, in Spanish, Heidi included in the curriculum many interesting activities with which to engage the students.

While Heidi generally felt good about her relationships with the students and was only somewhat concerned about student discipline, as the days progressed she became progressively more concerned about poor student attitudes toward learning; there was a widespread and general lack of interest in learning. As a subject-matter specialist and as a former honours student in high school, this was surprising and disappointing to Heidi; even the advanced debaters proved to be disappointing. Writing in her journal:

> The Varsity Debaters have grown accustomed to sitting around during class working on other things, arriving late to class, and not committing to completing assignments. 'This is how we spent last year,' [they say].

In general, and unhappily, Heidi found that the students expected her to 'spoon feed' them content and to entertain them; they pressured her to lower her expectations. Neither activity did she associate initially with teaching. Nor did she intend to 'spoon feed' the students; and, although she hoped to provide interesting activities, she did not intend to become an entertainer.

In addition to being bothered by the lack of student interest in learning, she was especially troubled by students who appeared to be self-destructive and felt compelled to try to do something about the situation to help them individually: 'I . . . care about them . . . . They're teenagers [and] life is hard. If they screw up now, who knows when they'll catch up?' She was surrounded by troubled teenagers needing help. Writing in her journal: 'I had to turn in a student I really like for snorting cocaine at lunch. I wanted to do it because I worry about him . . . ' And the same week:

> I caught . . . two 'Stoners' (students who use drugs heavily) during seventh period [who were supposed to be in my classes]. They both [cut] the classes they have with me. It was

an intense confrontation . . . . I [wanted] to shake the crap out of [them]. I wanted to shame them into coming to class. I really care about them but don't know if I can help. Others told me they aren't worth my time. Will I really [come to] feel that they aren't?

Later the vice-principal gave her this advice and warning: 'Don't get too stuck on these kids.' She ignored the warning.

As Heidi got to know the students better she began to be better able to anticipate their behaviour which helped her immensely when thinking about curriculum planning. In addition, she came to recognize patterns of belief and action that were tied to student-group affiliation. These groups, she noted, both complicated and simplified her work as teacher; Heidi ran headlong into categories and cliques tied to student music and life style. Heidi was not merely confronted by individual students but by powerful and organized student subcultural groupings[1] some of which, like the Stoners, the 'Hardcores' (Punkers), and 'Rockers' (students deeply involved in heavy-metal music), were hostile to schooling. Some groups, like the 'Wavers' (students heavily involved with 'New Wave' music and culture), 'Cowboys' and 'Skaters' (students who dragged skate boards around with them, while wearing brightly coloured shorts and T-shirts) were indifferent to schooling. Still others, like the 'Normies' ('normal' students), 'Nerds,' 'Preppies', and 'Jocks' liked school, although for quite different reasons. Recognizing the groupings, Heidi accepted them, although not entirely happily, making no pretence that she could or should change them but she hoped she might have some influence on individual group members. Any attempt to change the groups themselves was energy poorly spent; besides, such a responsibility was not the teacher's. Nevertheless, accepting the groupings and coming to terms with them as they manifested themselves in her classroom were quite different matters.

RESPONDING TO STUDENT GROUPS

Heidi's classes, like other public-school classrooms, contained a mixture of students. Most of Heidi's students would probably be Normies but sprinkled among the Normies were Nerds, Preppies, Jocks, Cowboys, Skaters, Wavers, Rockers, and Stoners (no Hardcores were ever seen in any of the classes). Normies, Nerds,

Preppies, and Jocks generally liked school, reflecting values contiguous to the wider community. Wavers, Rockers, and Stoners, in contrast, were little interested in or involved with school. Virtually all her classes were mixed, for example, in her third-period beginning debate class, a small class of only sixteen students. In the middle of the room sat two Wavers, a male and a female, complete with their baggy, mostly black uniforms; across the room near one of the six office-like practice debate rooms (which students would occasionally retire into to listen to music and to prepare their cases) sat a couple of Skaters, the apparent leader of the group, a male, wore a brightly coloured 'Brazilia Volleyball Tournament XII' T-shirt; and in the front of the class were a couple of Preppies who, before the buzzer, were excitedly talking about preferred colleges. The rest of the students would probably be considered by other students to be Normies, the buffering glue that keeps things together by keeping groups apart.

Members of some groups were clearly harder to work with than others. As noted, in one week Heidi had two run-ins with Stoners, members of a small group of students who were, as she put it, 'drug rejects . . . flunkies of a [drug rehabilitation program].' The student she caught snorting cocaine was especially worrying: 'He comes to my sixth period [class] after lunch just really weird and really hyper. He screams sometimes . . . . he's just out of control in class.' Despite this, Heidi, 'really like[d] him'. Although few in number, Stoners exerted an influence far in excess of their numbers. Heidi may have liked individual Stoners but as a group they presented serious problems to the teachers and the counsellors in the school, complicating Heidi's life and making teaching increasingly difficult. Their presence, and that of other group members hostile to schooling or indifferent to it, threatened Heidi's view of herself as a teacher-expert.

In debate the presence of Wavers presented Heidi with an especially bothersome problem. The debate teams represented the school in the various tournaments throughout the state. Prior to the first tournament, Heidi worried about how these students would present themselves and represent the school: 'I'm embarrassed to death to send them to a tournament.' But, despite her concern, she was willing to let them go. As it turned out, and had she known Wavers better she would have known this, she did not need to worry. To participate in a tournament students had to maintain a 2.0 grade-point average on a 4 point scale, with no more than one 'F'. The Wavers, not surprisingly, did not make the grade, no Waver apparently ever did. A more serious problem arose earlier when Heidi began to form debate teams. Students were very reluctant to cross group lines. When she attempted to pair a male Skater, who was quite serious about debate, with a female Waver who was very bright but seemed to be little interested, the boy remarked: 'I can't debate with a partner that has purple hair!' The students would not work together despite Heidi's efforts.

INCREASING STRESS AND ILLNESS

Aware of student groupings to which she tried to respond by developing a relevant and interesting curriculum, worried about and frustrated by students who were behaving in self-destructive ways, overwhelmed with paperwork and grading, swamped by the demands of four preparations that made it nearly impossible to plan very far ahead, and feeling guilty about neglecting her husband and their relationship, by November Heidi began to feel that she was nearing a breaking-point: 'I feel like everything in my life is out of control!' Her frustrations produced an uncharacteristically negative attitude toward students and toward teaching; and she found herself the victim of dramatic swings of emotion. Debate, for example, threw her onto an emotional roller-coaster over which she felt little control. When the students did well she was exhilarated: 'The students who worked the hardest last week had the most success at the tournament. Sometimes there are flukes and the hardest workers don't always reap the rewards. I was very proud of them. . .' When they did poorly, she was crushed, and struggled to displace some of the blame from herself and her feelings of inadequacy:

> Because I have an English minor and debated in high school
> . . . I'm supposed to be able to coach debate and speech?!?!?
> What did I get myself into? My debate students did not do
> well at a tournament last weekend.

At the end of the first week of the school year Heidi reported that she was extremely tired, physically and emotionally. Occasionally early in the year and throughout it Heidi tried to make time for herself by having the students do seat work and by having them grade a larger number of assignments, but these were but brief rests that did little to ease the demands of teaching on her time and energy. By Thanksgiving (late November) she was exhausted but, for a while, exhaustion was tempered by extreme anger at the discovery that as a debate-English teacher she was entitled, according to district policy, to two preparation periods, when in fact the principal had only scheduled her for one. Unfortunately, there was nothing she could do to alter the situation.

Her efforts to reach out and help troubled students only increased her difficulties. She discovered that because she was willing to listen to student problems, students talked, and talked, and talked; there was no escaping from them.

> Some ask me about college and learning foreign languages. Others talk about the debate circuit. Some want ideas for asking guys they like to [the] Sadie Hawkins [dance] and then they run to me after they have asked them and ramble [on] about how nervous they are to get the boy's answer. It goes on and on. I [missed] the assembly yesterday in hopes of getting some reading done . . . and couldn't get away from students.

The problem was that Heidi had let the students know that she enjoyed talking with them; she was of two minds: 'If I didn't ask them about their games every week they might not have come to chat with me. But they are so cute, I cannot resist being interested in their activities'.

There were other pressures as well: Heidi took graduate courses throughout the year in pursuit of an M. Ed. Here too, she had difficulty keeping up with assignments and readings and, especially, trying to maintain the high level of academic performance she and others expected. While trying to keep up with her job and her own academic work Heidi pushed herself to the limits of her physical endurance. She slept little. Rarely did she take time out to eat a nourishing meal and relied on fast foods and colas to sustain her. She spent little time with her equally busy graduate-student husband. And, she let her portion of the housework accumulate:

> My home life is really a scream. The bed hasn't been made for a week, clean clothes haven't been put away. Each morning we rummage through one basket, hopefully it is the clean one, to get dressed. Not only do we use paper plates,

but also paper cups [when eating]. I'm considering plastic silverware or not using any utensils at all! [My husband] is equally as busy but very supportive and tolerant of my life-style. Fortunately his mother wasn't an immaculate house-keeper (though I'm sure her home never got quite this bad).

With deepening exhaustion, Heidi fell ill. She had a case of the flu for the entire first week of October but missed only one day of school feeling that she 'needed' to be in her classes. She did not fully recover her health and even in the spring-time she was 'thoroughly tired' and battling a lingering cold. At the end of each school day she would be 'wiped out' and frequently would take short naps only to awaken facing more work. Moreover, into April her weekends provided little rest and relaxation, being taken up by debate tournaments throughout the state and in California:

> Those tournaments . . . run the week together. My kids, my debate kids, are . . . working hard. Thursday and Friday at the last minute [I'm running around] making copies [of material they need]. And [then] I remember, 'Oh Shoot! I forgot to get the excuses for them! . . . By Sunday I'm dead and I don't have any time to recover to start the next week.

In late November, Heidi's health, bad as it was, took a turn for the worse as she reported in her journal:

> Yesterday I began to have back spasms and by the time I got out of my car at home, I could not even walk. This has continued and I have to go to the doctor this morning. As much as I want to withdraw a bit from debate and have the debate students become more self-supporting, I am having fits about not being at school this morning. They have a tournament this afternoon . . . I tried to cover all the bases, but I'm so worried about them.

After visiting her physician, Heidi discovered that there was more than stress behind her physical problems; the physician told her she was pregnant.

Being pregnant and not feeling well, and being seriously overworked, Heidi looked toward Christmas break with great anticipation; she hoped to rest. Instead, Christmas proved to be emotionally an extremely trying time, perhaps one of the worst times of her life: she had a miscarriage just prior to the break. She returned for the few days before the break, despite being weakened and, as a way of coping, plunged herself into work with even greater passion than before, even putting aside for a time her graduate work. Feeling angry and bitter, she asserted, 'Hey, I'm really going to go Gung Ho for my career; bag this mother business.' Returning from Christmas Heidi worked as tirelessly as ever, pushing herself and filling every available minute with activity, in particular planning: 'I go home and prepare ahead. That's what I do instead of doing other things like doing the dishes ... or whatever; I just lesson plan.' As a result, she got well ahead in her planning in each class for the first time; and she caught up with paperwork and even cleaned up her normally cluttered classroom. Work was therapeutic: 'I'm working here because this is [a] place where I can succeed. You know, I can feel the success with the kids every day ... Other things in life are out of control; I just ignore them.' But she could not ignore them and felt troubled that, while totally withdrawing into work in order to heal, she was allowing her priorities to become even more unbalanced, and she lamented: 'I wish I were better at ... balancing things outside of school in my personal life; getting that together.'

A METAPHOR SHIFT

In response to the students and the pressures they exerted on her, her discovery that she enjoyed the students more than she expected, the difficulties of her teaching assignment, and the chaos of her personal life, Heidi's sense of herself as teacher changed. She began the year thinking of teaching in terms of demonstrating subject-matter competence: teacher is expert. Very early in the year this sense of teaching self was put into doubt especially by Heidi's teaching assignment. Clearly, for example, she could not function in debate as an expert, although for some weeks early in the year she sought to do so. In the first week of November, she remarked:

> I think what I'm afraid of ... is that they'll find out that they don't have everything they need [for the tournament] or that there's something I didn't tell them and that was my responsibility .... I just feel under the wire .... The kids know a lot more about the topic than I do .... I just can't do it.

Eventually, although at first somewhat unhappily, she came to terms with the problem: 'I've resigned myself to accepting the fact that I don't know everything' with the result that the debate classes became extended workshops, as noted. No other alternative presented itself.

Not being able to function as expert as she had hoped, and feeling somewhat uncomfortable with that role in any case, given her work context and the range of problems brought to the classroom by students who needed more of teachers than just content knowledge, for a time Heidi did not know quite who she was as teacher. Writing in her journal: 'Sometimes I am not sure who I am. Am I their teacher, their big sister, their mother, their friend, a police officer, a drill sergeant, a baby sitter?'

During this time of confusion she looked toward her students for self-confirmation and found in them her primary source of job satisfaction. It was in the establishment of friendly relationships with the students that Heidi found pleasure in teaching. The kind and quality of these relations came to define, for a time, who she was: a friend. Functioning as a friend, Heidi became increasingly open toward the students and involved in their lives; many students, in turn, reciprocated by confiding in her also as a friend. Quickly, however, she discovered that while she enjoyed somewhat the role of teacher-friend it was also troublesome; she had become overly friendly, too involved in the students' lives. Seeking to connect to her in friendly ways, the students invaded her space and consumed great amounts of time and energy that she so desperately needed for other activities. In frustration, she remarked: 'I don't want students to feel they can tell me everything, I don't want to know it!' They made other demands on her friendship and took liberties within the classroom, as well. One of the advanced debaters, for example, felt comfortable and confident enough literally to take over portions of one beginning debate class relegating Heidi to the role of Xerox copier and administrator. Feeling insecure about her knowledge of debating, and appreciative of what she thought to be his kindness in offering to help in the class, she allowed him to continue in his assumed teaching role. Gradually, however, conflicts arose as, for example, when she realized he was taking advantage of her in a variety of ways and that his work with the beginning-debaters had become nothing more than an opportunity for him to show off his knowledge and to exercise his power over younger students. The situation came to a head when, as a result of his having been late twenty-seven times for the advanced debate course during one quarter, Heidi gave him an 'unsatisfactory citizenship' mark which would appear on his permanent school transcripts as an indication of his having been a problem student. Calling on their friendship, he pleaded for her to change the mark which she did not; he had abused her friendship and trust. As Heidi discovered some of the limits to approaching teaching as a form of friendship, she withdrew somewhat from the students. The demands and the cost of friendship were simply too great.

In the midst of her struggle to find herself as teacher, Heidi attended a parent–teacher conference. The two-day conference proved to be an important occasion for getting feedback on herself as teacher, feedback which helped nudge her along in a direction that would eventually lead her out of confusion. Another role that included parts of her expert-teaching ideal and drew on the value she placed on friendship began to emerge, one that had deep roots. She spoke of the conference in her journal and of the students' responses to it:

> Tuesday and Wednesday nights combined totaled seventy sets of parents, almost half of my students being represented . . . . Several of the students whose parents should have come didn't show, but I wasn't surprised. I suspected that would be the case. The reports I had were not all good news, I was honest, and tried to let the parents know that I will do whatever I can to help their child succeed. With one exception, the parents were extremely pleasant. My gut feeling is that the experience was more beneficial for me than for the parents . . . So many of them said that their student really enjoys me and my classes . . . . I realized how important it is to me that I can contribute some enjoyment for my students in school . . . .
>
> The students' responses to the conferences were very negative. In each class I told the students how much I enjoyed meeting their parents and that I was able to say some good things about each of them without having to fib. The main consensus of the students was that their parents are deaf to positive comments from teachers. They can hear the

negative remarks which result in groundings, daily or weekly progress reports, and not a moment's peace when they are home without their noses in a book.

The tension Heidi noted between the adult world and that of the child was to become a key element in the teaching metaphor she eventually formed and lived out. Additional elements came from the students themselves. While she came to care deeply about the students, some of them behaved in ways that were very irritating. In particular she found students who refused to work, who refused to exert any effort on their own behalf in order to learn, extremely frustrating: 'The one's I'm hard on – some of them I like – but they're so lazy! They don't do anything. I don't want them to think I'm a softy; it's hurting them. It bugs me!' Some of these students were Rockers, some Wavers, some Stoners. She came to value effort above performance in grading in contrast to her practice-teaching experience where performance counted above all else. Gradually, Heidi began to perform a kind of triage on students: those willing to work she would meet half way and invest energy and time in them. If they worked even harder, she would put additional effort into helping them learn. For example, she decided in her beginning debate class that two of the students in the class, Wavers, were not worth her continued efforts to get them to learn; they would not meet her half way: 'I just won't waste my time with them . . . . They're not going to perform for me in Debate.' Heidi invested her energies elsewhere, concluding that 'I don't think I can change [them].' And yet, the 'Stoner' about whom Heidi was warned by the vice principal, and despite his group affiliation, met Heidi half way after she had gotten tough with him and confronted him for sluffing. He came to class and worked with the result that she made even greater efforts to help him. During one observation of the beginning Spanish class within which the Stoner was enrolled, Heidi's efforts to help were quite evident. Shortly after giving the class assignment she wandered by his desk to see how he was doing. In a very casual way a few minutes later she checked on him a second time. Two minutes later he raised his hand indicating he needed assistance and she gave it. Twenty minutes later she walked by his desk yet a fourth time, chatted briefly with him, tapped him affectionately on the back, and asked him to encourage his girl friend to begin attending class. By January, this student, despite being a Stoner, was a fully contributing class member. As with the Stoner, Heidi would meet other students half way, but no more until they proved themselves deserving. In this way she conserved energy and time, and yet found outlets for her desire to connect with students in caring ways.

An additional element of her emerging teaching self was tied to Heidi's belief that caring for the students meant at times being hard on them. It was all right to be tough; being easy was not doing them, or herself, a favour. There were numerous occasions which illustrated this development, for example: in Spanish, Heidi began giving students frequent tests to encourage them to do their reading and homework: 'I'm tired of worrying about them; it is time for them to be concerned about their own performance.' At the semester break she removed from her beginning-debate class all students who had not put forth a reasonable amount of effort, and encouraged them to take other classes that were required for graduation:

> Apparently you're having problems with grades in your other classes. This is an elective course. You need to be in a course where you'll get some substantial credit [toward graduation], and [you can] take Debate when your grades are under control and you can afford an elective.

She also generally increased her work requirements having decided she would no longer be a 'Gift Fairy . . . when it comes to grades'. Similarly, when a student failed to get her work in on time in order to count for the term's grade, despite an agreed-upon extension, Heidi failed her despite the loud and threatening protests of the girl's mother: 'I should hate for [my daughter] to not be able to walk down the graduation aisle because of one stupid debate class!', the mother exlaimed. In response to the situation Heidi spoke at length with the vice-principal who, in effect, hinted that she should pass the student, everyone else had, but Heidi refused:

> I went down to the vice-principal and [told him about] the situation. I [said I] don't want to back down. He said, 'Listen, you're not going to teach her a lesson. I'll support whatever you decide [to do], but if you want to back down [I'll understand]. Just realize, you are not going to teach her a lesson'. That . . . bothered me . . . . [This has] happened since 8th grade . . . . People just said, 'Let her go, it's not

worth [the trouble] . . . . Her parents . . . don't expect [her]
to live by the rules.

Being tough, however, did not mean Heidi was uncaring; indeed,
caring meant being tough, but fair. With the students who did
their part, those who met Heidi half way, she maintained warm
relationships and classes were frequently fun, a quality Heidi came
to value greatly in her selection of activities as a means for
increasing student motivation to learn. On their part, the students
recognized that Heidi was caring, and respected her for it:

> I've had a couple of kids say that. . . '[You're] different from
> a lot of my teachers because you really care about us. We
> know that you like us; that you want us to have fun [and] want
> us to learn something.'

For Heidi, becoming a teacher came to mean being a fair-minded,
caring adult: teacher is caring adult. As noted, many factors played a
part in nudging along this particular self-understanding but one
influence remains to be considered briefly: the terrible emotional
strain caused by the miscarriage. Her response to the miscarriage
seems to have moved her more quickly than anything else down
the road toward becoming the caring adult teacher. For example,
Heidi mentioned two months after the miscarriage that she felt
'quite different' as a result of the experience, less inclined to do
what other 'people think I should' and less inclined to try to
please; she was less disposed to define herself through the eyes of
the students or anyone else, for that matter. She turned inward,
seeking to locate sources of satisfaction and of self-worth that were
genuinely her own. Some aspects of life, she said, were simply
beyond her control and she would have to accept that but school
was a place where she could have a high degree of control and
could 'succeed'; in school 'things work'. Success at work made it
somewhat easier to bear the grief she felt and to blunt the anger
produced by the miscarriage. Succeeding meant having friendly
and warm relationships with the students and caring for them, but
not being friends with them; friends share pain, and this she could
not do. It meant getting the students to perform adequately, at
least those who were willing to try, and this required a tightening
up of standards so that they more nearly reflected the
subject-matter values she brought with her to teaching. And it
meant giving students whom others had written off an opportunity

to perform in the hope that they would take it. A few did, like the Stoner mentioned earlier, while others did not. In the success of these, and other students, Heidi found confirmation of her values and of her worth as a teacher.

AT YEAR'S END

At year's end Heidi had settled into a comfortable role, one that reflected accurately what she valued, and who and what she was as teacher. She felt as though she was being herself – her inner self and teaching self meshed – and no longer actually playing a role at all: 'I catch myself in class being . . . more . . . [relaxed] . . . . I'm loosening up a little in class when it comes to [expressing my] personality . . . but, I'm still pretty tight on the work.' She genuinely enjoyed teaching: 'I enjoy it . . . . It's not like work anymore. It's not like punching in at the office and putting in my time . . . It's kind of recreation, sometimes.' And, although bone tired, she felt much less stressed and more in control of both her personal and professional life: 'There are days that I go home that I don't take anything with me. I just go home. That's strange, [to me] . . . . [I feel like I'm] much more [in] control.'

IN SUMMARY

Heidi began the year thinking of herself as a subject-matter specialist. Within a matter of a few weeks after the start of the school year this conception of herself as teacher was put into jeopardy. While she was an expert in Spanish, she was clearly a novice in debate, and found herself unhappily dependent on the Varsity debaters for help. Furthermore, she found that the time demands of teaching, particularly of paperwork, made it impossible for her to make up the ground necessary to achieve a desired level of expertise. Despite working very hard, by mid year she was still not able to plan more than a day or two ahead. The students also challenged her view of herself as teacher. Many of them, she discovered, were little interested in learning, quite unlike her own experience as a student. And yet she enjoyed the students more than she had expected and found in her association with them a source of genuine personal satisfaction.

As her problems mounted, and as her grip weakened on the teacher-expert metaphor, for a time Heidi felt lost and uncertain as to who she was as teacher. For a brief period she sought to befriend the students but, as they responded to her, she found the demands of friendship to be excessive. The students got too close to her, expected too much of her, and occasionally took advantage of her good will. While seeking to redefine herself, for a time, Heidi felt out of control and highly vulnerable: 'I feel like everything in my life is out of control!' These feelings deepened as her health deteriorated, culminating in the miscarriage and in a depressing holiday break, when a respite had been so longed for.

Following the Christmas break she plunged into her work and caught up on a myriad of tasks that had formerly been left unfinished. But, more importantly, she began to identify more clearly the kind of relationship she wanted with the students. A number of incidents helped focus her vision, among them parent-teacher conferences, where she recognized as never before the size of the gulf separating the adult and adolescent worlds and the difficulties young people encounter as they cross it. Heidi came to think of herself as someone with a special charge to help young people make this crossing as successfully as possible but, to do so, required that they be willing to accept her help. Her task was to help them to help themselves; students who would not make the effort were discarded but she did not give up easily on anyone, even a 'Stoner'. To help them meant that she needed to be more demanding, which she was, and to be tough at times, but always fair. For Heidi, to be a teacher came to mean being a 'caring adult'. With this redefinition of herself as teacher, Heidi felt as though she had found herself and this new feeling spilled over and influenced other aspects of her life:

> I think my whole attitude about my life and everything I'm accomplishing is much more positive [than it was a few months ago]. I'm happy. I enjoy what I do . . . . I feel like I'm *really* a teacher.

8

ALWAYS A TEACHER

Kay, an optimistic, soft-spoken, married, 37-year-old mother of five children, 'always wanted to be a teacher'. No other career ever appealed to her: 'I can really say that it's always been the only thing I've ever wanted to be. . .' Even as a small child of 8, she wanted to teach. Often she role-played school, looking forward to the time when she would actually have her own classroom: 'I was the kind [of child] that had my dad put a desk in the closet in order [for me] to have a [classroom] to teach my [siblings and friends].'

Kay's intense interest in teaching was a little surprising; no one in her family had ever been a teacher. Her mother was a 'housewife' and her father owned a grocery store in the small rural community within which Kay grew up. And neither parent attended college, although both graduated from the high school Kay later attended. Growing up she admired teachers but, more than anything, it was her 'love for children' and the pleasure she found working with them that made teaching so appealing. She began college fully intending to obtain teacher certification but following marriage quit school to raise a family. While raising her own children she taught pre-school as a way of partially realizing her dream and of supplementing the family's income, all the while hoping to return to college. When four of her five children were of school age, she re-entered the university and single-mindedly pursued her dream.

Kay's return to college signalled a dramatic change in the family's life together. Her husband, a successful engineer for a large utility company, was away frequently from home on business. Like the children, he had grown used to having Kay home and was heavily dependent upon her. She was the force that organized the family and kept it together. The adjustment necessitated by Kay's becoming a student was very difficult, especially for Matthew, the youngest child, who suddenly found himself in a day-care centre. It was also difficult for Kay who, at times, felt she had selfishly abandoned her family. Despite this feeling, however, she was determined to realize her life-long ambition: 'I do have feelings of guilt [but] I am enjoying this new way of life. [The family has] to adjust to it . . . . This was something I had to do.' Nevertheless, despite Kay's determination, throughout her time in college and the first year of teaching, balancing family needs and responsibilities with her professional ambition and duties proved troubling. We will return to this topic later.

As a student teacher Kay taught a class of first-graders (ages 5 to 6) much like those she was to teach in Morrison Elementary School (fictitious name), a suburban school near her home within which she received employment. The students were well groomed, healthy looking, and generally eager to learn. Kay was an extremely effective student teacher and received high ratings and very positive evaluations from her cooperating teacher and university supervisor. Following practice teaching Kay graduated with a degree in elementary education and shortly thereafter signed her first teaching contract. Kay's children and husband were delighted she had finished school and were proud of her accomplishments. And they were pleased she had received a contract to teach at a school so near to their home. The long commutes that had consumed Kay's time while attending the university and, especially while student teaching, were finally over. They looked forward with great anticipation to a return to something approximating the normal family life they had so long been used to.

WORK CONTEXT

The faculty of Morrison Elementary enthusiastically welcomed Kay to its ranks. The principal and the faculty were very supportive of her and were committed to help her succeed. For example, before the beginning of the school year she was assigned a mentor, one of three other teachers making up the 'First Grade Team', who quickly befriended her. Throughout the early part of the year the mentor met daily with Kay to offer support, answer questions about the operation of the school, and to share teaching materials and ideas. On his part, the principal made a point early and throughout the year of periodically checking in on Kay to see how she was doing and to let her know that he valued her work. It was a close and caring faculty, Kay thought.

Like the other teachers in the school, Kay faced the formidable task of teaching virtually all subject areas: reading, math, writing, social studies, music, physical education, art and so on. Kay's favourite subjects were among the least valued by the formal curriculum: the arts, including drama, and music. She especially enjoyed music, having performed classical music as a vocalist.

Prior to her arrival the First Grade Team had committed itself to using the methods and philosophy of the 'Workshop' programme, a popular approach to organizing the curriculum of the early grades. Several key phrases capture the Workshop philosophy: 'No one has to know everything; it takes courage to risk; it is okay to make mistakes while learning.' From an instructional perspective, Workshop provided a structure and routine for each morning of the school day: in the morning students would enter class and look at the board which contained a listing of the order of the 'workshop tasks' which eventually numbered eighteen by year's end. Once the school day began and announcements were made, students, when routinized, would go to the appropriate location, select the materials they were to begin working on, and proceed at their own pace through each of the workshops. Meanwhile, the teacher would sit in the back of the room at a table and, while monitoring class behaviour, listen to individual members of the various reading groups (Kay created three groups: pink, red, blue) as they read passages that had been assigned the previous day. The tasks, which changed daily and varied somewhat among ability groups, included a variety of activities such as word games and worksheets as well as physical activities such as 'walk the line,' where a child would leave his desk and walk along a metal carpet-edging strip that ran the length of the room, much like walking a thin balance beam. Activities like this helped break up the monotony of seat work and had the benefit of helping the children improve their large motor skills. Early in the year some workshops required that special instructions be given to the class as a whole so that the students would understand what was required; later in the year, individual students would go automatically to work if well routinized.

INITIAL TEACHING METAPHOR

Having long thought of herself as a teacher, Kay took it for granted that she was one, and a good one. As a result, early in the year Kay found it difficult in interview to articulate the values driving her thinking about teaching and herself as teacher. Simply put, she had not thought much about it. She was certain about some values, however: above all else, what mattered most was that she do her best to help students feel good about themselves, and to be happy, and to learn. Nothing else really mattered. In taking care of the students' needs, she would take care of her own professional and personal needs, she asserted:

> Their success is my success. I like to see them happy and learning and growing and doing and learning things. I . . . feel good that my ability [as a teacher] is helping them [to learn].

Seeking these ends, Kay intuitively and spontaneously responded to the students.

Other values were less apparent, being implicit and deeply embedded in her experience as a mother, a preschool teacher, and a student teacher; these values were difficult to put into words. When explaining how she thought about herself as teacher, Kay found it easier to articulate what she *did not* want to be in the classroom rather than to state what she *did* want to be. She did not want to establish a mother–child relationship with the students, this was certain, and yet, given the children's ages, she recognized that they would likely 'look on the teacher as a mother'. The distinction between a mother and a teacher was an important one to Kay, a distinction the students would have to learn as she sought to move them out into the broader world of relations:

> [It is important] for them to know the difference between [a] teacher and a mother. [With] the teacher there are certain lines they can't cross. They have to know [that]. They have to know that sometimes they [will] fail. [Teachers must set] boundaries – sometimes moms have a hard time drawing [boundaries] because of the love [they have for their children]. Even though as a teacher I begin to love them too . . . they have to know my role [is different from their moms']. They have to learn to take another step [away from mother]. I can't just be a mother figure [for them].

Kay was also certain she did not want to be like some of the teachers she had come to know throughout the years. Too many teachers, she said, 'were overly structured and dependent on text-books'. She hoped to be different, but thought the organization of the public schools would make it difficult to be so. She expected to have to compromise her values. Moreover, she was troubled by how inefficient the schools were and hoped to have little wasted time in her classroom. There was, she thought, much wrong with American education; she intended for her classroom to be different:

> [I value] hands-on experiences [most. But, hands-on experiences are] not practical in the school setting . . . There's no library with manipulatives (materials for the children to manipulate) . . . . [Schools are] so structured; [everything] is out of [textbooks] . . . . Also, there's so much . . . wasted time in our school system . . . . I bet if you were to count up how much time you actually spend instructing it would be [about] 45 minutes a day.

Kay was certain that she did not want to be a mother to her students but she did want them to be happy. Nor did she intend to be a textbook teacher. To the contrary, she wanted a programme that was 'active', 'creative', 'imaginative', 'up-to-date', and 'effective'. Ultimately, her fantasy was to create a classroom within which the students would be happily engaged in learning and she could stand by and watch having created an environment they found enticing: '[In my ideal] I would be floating around [the classroom], watching children doing things [and] watching them learn as they do [them].' While she rejected this vision as unrealistic, even laughingly naïve, early in the year in those areas of the curriculum over which she had a significant degree of control, she created a curriculum that was, in fact, active, creative and imaginative, just as she had hoped it would be. In these areas, such as art, science, and social studies, the students engaged in innovative and unusual activities including, for instance, a talent show and the hatching and raising of chicks.

As the year began, and as Kay started to express in practice her understanding of herself as a teacher, values and understandings in addition to those mentioned became evident. Of particular importance was the discovery that not only did Kay like to see the children happy, she also liked to please others in the school, desiring to fit in quickly and to avoid conflict. She looked outward for her self-confirmation and self-worth; and she did not like to disappoint others.

Initially, Kay's conception of herself as teacher was tied to two implicit and interrelated metaphors. The central metaphor that gave coherence to Kay's teaching and that was deeply and firmly embedded in her biography and her teaching fantasy was 'teacher is facilitator'. A second and closely related metaphor, one that gave a particular flavour to Kay's understanding of facilitator, was 'teacher is public servant', one who finds pleasure and meaning through service to others.

GETTING READY FOR SCHOOL

One of Kay's first planning tasks was to become familiar with the Workshop programme and then to organize her classroom and morning curriculum around it. Additionally, she had to plan each of the other content areas not included in Workshop, as well as additional language, arts and mathematics activities to supplement the programme. And, as she knew from her practice teaching and preschool teaching experience, she needed to plan carefully for classroom management to make certain the students were quickly routinized. She brought to these tasks the teacher identity noted above.

After signing her contract, Kay began thinking about her programme in general terms: 'I've just thought about it and laid it out in my mind. It's only the last two weeks [before the beginning of school] that I've really hit [planning].' She began her planning by reviewing the state core curriculum for the first grade. She 'made files for each [subject matter] division' and placed in them the materials she had gathered over the course of her teacher-education programme and from her preschool teaching. As the first day of school approached, she prepared her classroom which became, under her hand, an inviting, colourful, and interesting place, complete with a large birdfeeder outside one of the two windows, two large plastic blow-up dinosaurs, and a comfortable rocking chair within which she would sit while reading with the children gathered around her. During this time she also attended a two-day school-district-sponsored orientation meeting. While Kay intended to create her own programme, following the orientation meeting she concluded that she needed to build her programme around the required state and district curriculum. She dared not deviate. Accordingly, some of the materials she gathered and organized in files would be used with Workshop Reading and Mathematics, the rest would be used elsewhere, making certain that each of the core topics was covered. This said, Kay doubted that it would be possible to teach all that was required to be taught, at least 'not to any great extent'.

Despite having the desire to develop her own programme, Kay found comfort and security in stepping into a teaching situation with an established set of curricular guidelines and agreed-upon approaches to instruction. She was excited about Workshop, seeing in it a philosophy and approach to instruction consistent with her own desire to build a programme emphasizing student activity and creativity. And, despite her critical comments about the use of textbooks, she intended to follow them as did the other teachers in the team, supplementing them with her own materials and using those from other teachers in the team that she found desirable.

Much of the curriculum would be organized around seasons and holidays, an approach common to the early grades. Kay intended to do this as a way of tapping student interests and of extending them. Moreover, she said, 'children have to have something to hang on to.' Reviewing a calendar of the year and filling it out, she identified topics and objectives that would fit a particular event. For example, she planned to link the topic of maps, a central part of the required study of geography, to Columbus Day: 'I could fit [maps] into Columbus Day . . . We can get some paper bags and cut them up like an old time parchment map and do some map work. That interests them.' During Halloween, the class would study skeletons and bones. The curriculum of first grade, she said, was 'pretty cutsy' (cute and simple). But, she believed, a 'cutsy' curriculum was necessary. Children 'can relate' to such a curriculum, while at the same time, and speaking as a facilitator, it was a way by which to 'move them from what they know to what they don't know'.

Knowing young children well, Kay planned carefully in anticipation of discipline and management problems. In particular, she knew she would have to give the children a great deal of practice in order to routinize them into the desired behaviour, especially if Workshop was to be effective. She intended to have the students practise procedures, and review rules often, and then periodically to return to them to refresh their memories until they became almost second nature. There would be procedures for calling the children to attention – the ringing of a small bell or clapping her hands, for example – for making transitions between activities, for requesting teacher assistance, for going to recess, assembly, or to lunch, as well as for beginning and ending the school day. The fact that she would have a class of twenty-six first-graders underscored, for her, the importance of giving careful attention to routines, which she did throughout the year. To encourage them in task behaviour Kay planned to reward students with 'chips' that would be placed in a large jar where the children could see them. Once enough chips had been accumulated, the students would be rewarded with a 'big party'.

Kay worried that during the first week of school she would mistakenly break a school rule or disrupt a routine and cause difficulty for other faculty members: 'I know there are a lot of things that everybody [on staff] knows that [I won't know] . . . . [For example], I'm afraid I'll mess up [getting the students to] lunch . . . I've had nightmares that I miss [the time for lunch] and [my class is] running down [to the lunch room]. Everybody is mad . . . That [worries me].'

THE FIRST WEEK OF SCHOOL

Following the lead of the first grade team, Kay organized the school day this way:

8.50–10.15	Reading groups
10.15–10.30	Recess
10.30–11.10	Phonics, handwriting, spelling and continuation of the reading groups.
11.10–11.30	Choral readings
11.35–12.20	Lunch
12.20–12.40	Language arts
12.40–1.40	Math
1.40–2.00	Music and art
2.00–2.15	Recess
2.15–3.10	Science, Social studies, physical education, health
3.10–3.25	Clean-up

The first week went much as planned. From Kay's journal:

My first week of teaching has ended and, as my mentor teacher said, 'This is a real milestone. If you can live through the first week, you can live through anything.' My main concern this week was to get classroom management rolling. I concentrated on communicating rules and procedures and on helping learners feel comfortable in the [classroom] environment. I felt a sigh of relief from the children as, at the end of the first day, I explained what they should do as soon as they came to school the next day. The sign of relief came as I announced: 'If you forget and make a mistake tomorrow, is it all right?' 'Yes! It is all right to make mistakes while we're learning'.

To help the students feel comfortable during the first days of school, to begin building group identity, and to help her know the children, Kay sent notes to parents before the commencement of school requesting that they send their children to school with shoe boxes containing their 'favourite things' to be shared with the class. From the very beginning, she organized sharing time so that the children were responsible for it. Each day a 'student leader' was appointed who called on students 'to share'. This activity, like most of the others planned for the week, achieved its desired results: 'All the children participated and were comfortable sharing with the rest of the class.'

THE SECOND AND THIRD WEEKS

The second and third weeks of school also unfolded as intended. Kay continued to emphasize rules and procedures but also made a concerted effort to get to know the students and their ability. While teaching as she had initially planned, she tested the students in math and in reading. In reading the students would be grouped according to ability. She was disappointed with the students' performance on several early assignments and adjusted her instruction, hoping, in particular, to communicate better with them so they might understand the assignments more clearly before beginning. Delightedly she observed that student performance improved. They performed 'wonderfully' on a test at the end of the next unit. 'I felt good about it . . . . I passed the test out and didn't explain anything. I said this is what we've been doing for the last two weeks. Let me see how much you know. Very

149

few of them missed more than one. Most of them missed none . . .
They got it. I thought, maybe it was [my] teaching [that made the
difference in their performance].'

STUDENT PRESSURES

Kay entered Morrison Elementary School very interested in and
sensitive to children. Serving children and seeing them actively
engaged in learning was what she most enjoyed. Accordingly, she
got to know the students very quickly and well. She was responsive
to subtle changes in their moods and rapidly came to recognize a
variety of differences in how they learned and in the problems they
encountered while learning. From her journal during the first
week of October, for example:

> Blue group is having difficulty decoding. I need to work on
> vocabulary. Immaturity seems to be the cause of slow-down
> for Aaron and Zeke (fictitious names). I'm not so sure about
> Sandy and Rebecca. Darren is coming along fine; [he] seems
> comfortable in this group . . . . I may need to make a fourth
> group. The Red group, I think, is well placed, but I will
> continue to observe [them]. Sandy is still physically reacting
> to problems; she scratched Zeke's eye and was punished . . .

On their part, the students responded to Kay's efforts to help them
with love and affection. The only adult female role that they
understood well was that of mother, and they responded to her in
this way as she anticipated that they would. They came to her with
many of their problems seeking assistance. From our observation
notes:

> Before class was to begin following lunch recess five girls are
> in the room awaiting Kay's return. As she walks in [a student
> yells]: 'I couldn't find my coat.' '[My] ear aches – someone
> yelled in my ear.' Kay responded by trying to encourage the
> students to go outside to play: 'It's so beautiful out there,
> that's where I would be if I could be.' Another child:
> 'Teacher, could I have a certificate for getting my ears
> pierced?' (Kay gives certificates to students for losing a tooth,
> thereby acknowledging that they are maturing.)

Endlessly, the students sought her attention and approval and,
endlessly, she tried to give it, wanting them to be happy and

productive. She tied shoe laces, put on coats, bandaged cuts, found lost articles, stopped disagreements, acknowledged accomplishments, passed out treats, hugged and comforted upset children, soothed hurts, listened to stories, helped a girl change her wet panties, helped administer medicine, and even tended the baby sister of one of her students when the mother came in weekly to read to the children. Virtually everywhere Kay turned, there were children letting her know that they liked and wanted to be with her. 'Why can't you sit over here?', she said one day while reading from the rocking chair to the students, trying to spread them out more. 'Because,' one student remarked, 'we like to be by you.'

Despite her initial desire to avoid being placed in a mother's role, as the weeks progressed, Kay found herself frequently falling into that role as she sought to make the children happy and nudged them along in their development. She discovered that what made them happy and secure was to be mothered. Some situations and some students, in particular, called out the mother in her:

> Helena's [fictitious names] sister went in for surgery today. The doctors say it's only a matter of time [before she dies] . . . Helena has a 'proud' attitude about the situation. She almost seems to run away from her real feelings and has a 'matter-of-fact' attitude. I watched her dad outside our room as he waited to explain to Helena that the time had come to take Lorie [to the hospital]. The weight of the world was in his eyes, yet I watched how he handled little Helena in a calm and reassuring way.

And a month later:

> I don't think there are many people who could handle Sandy the way I do . . . . [From my experience as a mother] I know how to handle her, when to ignore her, when to let her think she can get away [with] something.

The students were exceptionally demanding. Kay cared deeply about them but by December remarked that she was 'tired' of caring and yet, she discovered, that despite herself, she was mothering many of the students in response to their demands.

> I'm afraid [teaching] is turning into [mothering] for me . . . .
> [I'm] trying not to [let it be] but I'm watching myself more

151

and more [get close to them and] know them so well
that . . . I see myself falling into that role [which] I fit [very]
well . . . .

She struggled with this role and self-understanding and found
herself by Christmas mothering the children while simultaneously
attempting to 'push them away'.

PROBLEMS

During the first weeks of the school year classes went very well.
However, gradually problems began to emerge that, when coupled
with the pressures of the students to mother them, had a dramatic
impact on Kay. Taken individually, they were of relatively minor
consequence, but when taken together they proved threatening.
Writing in her journal: '[I'm] feeling extremely exhausted and
questioning my effectiveness as a teacher'. Some of these were the
result of Kay's increasing sophistication at recognizing what was
transpiring in her classroom and her greater knowledge of the
students; she began to note aspects of her performance that
needed improvement and required attention. Others arose
because of Kay's inability to meet her personal and professional
expectations. Still others arose because of the nature of work
within Morrison Elementary School and of simply being new and
unfamiliar with the setting, and of needing to fit in. Each of these
problems was evident as early as the third week of school as
illustrated by journal entries made during that time. A few selected
entries illustrate the cumulative effects of these otherwise small
problems:

It is so hot and miserable in the afternoon; I don't know how
we survive [in the classroom] . . . . [I'm] trying desperately to
find my place on the 'inside' [of the faculty] . . . . [I] stayed
late to prepare . . . [It was] not a good day for classroom
control – lots of headaches and 'when do we go homes?'
[said by the children] . . . . [I'm] feeling pressured. [I] need
to get further ahead in my planning so I can take a few
moments to 'veg out' [and relax]. Family pressures are piling
up; [My] teenagers [are] resenting the amount of time I
spend at school [and] I miss the children.

Problem recognition

Given Kay's desire to see each child develop and be happy in her classroom, it troubled her, particularly in reading, to see a few of the students having serious difficulty. In response, she spent additional time with these students, worked harder to adjust assignments to help move them along, and worried about what to do for them:

> I want to do a good job [but] I'm really struggling [with] my reading program. I can see the kids growing. Some of them are doing very well. Others – I can see their interest waning because they're not able to keep up . . . . I'm trying different things [hoping] to interest the ones who are ready [to move along] and not discourage the ones that aren't. That's worrying me . . . . Even though the [Workshop] programme is that you make sure [the students] know that it doesn't matter where anybody is [compared to anyone else], it only matters where they are – I continually stress that—but [the feeling of failure] is still there. I'm afraid of losing two of them . . . I've got to do something quickly [but] I don't know [what].

Personal expectations

> [I have] a personal problem because of my desire to be a good professional [and] my desire to raise a family . . . For many years I have concentrated on [building my] family . . . Now, I'm concentrating on [teaching]. The problem is . . . to find a medium point and still be effective in both places. Right now, my emphasis is professional. That causes some real adjusting on this other end . . . . [My family thinks] I'm spending too much time at school . . . . They thought [once I finished school] I'd be around more because I was working closer to home [but] it hasn't worked out that way, yet . . . I know it will, I just know it will.

Kay expected herself to be an outstanding beginning teacher – for the sake of the students and for her own sake – and to continue to be the exceptional mother that she had long been to her children. Anything less than superior performance was unacceptable. She found, however, that it was impossible to achieve both ambitions simultaneously and compromises had to be made. These compromises proved to be a major source of difficulty throughout the year but especially during the first several weeks of school as she watched her husband and children adjust once again to her absence. The situation was compounded by her discovery that teaching was not quite what she had expected; there was no end to the demands of the classroom:

> I was shocked [to find out how much of a] commitment teaching really is. I really felt like [I] might be finished at some point. That [I] could have a day of teaching, prepare for the next day, and be done. [But I] never [am]. [I] have to live with that; it's just never done .... Never ...

Despite this discovery, Kay held firmly to the belief that a reasonably satisfactory balance between family and work expectations could be achieved. All that was necessary was time to get on top of teaching: She explained to her family, 'It takes some time. Please give me until Christmas to get this really rolling'. The attempt to achieve the desired balance, however, was often very painful. For instance, on the way to school on the first Tuesday of October her young daughter remarked that she 'remembered when [Kay] used to stay home,' as though it had been many years before. Moments like this forcefully reminded Kay of the impact the decision to teach had on her family. She never regretted the decision, but she regretted the difficulties it had caused her family and she worked herself to near exhaustion to soften the blows and to avoid disappointing the children and her husband further.

Problems of working in Morrison Elementary School

By school-district policy, elementary-school teachers taught only half day on Mondays. The other half of the day was preparation time. Kay desperately needed this time to prepare but quickly found out that she could not count on it. Meetings were frequently held on Mondays, including in-service meetings, and Kay was expected to attend. Wanting to fit in and to be professional, she dared not miss. The result was that she had to find additional time for planning and preparation elsewhere and the only place it was available was by taking it from her family. She completed her detailed weekly planning Sunday nights at home, and stayed late after school, especially on Fridays and Mondays. From Kay's journal:

[I] introduced [the topic of] nutrition, practiced the play, and got several pages of math [completed today]. [One of the teachers in the team] suggested we . . . make Indian beads. I called her in the evening to find out how many batches of clay to make [and made the clay that night at home].

Working with the First Grade Team was both a source of pleasure and of frustration for Kay. Facing the three teachers in her team, whom she liked and respected, Kay felt pressured to please and to conform to their expectations. She felt unable to vary Workshop, for example, even though she noted early in the year that some of her students were having a very difficult time adjusting to the programme. Some students wandered about the room, needing constant surveillance, while others would quietly sit at their desks but do little work. Moreover, the programme emphasized quantity, not quality of work, which was troubling. Similarly, Kay stuck closely to the mathematics and reading programmes but, given her view of teaching, was unhappy doing so. As she felt more knowledgeable about the curriculum and comfortable with the children, her unhappiness increased with the 'steady diet of . . . textbooks', even though she had enriched the diet by including a wider variety of activities in the other content areas.

Additional pressures to conform came from the school-district requirement that she be evaluated twice during the year by the building principal as part of her probation. Facing this situation, and wanting a positive evaluation, Kay dared not take any instructional risks. In frustration, she wrote of her experience in her journal:

> I decided against any kind of . . . lesson for my evaluation [where] the boundaries [weren't] clearly marked . . . [F]or observations you lean toward [choosing] subjects that will *definitely* measure the child's understanding when the lesson [is] completed. [My lesson] objective was clear, the teaching methods varied (book, flannel board story, whiteboard discussion, folding paper visual aids, games, individual matching packets, and worksheet) and the measure was obvious but [the lesson] was not creative, not interesting, not exciting, but I followed all the rules.

Kay was also troubled by paperwork, the constant interruptions

155

during the day, and the trivial demands placed upon her by virtue of working within a complex bureaucracy. For example, 'bus duty' (monitoring the hallways while children embarked on and disembarked from the buses) was irritating, and she disliked intensely the requirement that she collect lunch money. Respecting the latter, her dislike was intensified when, early in the fall, she came up $1. 50 short. One student's lunch money was missing and Kay felt responsible: 'I feel like . . . I didn't do enough to make sure [all the money] was there.' She had let someone down.

Finally, Kay found it extremely difficult to manage her curriculum in the various subjects and simply to keep track of all the other activities going on in the school that impinged on her and her class time. There was simply too much going on. For example, during one Friday early in September a specialist in the teaching of thinking visited her class 'to do some creative thinking, "Brainstorming" was the topic. Some children were creative, others silly. The children enjoyed the session but I'm not so sure they learned anything.' Writing in her journal, Kay reminded herself that she 'must extend the discussion' if any good was to come out of it. The following Monday, the parent-teacher association initiated an 'Arts in the Park' programme. Inspired by a discussion of Paul Klee's work, the class 'painted tree houses', which 'looked great! I was pleased to see them hanging proudly on [display].' Later the same day, Kay attended a two-hour in-service course offered in the school on science and the core curriculum. Kay valued these activities, but felt nearly overwhelmed by all that was going on around her and by all that she was required and wanted to do:

> Sometimes I feel weary trying to deal with all of the different variables there are to teaching: from parents, to faculty, to administration, to children. [There are] so many different lives [to which to respond] . . . . The logistics of teaching are even hard to keep up on . . . . [There are] so many things to try and fit together . . . and [to] understand.

AN ILLUSIVE BALANCE

As Christmas approached with its promise of an extended period of time to be spent with her family, Kay found that it was unlikely to be the watershed she had hoped for; the balance between home and work remained illusive. In many respects teaching had become more, rather than less, complex and demanding. To be sure, the class was now highly routinized, almost too routinized, Kay thought, and the students were extremely well behaved and productive as a result. A clap of the hand, or a ringing of the bell she kept on the reading table, produced in the children the desired responses. But, there was still planning to do, and whatever time was freed up by her increasing teaching skill and knowledge of the school and of curriculum, was expended on other teaching demands and seeking to meet other expectations sometimes posed by the team or the students, sometimes presented by Kay as she sought to realize her image of a good classroom with herself in it functioning as facilitator. For example, during November and early December, Kay organized a variety of arts activities that, while being exciting for the students, were extraordinarily demanding of her time and energy. In November Kay's class put on a 'Turkey Tale' for the other three first-grade classes and later performed it for the parents. The December activity was a 'Nutcracker unit' involving making Christmas-tree ornaments, story telling, drama, music, and dance. The unit culminated with the students viewing a video-taped performance of the New York Ballet's production of the *Nutcracker Suite*. And too, working with the faculty had become increasingly complex as she became more involved in teaming and as she was placed in the position of having to make decisions about who within the First Grade Team she would work most closely with. For instance, early in December her mentor came to Kay to tell her that she was hurt that Kay had become so involved planning with another first-grade teacher. The mentor felt shut out. Kay became upset, realizing that she had to pay greater attention to faculty politics; in pleasing one teacher, she had inadvertently offended another.

Kay continued to drive herself. By October, the principal and mentor told her she had better slow down and take better care of herself. They told her to 'just lay back a little [else teaching] will burn [you] out'. The principal's concerns increased and in December he expressed his concern to Kay, asking whether or not she was 'home enough'. Moreover, she was not taking very good care of herself physically. She had stopped exercising in order to save time and would skip lunch on some days. Her husband and a few friends also urged her to slow down: 'I've had lots of friends tell me I've got to [slow down] or . . . by March, I'll be a basket case.' She thought their advice to be sound but felt unable to take it:

> I am doing things even though I don't have time to do them
> ... This is what is infringing on [my family life] ... [But] I
> want to do this well [although I know] I've got years to do it.
> [I've got to accept that] it just is not going to be wonderful
> this year, but it will be sometime ... [And yet] I don't think
> I'm getting much better [at balancing the two].

Although December did not turn out to be the watershed Kay had hoped for, it did prove to be an important time of decision. Tired, and with deepening frustration at not being able 'to do both things well', she accepted that something would have to give and that it had to be her overwhelming commitment to teaching. The problem was that she had not found a way of making a minimally satisfying compromise between the two. Facing these pressures, Kay increasingly and critically scrutinized her taken-for-granted understanding of herself as teacher. Kay became increasingly introspective and self-critical which resulted in a shift in self-understanding.

FACING AND FINDING SELF

As Kay got to know other teachers well, and shared with them her concerns and frustrations, several offered advice. They, like her, recognized that the first year of teaching is inevitably difficult but that there were ways of alleviating the difficulty. In effect, their advice was for her to stop working so hard and to look toward the future to realize her ambitions more fully. What Kay observed, however, was that the way in which they had achieved a balance was by relying on textbooks and routines to carry the burden of instruction: 'It's a job ... for them ... it's [only] a job.' In contrast, for Kay it was a 'calling', something that she had always wanted to do. In effect Kay was being told that the type of teaching she found most disappointing professionally was the most sensible personally. She was urged to stick to the routines accepted by the established first-grade teachers and to minimize the imaginative and creative activities, like the Nutcracker unit, that she had invested so much energy in producing. Stop trying to be a facilitator, give up being a public servant, she was told, and become a textbook teacher.

Over the Christmas break Kay began jogging again. While on her runs she began to think about the advice she had received and about herself as a teacher in ways she had not thought of before.

To this point, she had taught, and taught well, to be sure, but the costs had been very high. She needed to make some decisions about the kind of teacher and mother she would be. While jogging she made comparisons between running and teaching as a way of better understanding her experience which proved to be a powerful metaphor. Writing in her journal a few days after Christmas:

> [I] began running again today after a long lay off. I like running in the snow more than in the summer heat. I don't notice the cold after the first mile. No matter how 'cool' I dress, the heat gets worse with each mile . . . I was aware of the . . . comparison [between running and teaching] as I ran. I ran laps and it had just snowed enough to cover the road with a light skiff of white stuff. When I ran the second lap, I followed my own footprints, once in a while trying to match them up. The third lap . . . [and] fourth lap prints left the impression that the junior high track team had been running the park that morning. I thought about the first set of nice clean footprints and how I couldn't match those exactly the same way on the second lap. A day of teaching sometimes leaves a nice, clean pattern but most days are filled with a road of junior high track team prints. I wondered if after a year of teaching I will be able to glean a set of nice, clean prints to follow.

And a few days later she wrote:

> Woke up thinking this morning: [I realized that] those footprints in the snow, the mixed up, myriad of footprints, are like this first [half] year of teaching. I have been trying to make sense out of a lot of complicated new routines, new roles, and new expectations.

Kay realized that she was breaking a pathway and finding her way as a teacher and that it was alright to admit that she could not possibly accomplish all that she expected of herself. What she had not done, she discovered while running, was to face herself, to recognize and accept her limitations, and to make some firm decisions about the kind of teacher she would be. She had taught as seemed natural and appropriate to her, she had responded to the environment and demands of teaching and had not controlled her situation; it controlled her: 'I'm afraid of knowing me [but] once I face me that's when the footprints will be like the first lap footprints, *clear*.' Kay could no longer simply trust that by working hard the conflicts and frustrations she felt would resolve themselves. And so, Kay found herself at a turning point.

Feeling 'all nurtured out' Kay began to articulate more clearly and then to scrutinize her teaching expectations and the values behind those expectations, and her sense of self as teacher. She explored the increased emphasis she had found herself giving to nurturing students, a role quite consistent with her public-servant values; that teachers should do whatever is necessary to assist young people. She made some telling discoveries. She had expected far too much of herself and had been working far too hard. Her own unrealistic expectations were at the centre of her problems. In the future she would seek to be more realistic: 'I think I can expect less of myself and get just as much from the children.' She recognized that she had been 'carried away with the flow' of teaching; she had been primarily reacting and responding to the situation and to others within it rather than directing her own actions: 'I'm tired of feeling like a reactor. Analyzing [my situation] makes me an actor, [which is what I want to be].' The spirit of this change was indicated in her journal: 'It's natural to jump into . . . teaching . . . and swim with the current. [But] it's smart to be able to stand up and let the water go by for a while . . . to take a look at what is really happening'. She recognized, as never before, the impossibility of satisfying all the demands placed upon her that she had accepted willingly. She could not please everyone no matter how hard she tried. In trying to do so, her life both at home and at school was essentially out of control: '[I must] get in control of my own situation,' she said. Nor could she cover all the required topics as she had at first thought essential: '[In the future] I'm going to decide what I can really teach and teach [it] well, rather than [go for coverage]. You can't teach everything – it's impossible.' Happily, she discovered she could have more control than at first she thought possible. She realized also that she had been trying to prove herself to the principal and the other teachers; she was overly dependent on them and the students for her feelings of self-worth. She discovered that deep down she was sick of trying to conform and to please: 'I'm a conformer and I've been raised to be . . . a wimp.' She needed to rely more upon herself and her own judgement as a basis of determining her self-worth, not on the illusive and often times fanciful opinions of others.

These conclusions were nudged along by the teachers in her team who, as noted, urged upon Kay their own conservatism; which she little respected, even though she had sought, and unhappily so, to conform. Her opinion of the teachers changed: 'There is not much of a chance for the First Grade [Team] to learn. [My mentor] is uninterested [in improving] and [the other senior teacher] is flaky.' She was also helped by the discovery that there was a large number of supplies locked up in a room that had been kept from her. Feeling she had been taken advantage of and revealing hurt and anger, Kay wrote in her journal: 'I've been *buying* all that [stuff], I've been furnishing all that and it's been in the supply room all locked up'. So much for collegiality! And too she was helped to become more independent by her growing recognition of numerous and rather serious weaknesses in the adopted curriculum, particularly in mathematics and reading, that her concern for the students would not let her long ignore. For example, Kay wrote in her journal about her problems with the math program:

> I am going crazy with the Holt Math. They introduce a new concept and give one page of work and then the children are supposed to have mastered it . . . When talking about liquid measure they don't use the word 'cup'. The 'money' unit was scant and the place value unit was [poorly done].

At the same time, she began to understand, articulate, and accept more readily some aspects of the mothering role she had unintentionally and almost begrudgingly adopted. In effect, mothering and nurturing young children was an expression of her desire to be of service. If mothering was what the students needed, then mothering was what they should and would get from Kay, but not all the time.

> I look at teaching as my compassionate service. It is what I can offer to this world to help out a little. I wasn't happy with [only helping] people in the neighborhood [and] I am not good at watching soap operas and having a lot of un-structured time on my hands. But I am good at nurturing and [caring for] children. I love [teaching]; I want to be of service.

There were limits to how far she would go to be of service, however. 'Moderation', she said, was the 'key'. She had been too responsive to the context – to the demands and expectations of students and of other teachers – and had not taken good enough care of herself and of her family.

As Kay explored herself as teacher, near year's end she expanded her self-understanding with the result that the facilitator metaphor earlier embedded in her thinking was made more explicit and, in the process, another metaphor, 'teacher is coach' emerged. Kay used this metaphor to think through the new role she was seeking to create – even while creating it. She said that the class felt like a 'team' to her. Further, she wanted to work with parents in a team situation, where they also would coach their children. In part, this view arose from her successes working with a few parents throughout the year, and her realization that they were an important resource necessary to the achievement of the educational aims she had embraced and held from before the start of the school year.

> A coach sets the plays and is the strategist and knows the kids better than they know themselves as far as . . . what is developmentally right [for them to do]. A coach . . . knows his players . . . and utilizes their best assets and that's what I try to do.

But, she would be a coach of a certain kind, one who holds to the values of nurturing and helps students 'want and love to learn as opposed to pressure [them to learn]'. Reflecting her growing awareness of herself as teacher, Kay's teaching metaphors blended, opening up new ways for her to think about and then direct her professional development.

YEAR'S END

With growing self-awareness and despite being extremely tired, during the spring Kay shifted some of her attention away from the students toward more or less systematically working to improve her teaching skills by seeking, in part, to become a more effective coach. In the improvement of her skills, she found a source of great satisfaction as well as a means for saving precious time: '[I] worked on pacing today. It went well. [I'm] feeling better and more rested.' She was, however, too tired to keep working at the pace she had been and began to 'let a lot of things go'. She could do this because of her earlier successes routinizing and organizing the classroom. She looked to her second year of teaching as an opportunity to build upon and refine the insights gained during the first year of teaching.

> I'm an organizer and I usually know exactly what I'm doing and when I'm going to do it, and I write those things down and keep track of them. [But] I have been so overwhelmed with this job that ... I [now] just live from moment to moment, from day to day, continuing to the end, just surviving. I hate [this] life style ... I don't think it's professional to be like [I am right now] .... I need a break ... if I just had a three-day weekend – I think that would [really help]. Right now, I really am burned out.

Despite being exhausted and feeling overwhelmed, Kay felt very good about the accomplishments of the year. She was at peace with herself and 'glad [she] did it'. It was the kind of peace felt only after having successfully met a genuine challenge to self. Kay felt good about who she was in the classroom and what she had accomplished:

> Being in school is like sitting by a warm fire .... on a cold evening. I feel comfortable teaching. I feel contented .... As a career choice, it was probably the best one I could have made.

Having survived the year, Kay felt renewed confidence as a teacher:

> I know I can teach and no one can make me feel differently about that .... I talked to a mom like I was a full-fledged professional today!

And, she looked forward to her second year of teaching with great anticipation.

IN SUMMARY

Kay had always thought of herself as a teacher. Having so long thought of herself as such, and having so long performed teaching responsibilities at home and at the pre-school, she simply assumed she was a teacher. Kay found it difficult to put into words the vision she had of herself as teacher. She just was one. She was certain, however, that she did not want to mother children and that she did not want to be a 'textbook teacher'. On the positive side, she thought of herself primarily in terms of responding to the 'needs' of children and of facilitating their growth. Two closely interrelated but initially implicit metaphors were deeply embedded in Kay's self-understanding: teacher is facilitator and public servant. It was through serving others that Kay found her greatest joy.

Both metaphors seemed to be well suited to the teaching context at Morrison Elementary School. The students loved Kay and responded positively to her efforts to nudge them along in their development and to help them feel good about themselves. But, since the only adult female role they knew well was that of mother, despite herself, Kay was frequently cast in a mother role by the students which proved to be exhausting and a source of inner tension; simultaneously, she would mother them while attempting to distance herself from them. Other problems also arose: Kay badly wanted to serve the children in every way possible but no matter how hard she worked, she recognized – especially as she got to know the students better and their particular learning problems – that there was always more to do, and yet she sought to do it. As she did so, and as she sought to create the lively and interesting curriculum she envisioned, she found herself spending extremely long hours at school and away from her family. Moreover, teaching proved to be more complicated than Kay had imagined. The burden of paperwork, for example, and of learning and managing effectively a new curriculum, also increased the demands on her time and energy. As she spent more and more time at school, family pressures mounted as her children resented the absence of their mother. Kay had expected, not only to continue to be an exceptional mother but also an outstanding first-year teacher and, she felt she was neither.

Kay relentlessly drove herself to serve fully her family and her students. In the attempt, her health deteriorated, she felt frustrated with teaching, and was deeply concerned about her family. Facing this dilemma, Kay was forced to turn inward. She critically scrutinized herself and discovered that she had not been controlling her life but, rather, reacting to what she thought others expected of her. Her own expectations were, she concluded, unreasonable: compromises were necessary. Several factors assisted her to accept compromise, among them her increasing dissatisfaction with the adopted curriculum, and her growing recognition of weaknesses in other teachers whom formerly she had sought to please. Through critically reflecting on herself and her values, a new understanding emerged for Kay and, with it, a new feeling of independence and strength. She would mother some children and continue to serve them, to be sure, but near year's end she had begun to explore a new metaphor, 'teacher is coach', and to establish a new relationship with the students and other teachers. In the future, Kay was determined that she would no longer 'be a wimp' but would gain control of her situation.

9

CHANGING METAPHORS: THE THREE TEACHERS IN RETROSPECT

INTRODUCTION

Barbara, Heidi and Kay each entered their first year of teaching with strongly held, but not rigid, conceptions of themselves as teachers: Barbara was a 'nurturer', Heidi a 'subject-matter specialist', and Kay a 'facilitator' and 'public servant'. These were deeply embedded identities, particularly for Kay and Barbara, formed over years of experience and confirmed, for the most part, by practice teaching. They were not, however, fully articulated understandings; rather, for the most part, they were taken for granted. Embedded within them were their teaching schemas by which the various aspects of teaching were made more or less sensible and through which problems were framed and solutions proposed and tested.

At the beginning of the year, and upon first entering the class-room as contract teachers, each of the three teachers displayed confidence that they would be outstanding teachers, although each had one or another cluster of concerns and self-doubts. Indeed, in their minds they *already* were teachers, and all that was lacking was a classroom within which to play out their conceptions of themselves as teachers. For each, the first days of teaching went well but gradually problems arose that, in varying degrees, challenged their conceptions of teaching and their conceptions of themselves as teachers: they encountered the reality of teaching and their schemas and the meanings attached to them were found to be wanting in varying degrees, but not primarily due to prob-lems with classroom control. Other aspects of teaching proved to be more challenging. Like the teachers in Weinstein's (1988) study, all of them had been overly optimistic in their expecta- tions, particularly of themselves as teachers and of their students.

166

Feeling threatened, all the teachers responded by holding more tenaciously on to their metaphors – their conceptions of themselves as teachers – and attempted to shore up their teaching schemas by a variety of means, such as abandoning parts of the curriculum and working even longer hours, among others. Eventually, however, some changes in the meanings associated with their conceptions of themselves as teachers and of teaching became necessary if they were to function productively in the classroom and, especially, effectively in their other life roles. How Kay experienced the challenge such problems presented is aptly, and metaphorically, illustrated by an entry from her journal:

> I was on vacation in Yellowstone [National Park]. I was running down Red Rock road and trying to cut my time, so I was really concentrating. When I looked up and saw something in the road. As I got closer I saw that it was a big bull moose. I was intent on wanting to see the canyon and run the distance. I started thinking, 'Oh, I'm sure he's afraid of me and will move out of the way when I get closer.' *Wrong!* As I neared the moose, he bellowed, stood firm, and looked rather angry. I'm sure I broke my mile record as I flipped around and ran the opposite direction. Teaching has been like that for me this year. Sometimes I'm so sure I can overcome the obstacles and [that] they'll move out of my way only to discover that I have to retreat and try a different path.

According to Anderson (1977), this is precisely the way a schema works: strongly held schemata are resistant to change. But, for a variety of reasons they generally do change, and if enough meanings change, a shift in self-understanding will occur. On the other hand, if the individual's schema is rigid and impenetrable and she is unable to alter the situation in order to make it more fitting, the outcome, like that of Louis Agassiz's response to the challenge of evolution (Gould, 1983), may be arrested development and perhaps growing incompetence.

Some changes are forced – somewhat like when facing a bull moose that blocks a desired course of action. Facing the moose, Kay altered her plans and direction. In these instances, strongly held meanings, like Heidi's conception of herself as subject expert, although initially resistant to change, are reconstructed and thereby made more fitting and useful for interpreting the situation and framing problems in productive and fitting ways. It is the lack of fit of a meaning or the difficulty and costs associated with establishing and maintaining an interpretation that produce the need for a shift in understanding. The latter arises in recognition that the essential external elements of a situation are unlikely to change and that in order to maintain a desired course of action meanings must change and, with them, new sources of satisfaction are found or created which in turn, recast the situation. Other changes are more gradual, and subtle, reflecting assimilation rather than accommodation to a new situation. And, still other changes are made in the context itself so that the meanings held become more fitting, as when Heidi removed from her beginning debate classes all students who refused to perform.

Thus, for each of these teachers, the story of their first year of teaching was one of building a more comprehensive, cohesive, fitting, and productive teaching schema initially and primarily through trial-and-error testing and adjustment of meanings, and of seeking metaphors and attendant images by which to define a teaching self consistent with the inner self. Eventually, these teachers' reliance on trial-and-error approaches to problem solving diminished as their knowledge about teaching and of themselves as teachers grew, and as their teaching skills, upon which the realization of their metaphors ultimately depended, improved. Through these skills they became better able to shape the situation to make it more fitting. As they moved away from dependence on trial and error and became more self-assured, at some point each teacher crossed the elusive boundary separating the survival from the mastery stages of learning to teach.

While attempting to negotiate a productive and satisfying place within the school, each of the three teachers encountered a variety of challenges to the meanings they brought with them to teaching. In response to these, their teaching schemas filled out, and in particular their conceptions of themselves as teachers and what they expected of themselves changed as indicated by the shifts in their teaching metaphors. While inextricably intertwined, the most significant pressures that encouraged reinterpretation and change were those associated with getting to know and responding appropriately to the students, the complexity of teaching, the fit or lack of fit of the teaching assignment, and the amount and intensity of the work and its impact on the teachers' families and on their health. Each area will be considered in turn and in relation to the conflicts produced and the teachers' responses to them that, for these teachers, eventually produced a satisfying and productive place within their schools and a fuller, more appropriate, and comprehensive teaching schema. Because of the importance of students to the success or failure of beginning-teacher role negotiation – an importance underscored by Riseborough in his description of the pupil as a 'critical reality definer' for teachers (1985: 262) – a rather extensive discussion of student culture and of its influence on teachers is provided.

STUDENT PRESSURES: BARBARA AND HEIDI

Each of the teachers came to know their students gradually, moving from recollections of themselves as young people, knowledge gained from siblings and in Kay's and Barbara's cases from their own children, and from student teaching, to the context-specific knowledge that came through working with the students at their three schools. Within the classroom they came to know individual students from whom they made generalizations, producing a kind of generic student image which, eventually, each productively used when confronting the problem of planning their classes.

Berliner (1986) notes that expert teachers possess just such an image, but fully fleshed out to include knowledge about common learning problems, among others, that can be then anticipated, as well as common interests and concerns. Such an image forms an essential component of a rich and complete teaching schema. Even before teaching, the expert teachers in his study 'in a sense believed they already knew all about [the students]. They did not have to delve very long into the assorted class records [provided to them] before deciding that these students were "like other kids" [they had taught].' (1986: 10). Expert teachers begin teaching with this image in mind and, we assume, adjust it as the situation demands, for, if they do not, their expert status is surely placed in jeopardy.

Student commonalities are the stuff out of which this image is created. It was while filling out their generic images of secondary-school-aged students that both Barbara and Heidi noticed that student groups were operating powerfully within their classrooms. Eventually they, like Larry as discussed in part I, identified these groups with differing student life-styles within which music played a pivotal role. Through interacting with the students during school, the teachers gained insight into what these styles were and, more importantly, the meaning group membership had for participants. In so doing they encountered a few of the common forms of American youth culture, attached to social class differences (Eckert, 1989), which proved somewhat surprising to both teachers, given their backgrounds. These are not isolated forms, only evident in a few schools, but rather are representative of a cultural phenomenon which many adults find disturbing but with which they nevertheless, as teachers and parents, must grapple. Allan Bloom, for example, harshly concludes that young people have embraced a 'worldview [that] is balanced on the sexual fulcrum . . . [It is a worldview within which] Nothing noble, sublime, profound, delicate, tasteful or even decent can find a place . . . There is only room for the intense, changing, crude and immediate . . .' (1987: 74).

STUDENT SUBCULTURAL GROUPS

Brief descriptions follow of some of the groupings that the secondary teachers encountered. These are included, along with a discussion of the importance of student subculture, because of the powerful influence of students on teachers, both positive and negative, in shaping how they come to conceive of themselves as teachers. It is, after all, toward students that teachers look for much, perhaps most, of their job satisfaction (Rosenholtz, 1989) and confirmation of the themselves as teachers (Knowles, 1989). The descriptions that follow are based primarily upon quotes from writings provided by Heidi's sophomore English class and from extensive observations conducted of her, Larry's, and Barbara's classrooms. It is worth noting that the students were very aware of the different groupings, although occasionally some of them confused signs of belonging. Additionally, descriptions of three groups are included from the study of Kotarba and Wells (1987). Finally, it should be noted that labels vary from school to school and that not all students fall neatly into one or another group, though these groupings appeared to capture most students in the three schools. Further, students do not hold to membership with equal tenacity; and some do not choose to belong but are assigned to groups by other students.

Normies

Students do not claim to be 'Normies', others label them that way. Some students enjoy the label, once given it, as one 'Normie' said,

> These people could [not] care less about the whole thing (all the groupings), like me. It's all very stupid [and] I'm sure that's what most high school students think. The junior high [school age student] is a little immature and they go by these [group] *rules!*

And another Normie remarked, 'like me, not really in a group, just have other normal friends, listen to pop music, sometimes a little rock. Just ordinary people.' The essence of the Normie spirit was nicely captured by a girl who said: 'I am . . . concerned about . . . my grades because I want to do something good with my life and go to a good college.' Obviously, teachers like Normies.

Nerds

'They are the ones which *other people* classify as scrounges. They wear clothes that are out of style, their hair (referring to female Nerds) is never curled, mostly straight, they're quiet, and always look unhappy about life.' Another student, a Rocker, described Nerds this way: 'There are nerds, they listen to music your grandma would like. They dress [for] floods (meaning short, poorly fitting pants)'. Nerds, like Normies, are outsiders, students who do not belong to tightly formed groups. Presenting no challenge to authority, they too are often popular with teachers.

Preppies

Kotarba and Wells nicely capture the Preppy in their description of the 'yuppie'.

> The yuppies may be best conceptualized as *proto-adults* rather than a specifically adolescent subculture. Put differently, the yuppies closely adhere to or at least aspire to middle- or upper-middle-class values and behavioral expectations. In a word, they like *Top 40* music, including a lot of dance music.
> (Kotarba and Wells, 1987: 408–9).

They are into money, clothes, cars, and 'getting ahead'. School fits into 'getting ahead'.

Jocks

The 'Jocks', mentioned frequently and generally negatively by their peers, were distinguished by their participation in athletics but, like the Normies and Nerds, not so much by their musical tastes. Aside from participation in athletics, what sets male Jocks apart is that they like to 'wear shorts, a lot', a letter jacket [indicating that they take part in school sports], and have short hair. One decrier commented that they are 'rich, walk bull-legged, wear Levi's and T-shirts, and act real tough. They think they run the school (which may not be too far from the truth!). Wear too much cologne [and] drive nice cars.' And yet another commented that they 'think they are better than the rest [of us].' Females who hang out with the male Jocks wear letter jackets or Levi jackets, tight, short skirts, and 'poofy' hairdos. For Jocks, but for reasons quite different from Nerds, Normies, and Preppies, school is very important; it is the arena of their triumphs. But, in order to participate in athletics, they must maintain at least a modest level of academic achievement, a point not lost on teachers who face the problem of motivating them to perform in class.

Cowboys

No one but Cowboys seemed to like Cowboys. Among other things, they have some nasty habits: Cowboys 'usually wear cowboy boots and chew, which has to be the grossest thing!' They 'listen to country [music], wear Wranglers, and chew tobacco and think that they're the greatest!' And, they 'drive trucks, wear cowboy hats,' and 'smoke and drink'. They are little interested in school.

Skaters

Skaters get their label from the skateboards so many of them drag around. Showing no lack of self-esteem, a member of this group described fellow members as 'just awesome, all around . . . . They're a lot better than any of the others.' Skaters wear bright, colourful, beach shorts, and colourful 'surfer' T-shirts, and 'vision street wear'. Their hair is 'usually bleached out . . . longer in front and one side kind of hangs in their one eye.' Skaters were generally considered to be rather poor students, not taking school very seriously: 'They could [be good students] but they just don't want to be.'

Wavers

Wavers, are the 'ones that pull their hair to the other side of their head, and wear it backwards. Dress in baggie clothes. Doesn't [sic] really care about school.' 'Their music is waver music.' A member of another group described Wavers as having 'their hair around their face and they listen to gross music like Talking Heads . . .' and 'Depeche Mode, Pet Shop Boys, Inxs and etc!' An out-group member commented that they 'like to wear black . . . . [and] dress all alike. . .' A Preppie female described them as 'strangely dressed people who listen to obnoxious music made by strangely dressed people.' Wavers do not care for school.

Rockers

Kotarba and Wells labelled these students, who are often from working-class backgrounds, as 'Metal Heads' and their description aptly fits the Rockers:

> [Their] tastes in clothes tend toward extremes, either simple black or very colorful and sexy . . . . but the most common attire consisted of black jeans and black T-shirts with heavy metal band logos printed on the front and back . . . . Female metal heads are inclined toward wardrobes that draw the attention of others, such as pants with leopard-skin patterns, tight fitting spandex pants, tight shirts, halter tops, and spiked shoes. Some female metal heads, however, prefer the plain, drab look of their male counterparts.
>
> (Kotarba and Wells, 1987: 404)

Non-group members described Rockers derogatorily. A 'Waver' said that 'They dress like slobs and listen to heavy metal junk *and* most of them smoke . . . and like to pick fights.' A girl commented that 'The boys have long hair, most of them smoke and drink! They wear Levis and T-shirts'. Another student said they have 'long hair, a rock group T-shirt, listen to heavy metal, [and] usually don't get good grades because they sluff a lot.' Their bands include 'Cinderella, Motley Crue [sic] . . . Metalica, Megadeath, etc.' These are the students who so troubled Larry.

Stoners

Although few in number, because they rarely attend school, Stoners were seen as a subgroup within the more general Rocker classification—a 'variation of a rocker'. What distinguished them was their heavy and consistent drug usage: 'they are into drugs and everything, [they're] worse than Rockers'. They were described as students who 'are always stoned or high on pot or some other drug, they look really bad . . . they like hard rock and acid rock [and] really hard stuff like: Led Zeppelin, Iron Maiden . . . and stuff like that.' And, they are thought to be people who 'party *hard*'.

Hardcores

Kotarba and Wells describe these students as 'punkers'. During our observations no Hardcores were seen in the junior highs and only a few in the high school. 'Punkers . . . often sport earrings and spiked, multicolored hair. They exercise a certain degree of creativity by transforming ordinary objects into fashion accessories' (1987: 407). On the American scene, Kotarba and Wells argue, 'punkers as a group are very bright, articulate, and success-oriented. They simply choose to act out adolescence in a rebellious style reminiscent of the beats and hippies of years gone by, but their angst is at least as existential as it is political' (1987: 408).

THE IMPORTANCE OF SUBCULTURE

These groupings, and others not mentioned, are of great importance to the young people who inhabit them. They provide young people with categories, meanings, and rules by which to structure their social world. Moreover, they are the means by which the young person attempts to make an independent place in the world outside dependency on parents. They represent, contrary to the commonly held view, highly organized ways of life, albeit generally defined in negative terms against adult values and against other subcultural values (Eckert, 1989). As Hebdige puts it,

> [there is a] symbolic fit between the values and lifestyles of a group, its subjective experience and the musical forms it uses to express or reinforce its focal concerns . . . each part is organically related to other parts and it is through the fit between them that the subcultural member makes sense of the world.
>
> (Hebdige, 1979: 113)

It is worth noting that the groups are not wholly the creations of young people. The categories and meanings of the group are presented to them through the media, which appropriate the culture and exploit it. Youth culture is commodified, turned into a commodity, and in the process the challenge it presents to the dominant culture is muted, although never completely removed, and the 'original innovations which signify "subculture" are . . . frozen' (Hebdige, 1979: 96). In the wake of commodification latecomers are left with styles which they more or less try on (Kotarba and Wells, 1987). Style includes a variety of 'portable symbols', most powerful among them those attached to 'clothing and adornment' but also 'books, radios, cigarettes, and sports paraphernalia [which are] effective indicators of social identity. . .' (Eckert, 1989: 50).

The place of music in student subculture is pivotal, presenting an 'ideological and expressive' centre (Lamy and Levin, 1985: 158). With music as the centre, 'most of the changes in youth culture correlate with changes in the form of rock music' (Snow, 1987: 334). To avoid a chicken-and-egg argument, suffice it to say that it is impossible to imagine a youth culture in a Western context separate from music. Indeed, music is ubiquitous. According to a study done by Leming, young people on average have about thirty 'hours a week of involvement with music', about equal to the time they spend in school (Leming, 1987: 374).

Since each subculture group reflects a different social experience, the relationships of subcultural groups to the dominant culture, and its institutions, vary. Groups 'can be more or less "conservative" or "progressive," integrated *into* the community, continuous with the values of that community, or extrapolated *from* it, defining themselves *against* the parent culture' (Hebdige, 1979: 127). From a teacher perspective these are important differences, signifying that they may be facing students in their classrooms for whom belonging to a group requires classroom disruption, withdrawal, or compliance.

Given that subculture groups have different social experiences, that they relate to the dominant culture and its institutions differently, and that they make the world meaningful in ways quite apart from how adults understand that world, teachers, but especially beginning teachers who are unfamiliar with these or similarly powerful groupings, face serious challenges. The temptation for beginning teachers is to act toward students in terms of the styles they assume and neglect the student beneath the category. Thus, being seen as threatening, Hardcores, Rockers, Cowboys, and Skaters may very well immediately elicit negative responses. What else are beginning teachers to do with students for whom school is educationally meaningless and about which they know so little? How they respond to this problem may in good measure be dependent upon the strength and appropriateness of the teaching self; their conception of themselves in relation to their understandings of the students they are to teach.

Facing this question, as a nurturer Barbara adjusted her planning to take the groupings into consideration, hoping to be able to establish the kind of warm family environment she sought and that was necessary if she was to realize her metaphor. Her curriculum focused explicitly on issues of interest and concern to the students and her approach to instruction placed a premium on encouraging and expanding interaction between students and across groups. By seeking to soften the boundaries between groups, she sought to encourage the students to conform more to her image of good students-children. For Heidi the encounter with so many students little interested in academic subjects proved to be very troubling. Her own previous experience as a student herself, as a student teacher, and her social class background had not prepared her for the problem. Eventually, as she gave up some of her academic ambitions and broadened her conception of teaching, Heidi responded productively to it by working hard to give each student the opportunity to perform but, when they chose not to take it, she would shift her energies elsewhere to students more interested in performing such as the Stoner discussed earlier. Students who would not perform were urged to withdraw from her classes and some were removed, particularly in the debate classes.

STUDENT PRESSURES: KAY

In the elementary school, Kay did not encounter groupings of these kinds which emerge in junior high school (Eckert, 1989). Her students were still adjusting to school and had not yet even fully become students, let alone members of student subculture groups. They generally sought to please teachers, as they would a parent or other adult. Nevertheless, as noted, she encountered student pressures of a different kind. These pressures arose from their expectations of teachers and of school. To be sure, her students' expectations were far less well organized and powerful, the children having had so little experience with teachers and with school. Kay's students subtly pressured her to assume a mother role, which she resisted but frequently found herself falling into none the less; after all, she was a mother. This is an experience common to women teachers, as Aspinwall and Drummond note: 'The working world of the primary school is riddled with events and equipment, demands and daily disasters, that seem designed to force female teachers straight into the stereotyped role of the effortlessly caring mother-figure, however sincerely they may wish to resist' (1989: 18). The students placed Kay in a difficult position: as a public servant she wanted to make the students happy and to serve their needs, the source of her greatest pleasure from teaching, but to do so meant mothering them. Resolving this dilemma proved to be very difficult. Kay discovered that her conception of herself as teacher was not quite fitting and that changes were in order; on their part, through Kay's actions the students would eventually come to see her as other than mother.

THE COMPLEXITY OF TEACHING

Each teacher began the year fully expecting to be able to master the work of teaching but, as the year progressed, the job itself became increasingly complex. They discovered that their knowledge about and understanding of teaching was but partial, based upon experiences as a student and student teacher, primarily. Some of the teachers' growing awareness of the complexity of teaching was tied to their increasing recognition of the needs of students; and some was tied to a growing recognition of gaps in their professional knowledge and skill. Like other beginning teachers, Heidi, Barbara and Kay would have to learn to teach while teaching. As noted in chapter 5, being a teacher, for beginning teachers, means doing all that teachers do, even when not yet able to do them.

The situation is further complicated by the length of the list of teacher responsibilities which continues to grow. Moreover, not only is the list a long one, but many of the items are vague and confusing, underscoring the current confusion over the role of teacher and the purpose of public schooling itself (Bullough, 1988b). And too, each responsibility, once recognized and assumed, brings with it a series of often complex and interrelated decisions that require a continuous reframing of the problem. Generally speaking, beginning teachers only become aware of these decisions as they assume the responsibility associated with them and start to face their consequences, to say nothing of the myriad of seemingly more minor decisions that are made, about every two minutes (Clark, 1988: 9), while teaching. Furthermore there is no fully adequate way to prepare beginning teachers to make these decisions or to fulfil the responsibilities they will face, as Schon (1987: 83) observes: 'The instructor . . . cannot tell the [teacher education] student what he needs to know, even if he has words for it, because the student would not at that point understand him.'

Each of the three teachers encountered just such difficulties. A few examples will suffice: thinking of herself as a subject-matter specialist, early in the year Heidi committed herself to do the majority of the grading of student work. This, she thought, was what teachers did. Soon, however, she found herself inundated by papers with no end in sight. It was only after considerable soul searching that she reframed the problem and decided that her initial decision was a mistake, she could not give the feedback the students deserved on their work, and that they would have to become more involved in grading. Heidi simply did not have the time or energy required to do the work and she altered the situation. Intimate involvement in the lives of students was a central component of Barbara's conception of teaching. By getting involved, she soon found herself sitting on the edge of a whirlpool facing the very real possibility of being pulled under by student demands and therefore she altered the situation. Necessarily, but unhappily, Barbara found herself backing away from the students. Once committed to developing an active, 'hands on' curriculum, Kay quickly found herself involved in activities that required extensive and time consuming planning and organization, as well as considerable personal financial expense. She liked to see the students engaged and happy. But their happiness came at the expense of her own family's contentment and her health. And, like Heidi and Barbara, she discovered that, no matter how hard she worked, there was simply no possible way adequately to carry out all the responsibilities that came with teaching.

Teaching was also made more complex by the three teachers' growing recognition of the politics of teaching and of their own vulnerability. An essential part of role negotiation is negotiating appropriate and satisfying relationships. Each teacher wanted to fit into the school and become a contributing member of the school community. What they found out was that fitting in is not always easy, especially when coupled with the desire to be themselves and to personalize the context. Sometimes, as Blase concludes from his study of teacher socialization, '"playing the game" and survival at work. . .' require unhappy compromises (1988: 130). Fitting in, as especially Kay and Barbara discovered, can be troublesome. Schools have established ways of doing things to which teachers and students are expected to conform. These are taken for granted by those within the school and are part of the school's culture. Fitting in means, for the beginner, appropriating and then conforming to some institutionally acceptable level the meanings of the culture. The process of fitting in is, therefore, inherently conservative and conformist in nature, although there is always a degree of wiggle room (Bullough and Gitlin, 1985), but beginners may not be aware of this. For Kay, the problem had several manifestations from the time of her decision to accept the First Grade Team's curriculum, to the hurt felt by her mentor when she began working closely with another team member, to her decision not to take any instructional risks and to meet precisely the principal's expectations when being evaluated as a probationary teacher, and to being encouraged to give up her desire to develop an active and creative curriculum by Team members. For Barbara, who as a single mother had little time to socialize with administrators or faculty members and so was necessarily limited in her involvement, the problem was most apparent when she taught the 'Love and Friendship Unit' involving *Romeo and Juliet* to the irritation of the department head.

And, for Heidi, who was in many ways left alone in the school to do as she pleased, as is so common to American high schools (Cusick, 1986), the problem showed up in her desire not to have her debate teams embarrass the school and in her refusal to change a student's grade to avoid conflict as subtly suggested by the vice-principal. Consistently, the press was toward conformity and conservatism, and away from risk taking. Little wonder that many teachers find peace and security in isolation and withdrawal (Bullough, 1987; Blase, 1988).

THE TEACHING ASSIGNMENT

As suggested in chapter 5 in our discussion of Larry, 'The difference between a positive beginning teaching experience and a mediocre or disastrous start can be decided before a new teacher even steps into the classroom' (Wildman, Niles, Magliaro and McLaughlin, 1989: 480). The importance of the teaching assignment cannot be underestimated in the development of each of the three teachers. It may be a major cause of increased teacher vulnerability or of security and confidence. Kay walked into her classroom already secure in her knowledge of the type of child she would be teaching. Not only were the students very much like those she had practice taught but they were much like her own children. Moreover, having practice taught first grade before, she was not a complete stranger to the curriculum. For Kay, the teaching assignment, as such, enabled her successful adjustment to teaching. Similarly, with the possible exception of her two low-ability classes, Barbara's assignment to teach English was generally a good one, one amenable to her conception of herself as teacher.

Heidi's teaching assignment, in contrast, proved to be a source of great tension. Neither in debate nor in English could she function as the subject-matter specialist she had envisioned herself to be. She was, however, generally comfortable with the students and able to maintain discipline in all of her classes and this gave her time to find her legs. Lacking subject matter expertise, Heidi found herself in the debate classes relying heavily on the advanced students for help with the beginning debaters. In English, she found herself barely keeping up with the students. For example, she would do assigned reading the same night as the students. While struggling to establish a productive role, she found herself beginning to establish close and caring relationships with the students who, as with Barbara, Kay, and perhaps most other teachers (Rosenholtz, 1989), soon became the major source of her personal satisfaction with teaching. While frustrated in her effort to play out one role, she successfully forged another one, with its attendant meanings and associated relationships, that was educationally productive and to her liking. Unlike Nancy, even when struggling most with teaching and herself as teacher, the rewards of teaching for Heidi outweighed the frustrations, a condition essential to professional growth and to maintaining commitment and interest in the job (Rosenholtz, 1989).

WORK PRESSURES AND FAMILY PRESSURES

Each teacher underestimated the amount and intensity of the work associated with being a full-time teacher. While they expected to have to sacrifice some time with their families, at least during the early months of the school year, they fully expected to be able to arrange a reasonable balance between home and work demands. What they discovered, particularly Barbara and Kay, was that, as Madeleine Grumet states: 'For those who sustain the emotional and physical lives of others, there is no time out, no short week, no sabbatical, no layoff' (1988: 86). Like other female teachers who were mothers, these women encountered extreme difficulty in reconciling their professional roles with motherhood (see Littlewood, 1989). Initially Barbara and Kay responded to the increasing pressures of meeting the demands of teaching and of family by sacrificing their time, energy, and personal interests. Such a solution, as Belenky and her colleagues note, is consistent with the sex-role stereotype common to women facing self–other conflicts: 'Conventional sex-role standards establish a routine for settling self–other conflicts when they occur. Men choose the self and women choose others' (1986: 46). In serving others, Barbara and Kay found great personal satisfaction. But, having limited physical and emotional resources and facing unlimited demands, both teachers eventually faced a moral dilemma that demanded a reframing of a very fundamental issue: they had to choose which interests to satisfy; and, like the teachers in Pajak and Blase's study (1989), they necessarily chose their families' over the students' interests. With Barbara this decision was eased by the growing disappointment she felt with some students who failed to express appreciation for her sacrifices on their behalf. In making this decision, both teachers compromised some of their personal and professional expectations; their views of teaching and of what realistically could be accomplished as teachers shifted somewhat. Ultimately, they would sacrifice themselves for teaching, but not their families. But, in doing so, both teachers, as is common especially among female teachers (Pajak and Blase, 1989), felt guilty.

Not having children and having an extremely busy graduate student for a husband, Heidi faced far fewer family pressures than either Barbara or Kay. Nevertheless, she too worried that, while being consumed by the demands of teaching and learning to teach, she was neglecting her husband and her share of the home duties. She was bothered, for example, that, because of her lack of time and energy, their apartment was cluttered, the dishes and clothes wash frequently piled up, and that relatively few meals were cooked. Heidi did not, however, have to make a choice between home and work. Although concerned about his wife being so consumed by teaching, and especially about her lack of attention to her health, a concern that grew as the year progressed and especially following her miscarriage, Heidi's husband was similarly engaged with his own work and studies and did not expect her to be any different. Following her miscarriage, Heidi found in teaching a welcomed escape from thoughts about children and family responsibilities. To save her inner self, she lost herself in teaching.

WORK PRESSURES AND HEALTH

Barbara, Kay, and Heidi each were heavily committed to succeeding in teaching. While Barbara discovered in teaching a niche, there was much more involved in her satisfactory performance than just playing out a fantasy. She needed the work and income in order to support her five children. For Kay, teaching was a calling, something that she had always wanted to do; by teaching she was realizing a life-long ambition. Although upon first glance Heidi's investment in teaching appears to be less than that of either Barbara or Kay, she none the less was dedicated to teaching, as we have seen. For each, much was at stake in her successful performance in the classroom and each was willing to pay a very high price to achieve it.

Deteriorating health was one of the prices paid. As noted, many factors associated with teaching and learning to teach made excessive demands on the teachers' time and energies. Their net result was that each teacher became progressively more tired and worn down, physically, emotionally, and mentally, as the year progressed. For women used to taking charge of their lives, and especially for Barbara and Kay, used to giving of themselves in the spirit of public service (Bullough, Gitlin and Goldstein, 1984) and to finding pleasure through the success of others, being vulnerable, somewhat out of control, and unable to continue to give, was a jolting and disconcerting experience. Through teaching they discovered new limitations on what they could and could not do. In response, expectations changed. Reflecting on the discovery of the limits of her endurance, Kay remarked in interview:

> [Next year I will] not try and do everything . . . [I will] simplify things more than I [have this year]. I think [that] more is better and I get lots of ideas and [try] them all . . . but I need to be more discerning about what I do. [I cannot do it all].

Of the three teachers, Heidi's health problems were most severe culminating in her miscarriage. While, in the aftermath of the miscarriage, she worked at a frenzied pace and even caught up in her planning as a result, this was surely no sign of either emotional or physical well-being; indeed, quite to the contrary. She was undergoing great emotional stress tied to, among other aspects of her life, confronting questions about her future as a mother, and even doubting whether or not in the face of the experience of loss she wanted children. Kay had lingering colds throughout the year and, after having given up jogging, put on additional weight. She looked very tired. On the surface, Barbara seemed to be the picture of health, although she too occasionally had a cold and from time to time was short tempered with the students. However, Barbara's view was that she masked her problems very well: '[I am] not, by any means, half as . . . intelligent, strong, and capable as the front [I] put up.' Occasionally in interview, the mask would fall and Barbara would openly sob and share her worries and fears especially about 'her babies' at home for whom she had to be 'strong'. Barbara was under tremendous emotional stress. Early in the spring, and in recognition of her need for a break, Barbara took three days off from teaching and took her children on a vacation. Like Kay, she found herself 'nurtured out' and needed a break.

GROWING AWARENESS

As noted, as each of the teachers' conceptions of themselves as teachers underwent change, their metaphors shifted and their teaching schemas filled out. Barbara's conception of nurturing shifted; Heidi came to think of herself as a caring adult; and Kay began to explore teaching through the metaphor, 'teacher is coach'. Clearly, holding strongly to a concept of self as teacher and then being able to play it out in situation are two quite different things. And yet, despite the changes that took place, for each of them, having a strongly held and relatively coherent but not rigid initial concept, which served as a basis upon which and out of which new meanings were built, was of great importance to the ultimate success of their role negotiations and undoubtedly played an important part in minimizing the discipline problems they encountered. They appeared to know who they were, and were able to act in relatively consistent and predictable ways within the classroom.

For each of the teachers much, perhaps most, of the process of negotiating meanings and relationships associated with the teaching role took place tacitly as part of the internal conversation noted by Blumer (1969) and in response to the teaching context and the quest to produce and maintain a reasonable level of satisfaction in teaching and at home. But, as the year progressed and through the constant and often subtle challenges to the teachers' teaching schemas and to how they framed and responded to the problems of teaching, progressively more of the meanings attached to them were made explicit. In this way, the experience of teaching became increasingly susceptible to the powers of reason (Polanyi, 1958) which is essential to choosing and justifying oneself as person and as teacher. This change was most evident with Kay and Heidi, and less so with Barbara. Kay saw in her increasing critical capacities and growing self-awareness a powerful means for increasing her control over the teaching context and a source of her growing independence from the pressure she felt to conform. In effect, she became a student of her own teaching, as did Heidi. As Kay put it: 'I'm tired of feeling like a reactor. Analyzing [my situation] makes me an actor.' As noted, one manifestation of their growing self-awareness was that each of the three teachers found themselves relying less frequently on trial and error approaches to teaching, as is common among beginning teachers (Dreeben, 1970; Lortie, 1975; Bullough, 1989a). Another, was that they began more or less systematically to work on specific aspects of their teaching to improve them as, for instance, when Kay focused on lesson pacing and sharpened both her understanding of the problem and of what solutions were likely to produce the desired results. The improvement of specific teaching skills played a central role in the ability of each teacher to realize in the classroom their images of self as teacher and was an important means for gaining increased control over the teaching situation. Kay's growing self-awareness was a clear indication of her having moved out of the survival into the mastery stage of learning to teach (Ryan, 1986). And yet another was the increased clarity, confidence, and sophistication with which they were able to speak in interview of themselves as teachers and of their teaching values and the problems of practice. At year's end, each of the three teachers knew who they were as teachers and were confident in this knowledge and in their abilities to teach and to direct their own development as teachers. Importantly, they felt like teachers, and their inner and teaching selves bonded. Each looked toward their second year of teaching with anticipation as a genuine opportunity further to elaborate these understandings, to strengthen and build better professional relationships, to improve their teaching skills, and, importantly, to shape the teaching context to be more to their liking.

10

TEACHER EDUCATION AND TEACHER DEVELOPMENT

INTRODUCTION

Generally speaking, beginning teachers enter their pre-service teacher-education programmes with partial, but often firmly held, conceptions of themselves as teachers and a teaching schema, developed over years of life experience including thousands of hours spent observing teachers as students (Lortie, 1975). The meanings attached to the teaching schema function as an interpretive lens through which beginning teachers selectively respond to the content and activities offered to them. Generally, their aim in responding is to seek confirmation of what they already believe to be true (Zeichner, Tabachnick and Densmore, 1987). Hence, it is not surprising that, given the limited intensity and short duration of most programmes, teacher-certification candidates leave pre-service teacher-education often little changed from how they entered (Crow, 1987). For those individuals who enter lacking a reasonably clear conception of themselves as teachers, pre-service teacher-education may provide the opportunity to explore a few alternative visions of teaching, perhaps those of cooperating or supervising teachers, but seldom the opportunity to test these visions in practice in more than superficial ways to determine if, and to what degree, they are appropriate and rewarding. Thus, like Larry and Nancy, such beginning teachers leave their teacher-education programmes expecting, in a sense, to find themselves as teachers while teaching and are likely to be extremely vulnerable to the contextual pressures of teaching.

During the first and, especially in the event of changes in the teaching context, perhaps the second and third years (Wildman,

Niles, Magliaro and McLaughlin, 1989), all beginning teachers engage in a complicated process of role negotiation. For teachers lacking a reasonably clear and consistent conception of themselves as teachers through which to begin thinking about and planning for teaching, the task of negotiation is especially complicated, and often it is merely an exercise in fantasy. This, along with holding to a very poorly fitting or contradictory teaching self, like Marilyn's, is a factor producing the survival stage of learning to teach discussed by Ryan (1986). Yet, even for teachers who hold reasonably complete and strong teaching schemas and conceptions of themselves as teachers, there is no guarantee that a smooth transition into the role of teacher is ahead, as Heidi discovered. The context of teaching and especially the teaching assignment can make negotiation very difficult and perhaps even impossible for some beginners.

From the studies presented here and others (Bullough 1989a, 1990a; Knowles, 1989; Wildman, Niles, Magliaro and McLaughlin, 1989) it is apparent that becoming a teacher is an idiosyncratic process reflecting not only differences in biography, personality, and in conceptions of teaching and how well or poorly they are developed, but also in school and school-community contexts. Saying this, however, does not mean that there is nothing to be done to help beginning teachers as they seek to negotiate institutionally productive and personally satisfying teaching roles. There is much of value that can and needs to be done but, in order to do it, a significant change must take place in much of our current thinking about teaching and teacher education. Perhaps the most serious impediment is the long tradition of teacher education as 'training', a tradition that has been with us since the days of the first normal school (Harper, 1939; Messerli, 1972), and is firmly entrenched in our thinking and embedded in our institutional structures and relations (Bullough and Gitlin, 1989), thus inhibiting appropriate and useful responses to the problems of role negotiation.

THE ASSUMPTIONS OF TRAINING

That teacher-education is firmly entrenched in a training orientation and approach is indicated by the ease with which the phrase, 'teacher training', flows from the lips of teachers and those who work with them and by the great emphasis upon the development of discrete and technical teaching skills; clearly, training dominates the language of education.

Some of the assumptions embedded in training views of teacher education and development are worth reviewing because of the mischief they cause. Consider a few of these assumptions and their implications: there is, at least operationally, a single definition of the 'good teacher', to which teachers must aspire, that centers on the demonstration of a list of narrowly construed teaching skills (see Florida Coalition for the Development of a Performance Measurement System, 1983; Hunter, 1984). This view is quite apparent not only in certification programmes but also in the dominant approaches to teacher evaluation (Bullough, 1988a, 1990b; Gitlin and Bullough, 1987; Johnston, 1989). Teaching is regarded as being synonymous with instruction, the process of ·mparting knowledge, and distinct from curriculum development which is done by someone else: the dominant metaphors are 'teacher is instructor', and 'teaching is telling'. Broadly speaking, from this assumption, teaching, as Friere (1970) describes it, is a process of 'banking' knowledge in the presumably empty heads of young people. This same assumption informs the instruction that takes place in teacher-education programmes where teacher-education students are viewed, like the students they will eventually teach, as 'empty' and in need of filling. From a training view, there is no reason for teacher-education programmes to attend either to personal biography or to teacher self-conceptions – all potential teachers receive the same 'treatment' – which, ironically, assures limited programme impact. Moreover, the training orientation brings with it a tendency to view clear-cut endings and beginnings to education both pre-service and in-service. For example, once 'trained', the 'trainee' is a teacher; although often only provisionally certified.

Following pre-service education, the 'teacher' is dropped by his or her professors on to the job market and only rarely is there any attempt to help either with placement or, once a job is secured, with adjusting to the new situation. Pre-service and in-service training are sharply demarcated. One result of this separation is that very little attention is given to teacher development and to establishing the conditions necessary for optimal development to occur. Instead, like the current tendency among American businesses, virtually all capital resources are put into achieving short-term gains, which are often those most easily attained but of

188

least importance or enduring value. It is little wonder that so much of the content of teacher-education is superficial and simple-minded. Finally, training is expert-driven and hierarchical; teachers frequently are viewed not only as lacking in expertise but, because of this lack, in need of constant supervision by those presumably possessing such expertise (Bullough, Holt and Goldstein, 1984). In sum, the model of teacher-education as training encourages teachers to be dependent, conservative, conforming, intellectually passive and withdrawn, and insecure and distrustful. And it celebrates individualism. Obviously, these are not the qualities of a vigorous profession likely to attract and keep talented persons; nor are they desirable qualities to be developed by beginning teachers.

AN ADDITIONAL PROBLEM

A second prominent source of difficulty, closely related to the assumptions of training, is the tendency among educators to focus school improvement efforts on altering attitudes and beliefs without altering the organization and structure of work to effect different kinds of relations: meaning is separated from context. As Kliebard (1988) has observed, the failure to alter the structure of schools to support desired changes in understanding and behaviour is a major reason most innovations are short-lived. Thus, and consistent with the tenets of symbolic interactionism (Blumer, 1969), those who would assist beginning teachers in their quest to negotiate productive and satisfying teaching roles must attend carefully to context and to influential context variables. Clearly, as the cases presented in *Emerging as a Teacher* illustrate, some organizational and structural arrangements of work inhibit, while others enable beginning-teacher development; some foster with-drawal, while others encourage making links with other teachers to explore issues and concerns. An alternative understanding of teaching, and of teachers and their development, must be forged and a parallel institutional structure developed: new wine, new bottles.

AN ALTERNATIVE VISION

The challenge before us is clear: Beginning teachers need to be helped to come to a reasonably full awareness of the conceptions they hold of themselves as teachers and of the origins of the meanings they hold; they need to recapture their histories. As illustrated in the cases presented, many of these meanings are unarticulated and taken for granted; they find expression in the teacher's 'common sense' (Woods, 1987). Becoming aware of them is necessary for them to be remade and represents a first step toward helping beginning teachers become, in Kay's words, 'actors' rather than 'reactors' in the induction process. They need to be helped to become simultaneously students and architects of their own professional development. They need assistance to develop frameworks for thinking contextually and reflectively about their development; they need to become students of schooling and those aspects of institutional life, school practice, and interpersonal relations that are likely to enable or inhibit their development as professionals. Moreover, they need to be able to recognize and utilize school resources that will enable and enhance their development. In sum, and quite contrary to the assumptions of training, they need to recognize themselves as centres of meaning-making, as producers of legitimate knowledge that is worthy of being shared and deserving to be acted upon (Bullough and Gitlin, 1989).

In addition, the contexts within which beginning teachers struggle to come to terms with teaching need to be changed so as to provide them with a reasonable possibility for success. In saying this, our concern is not primarily to urge that beginning teachers be assisted to make a smooth transition into schools, especially into institutionally acceptable teaching roles and relations like that of 'policeman' as encountered by Larry. Rather, our aim ought to be to maximize the control of the beginning teacher over the process and outcomes of role negotiation and the autonomy necessary to achieve a successful negotiation; the structure ought to help empower the beginning teacher to choose the kind of teacher he or she will become.

A central part of negotiating a teaching role is the negotiation of a place within the school and wider professional community (Bullough, 1989b). In thinking about structural changes that will assist negotiation, careful and critical attention needs to be given to the kind and quality of roles and relations characterizing the school community to which the beginning teacher seeks membership and the norms and assumptions, which are embedded in the community's language or discourse, upon which it rests. Clearly,

190

while we have argued that each teacher is a centre of meaning-making, meaning is made within context (Mishler, 1979) and through interaction, and shared contexts tend to produce shared problems and issues as well as understandings. Sadly, many school communities offer little help to the beginning teacher as he or she strives to negotiate a satisfying and productive role. Indeed, withdrawal from the school community into the security of the classroom and the reliance on 'private survival strategies' (Sikes, Measor and Woods, 1985) may well be a reasonable response to the presence of an unhealthy school environment.

Ultimately, the teaching role that is negotiated by the beginner reverberates outward into the wider professional community, carrying to others interested in the education of young people a statement of ideals and implicit beliefs about teaching as a profession. Actions intended to assist the beginning teacher negotiate a role ought to be guided by recognition that, for good or ill, induction involves not only a process by which the novice is linked to both school and professional communities but also is the *means* by which those communities are sustained, perpetuated or remade. Participation in and the building of communities – communal relations, understandings, and commitments – consistent with the aim of teacher empowerment, and not simply the adoption of an institutionalized role, ought to be a central concern of those seeking to assist the beginning teacher establish a productive place within the school.

The wider professional community into which the beginning teacher seeks membership is not a very healthy community, however. And this needs to be recognized. At present it is deeply fragmented (Soder, 1988), as is indicated by the gulf separating the university and the schools, and dominated by 'an enveloping bureaucracy' (Boyer, 1983: 225) that devalues human action and agency, and by the training mentality, for example. Despite these problems, as severe as they are, the core values of teacher professionalism that arise out of the history and practice of teaching, and the kinds of relationships encouraged by these values, are relatively clear and it is these that bind teachers together and inspire their commitment. At the centre is the value of student learning and development and a powerful ethic of caring (Noddings, 1984). In part, the ethic of caring originates from the domination of teaching by women and in the motives that inspire them to teach (Belenky, Clinchy, Goldberger and Tarule, 1986; Grumet,

1988). Enhancing and extending the ethic of caring, by building caring relations in the school community, are essential to helping the beginning teacher to negotiate a productive and defensible teaching role, just as it is fundamental, more generally, to creating an authentic teacher professionalism (Freedman, 1987).

Rather than looking to law and medicine as exemplary communities to be emulated and for professional practices and ideals to guide and inspire action, as is widely being suggested (see Holmes Group, 1986), the gaze should be directed toward others who in particular share the ethic of caring, such as the religious ministry and ministers (Mattingly, 1975; Jackson, 1987). And especially the gaze should turn inward to historical and currently vibrant school communities, and to exemplary members of the wider professional community, some of whom, like the 'distant teachers' mentioned by John-Steiner (1985: 36), are no longer living (see Board, 1991; Broudy and Palmer, 1965; Bullough, 1981; Cremin, 1988; Jewett, 1988; Peterson, 1946; Winetrout, 1988). When thinking through specific efforts to assist the beginning teacher negotiate a role, attention ought to be given to this more general level of becoming a teacher.

Gazing inward may produce some surprising and pleasing results. For example, from their study of 105 teachers who felt positive toward teaching, Zumwalt and her colleagues identified four 'themes' that not only represent some of the characteristics of vibrant school communities and relations, but also help define teacher empowerment. Central to these teachers' positive attitudes were:

> (a) the freedom to be creative and innovative; (b) their capacity to influence and impact students; (c) opportunities for feedback, recognition, and support from adults and students; and (d) opportunities to share and work with other adults . . . . These teachers were involved, on a problem-solving level, with other teachers in small and large groups working on school-related problems or projects.
>
> (Zumwalt, 1988: 156)

While a much longer list could easily be produced, clearly these factors and the part they play in making teachers feel good about their work present a rather clear vision of teacher professionalism and the high value placed on student learning and on caring. Moreover, they are illustrative of some of the discoveries that come

from gazing inward toward those within the community who possess and maintain a lively sense of being a teaching professional.
Such discoveries can and should play an important part in giving
direction to efforts to revitalize the wider professional community.

The phrase, 'empowering teachers', is in one important respect
problematical. It seems to imply that others who enjoy power over
teachers will willingly share it with them. Besides representing a
remarkably naive conception of power and its operation
(Cherryholmes, 1988), by encouraging teachers to look toward
others to resolve their problems such a view is inherently
hierarchical and supportive of teacher passivity and conservatism.
Thus, a residue of the training orientation persists even in talk
about empowerment! As is illustrated by the cases included in
Emerging as a Teacher, the challenge to training views of teacher
development, if it is to be successful, must be built upon a clear
understanding of the central role of the individual in his or her
own development; in a very real sense, teachers cannot be
empowered, they can only empower, or choose, themselves,
although others may be of some assistance along the way (Giroux,
1983; O'Loughlin and Campbell, 1988). As Lashley puts it, 'Power
is never given; it's taken' (1989: 2).

ASSISTING NEGOTIATION AND BECOMING PROFESSIONAL

Where do we begin to create conditions that will enable a different
kind of teacher-role negotiation and development from that
common today; one counter to the training model and consistent
with the image of teachers as knowledge producers (Duckworth,
1986) and active members of a professional community in need of
reconceptualization? Pre-service and continuing teacher-
education are two places where changes can and need to be made.
In addition, school principals can do much to nudge along
successful negotiation as can experienced teachers. When
considering pre-service teacher-education we will draw on our own
experience and practice that reflect insights gained from the
research presented in *Emerging as a Teacher*, as well as from other
studies (Bullough, 1991). We do not offer our work as an
exemplar, something others ought to follow, but only as
representative of a few of the many alternatives possible in the
hope that by doing so we will encourage the explorations of others

who share our interest in and concern for beginning teachers and who are troubled by the domination of teacher education by the taken-for-granted language and values of training. We believe the suggestions that follow are modest ones, well within reach of those interested in and involved with beginning teachers.

PRE-SERVICE TEACHER-EDUCATION

As noted, when considering directions for pre-service teacher-education that will challenge the 'training' model and facilitate the building of a professional community and empowering relations, it is important to attend carefully to programme structure and organization. We begin, therefore, with a brief discussion of some aspects of programme structure which is followed by a discussion of process-related issues.

Structure

The aim of building a professional community that embraces an ethic of caring and honours the central teacher value of student learning necessitates that teacher-education be organized communally and that it stress interaction among participants. Such an organization facilitates the development of caring relations. In our own work this aim has found expression in the development of 'cohorts'. A cohort is a small group of about twenty students who proceed together through their pre-service teacher-education coursework with one or two instructors who function as 'cohort leaders'. The leaders stay with the cohort throughout the entire programme and serve as instructors, advisors, and facilitators. We have found the cohort to be an essential structural condition for the building of community and for the establishment of a level of trust essential to the development of critical teacher reflectivity where values can be openly and honestly explored. To expand the community, the cohorts are intimately linked with one or two schools within which all field work is carried out; they get to know one or two schools and a small group of faculty members very well over the course of a year in secondary education or two years in elementary education. Work in the schools is continuous throughout the programme. It should be noted that eventually our hope is that the schools we work with will function as fully fledged professional development schools (Holmes Group, 1991) but this ideal is still in the future for the secondary schools where its implementation has proven to be much more complicated than in the elementary schools.

To facilitate the development of interpersonal reasoning (Noddings, 1991) and critical teacher reflectivity, practice teaching runs for one half-day for two quarters and is linked to an ongoing and required problem-solving seminar. By limiting practice teaching to one half-day, pre-service teachers are given the time essential to consider their work in ways prohibited when practice teaching occupies all of each day (Wildman and Niles, 1987) and pre-service teachers are dominated by the concern for personal and professional survival. Within the seminar the expectation is that the students will engage in the study of their own practice and development and assist others in their efforts to become teachers.

Processes: life history

A consensus has emerged in much of the recent work on teacher reflectivity that beginning teachers ought to engage in reflection in three areas, or at three levels:

(1) the pedagogical and curricular means used to attain educational aims, (2) the underlying assumptions and consequences of pedagogical action, and (3) the moral implications of pedagogical actions and the structure of schooling.

(Liston and Zeichner, 1987: 2)

Surprisingly, as important as these areas are, they may not directly address the meanings about teaching and about self-as-teacher held by the beginning teacher and make no room for the consideration of the biographical origin of these meanings. The challenge is clear: 'Teacher educators must . . . explore new ways of permitting student teachers to explore problematic aspects of their life-world without, at the same time . . . heightening the already great anxieties many of them feel' (Young, 1990: 164).

As we have argued, effective teacher education must begin with 'who' the teacher is and with 'how' he or she conceives of himself or herself as teacher – the inner self and the situational self. The recent focus on writing life histories is a promising avenue for beginning such an exploration and nudging teachers toward self-awareness (Butt and Raymond, 1987; Pinar, 1980; Woods, 1987). With our focus on pre-service teacher education, however, our aim for life history is necessarily much less ambitious than that of Goodson (1981), for example. Our point of concern is more narrowly with education-related life histories. There is nothing mysterious about the writing of education-related life histories. They are just as the title suggests: histories of how the beginning teacher experienced school and learning and of how these experiences are related to current understandings of themselves and of teaching.

Typically, cohort leaders begin by asking the pre-service teachers to write life histories which become texts subject to continuous elaboration for study and analysis, especially in relation to classroom practice once student teaching begins. Analysis takes two forms: individual and group. For the individual, the writing of a life history is frequently illuminating and serves as a basis for future thinking about teaching as biases and assumptions that underpin and permeate interpretation are identified and linked to past experiences. It is a means for getting in touch with how one learns and creates meaning and how one develops over time. And too, for some pre-service teachers the act of writing itself is therapeutic. Collectively, through the sharing of life histories, common themes are identified and explored, which become focal points for readings and group examination. For example, the theme of being victimized by school and feeling powerless arose from the analysis of the life histories written in one of our recent classes:

> We were practicing a song for a PTA performance. We had sung this song over and over to the point where I had it memorized. At one point the music teacher saw me not reading the words and she stopped and told me to pay attention. I told her I didn't need to look at the words because I knew the song by heart. She then asked me to sing the song by myself if I knew it so well. Well, I was not about to sing solo – I was too scared and embarrassed. She then said, 'I knew you didn't know the song. Don't let me catch you not paying attention again.' This was disturbing to me because I felt as though I was misunderstood, that I was treated unfairly, that I was not trusted. A similar thing happened to me in seventh grade. I was accused of getting into a kid's

locker next to mine. The principal called me into his office and asked me why I did it; he did not ask me if I had done it. Well, I denied having done it and he told me I was lying. Then I lost it, I couldn't stop crying; I sobbed so hard I couldn't talk. I was mad, humiliated, afraid. I felt like a victim, and there was nothing I could do to change things.

Being a victim had a powerful influence on how this individual thought about himself as a teacher and especially shaped his thinking about the kind and quality of relationships he wanted to establish with students. Others shared similar experiences which impacted their thinking about student–teacher relations. These experiences were explored in relation to the culture of teaching and the structure of schooling as a means for identifying contextual factors that influence meaning-making. One of the insights gained was that in bureaucratically organized institutions students are not the only ones victimized; teachers (and administrators) suffer too.

Processes: metaphor analysis

To help beginning teachers to think about their development as teachers, over the course of the programme they are encouraged to identify and explore their personal metaphors for teaching (Bullough, 1990a; Bullough, 1991). The virtue of metaphor analysis is that metaphors simplify complex phenomena and thereby make them analytically manageable (Dickmeyer, 1989). While we have approached this assignment in a variety of ways, most recently the assignment was made directly: 'Drawing on your life-history, identify a metaphor that captures the essence of yourself as teacher.' As the pre-service teachers work through the teacher-education programme they encounter a variety of challenges to their initial conceptions of themselves as teachers, especially once practice teaching begins and they start to engage in action research (to be discussed shortly). Periodically, we return to a consideration of their teaching metaphors, which are typically multiple, seeking to identify if and in what ways their thinking about themselves – their story – has changed and what experiences, specifically, have encouraged the changes. In this way they are helped to locate aspects of their self-understandings that are contradictory or partial, and are helped to identify the types of contextual factors that most dramatically influence them and their understanding of themselves as teachers, with the aim being that of assisting them to increase their understanding of and control over their development. Put differently, the aim is to help the teachers recognize more fully how they author their own stories and to identify within the stories the potential for development lying latent within them.

Sometimes the discoveries made about self have been painful, and the results distasteful, necessitating serious soul searching on the part of the beginning teacher:

> I find there is a lot more parenting in my teaching metaphor than I would like. Perhaps because I am a parent and have chosen the parenting metaphor in other areas of my life and that metaphor is so very strong [that] it reaches over into the teaching area .... I don't want to permanently parent anyone other than my own children. Thus, I fight against becoming so involved with any student that I am personally affected by his behavior.

Other times, the process has been gratifying as the beginning teacher begins to realize that progress has in fact taken place. And for many, metaphor analysis has proven to be a useful means for thinking about who they are, as teachers, as one pre-service teacher's comments illustrate:

> This whole idea of [producing] a teaching metaphor has really been a powerful [vehicle] for [thinking about] myself ... It comes at a time when I am experiencing a personal crisis over the age old question of 'Who am I?' Just when I thought that my [teaching] identity was fairly secure and well established, I am being subject to yet another identity crisis.

Processes: classroom ethnography

Early in the programme an ethnography is written of the classroom within which the beginning teacher will eventually be practice teaching. Two purposes guide the ethnographies: first, from a practical standpoint, to identify how classrooms are organized by teachers for learning; and second, to explore the assumptions underpinning that organization. The second purpose is embedded in the more general aim of developing critical teacher reflectivity whereby the beginning teacher learns to 'read discourses critically, including interests, ideologies, and supporting power arrangements' (Cherryholmes, 1988: 94). In the ethnography the beginning teachers explore how relationships within the classroom, which form the classroom environment, are ordered and justified and the parts played by the teacher and students in providing and maintaining that order. Specific attention is given to identifying patterns of interaction, in particular routines, and to the formal and informal rules underlying them. As with the life history and metaphor analysis, the ethnographies become part of the text of teacher-education. Through writing and sharing the ethnographies the beginning teachers are assisted in their efforts to think through the kind of learning relationships they wish to create, and in relation to the politics of teaching and learning and to the teaching skills necessary for actually establishing such relationships. In addition, they become increasingly sensitive to how context influences meaning-making and teacher behaviour. Through the sharing of the ethnographies, once again, common themes and issues are identified for further exploration.

Processes: action research

Based upon the belief that 'The most effective evaluation for learning is self-evaluation' (Johnston, 1989: 523), throughout practice teaching – and we hope into their first years of teaching – our pre-service teacher education students engage in a variation of 'action research'. For example: they are assigned to audio- or video-tape lessons in a single class or subject area that they find to be of special interest. They do this a number of times over their teaching experience. The purpose of the first few tapings is to provide data from which a rich picture of what is going on in the classroom can be formed for analysis. The first task, then, is interpretative and descriptive. In addition, the teachers identify any aspects of the class sessions that proved to be surprising. Next, based upon their analysis of the data gathered and their written descriptions, they seek to locate and then frame for study a problem that is of interest or importance to them and their development as teachers. Since many of the problems identified are shared ones, collaboration is encouraged. At this point, the

'Action Research Spiral' suggested by Kemmis and McTaggart (1988) is loosely followed: a plan of action is devised, the plan is implemented, observation of the effects of the action takes place, and the beginning teacher reflects on the effects and writes up an analysis for sharing with others in the cohort looking toward another spiral. Sharing of the plan and results is extremely important inasmuch as many of the problems identified are common ones and the beginning teachers are able to assist one another in their development as members of the cohort community. In seeking solutions, appropriate readings are provided which often are directly related to acquiring desired teaching skills which at this point in their development is of paramount concern.

The influence of action research on teacher self-conception and on the improvement of practice has been dramatic. Through action research the pre-service teachers have had the opportunity to consider in powerful ways the relationship between their teaching identities and teaching contexts which has enabled the identification for some of more productive ways of being and working in the classroom. Minimally, there have been many surprises, as one pre-service teacher observed:

> This particular group always seemed to be on task. When I approached them they were [always] diligently working. Or so I thought! The tape recorder does not lie! The conversation while I was away [from the students] was anything but on task, but as I approached, it miraculously changed to exactly what I wanted to hear. What was more embarrassing was the way in which the kids made the transition. In midsentence and even in mid-word, they were able to change the topic without missing a beat. Moreover, as soon as I walked away they switched back to their own conversation without leaving so much as a clue for me to discern. These students were experts at this kind of deception!

Some discoveries about self were painful, although ultimately rewarding. For example:

> Instrumental to changing my outlook on student teaching was . . . the examination of my teaching by way of recording and then analyzing [audio] tapes. This allowed me to step back a little and look at myself and my students more from

the perspective others had. During this time I discovered that what others had been trying to tell me, [that I had serious problems], was true. The acceptance, and then the overt attempts at improvement, required some soul searching and painful self-analysis, but the rewards [have been] at times astonishing.

By having pre-service teachers concentrated in a few schools, peer observation becomes a possibility, yet another aspect of action research that complements the effort to build community and weaken individualism. The benefits of peer observation, aside from providing additional sources of data useful for analysing practice, are readily apparent, as Johnston observes:

when two teachers observe each other teaching and talk about their experience, some important things tend to happen. That each watches the other reduces power differential – both are at risk. When I watch another teacher I see specific examples of teaching activity that will or will not fit into my theory of teaching. When the other teacher watches me, to the extent that I know that teacher, I view what I am doing, as I am doing it, through his or her eyes. In many cases, simply doing that is enough to produce reevaluation and change. In a way it gives stereoscopic vision. The dialogue that stems from these experiences, and their explanation, is likely to produce a reevaluation of the activities and of the theories, provided there is security within which to contemplate disagreement.

(Johnston 1989: 524)

These activities and others, such as journal writing, are intended to help the pre-service teachers become more self-aware of who they are as teachers, and how they understand teaching, and to face themselves squarely and critically. Moreover, they are intended to assist the pre-service teacher become a student of his or her own development in order to direct that development more effectively and intelligently in the belief that, as Zumwalt (1988: 170) states, a 'self-analytic stance insures continual professional growth.' And also our intention is to encourage them to begin thinking about themselves in relation to various, and specific, aspects of the work of teaching and the teaching context; and to realize the importance to their development of others. Finally, through openly sharing experiences and critically reflecting upon them, it is hoped that the development of professional community is furthered. Obviously, however, there are serious limitations as to what can be accomplished in pre-service teacher-education. If an alternative vision of teacher induction to that informed by the assumptions of training is to be realized, efforts must continue into the first few years of teaching. Otherwise, whatever good is accomplished in teacher education may very well be 'washed out' (Zeichner and Tabachnick, 1981).

CONTINUING TEACHER-EDUCATION

Frequently, once a teaching position is assumed, the beginning teacher finds himself left alone to 'sink or swim'. Although possessing very limited resources, to help prevent this possibility from becoming a reality for some of our graduates we have been exploring the place a seminar or support group for first-year teachers may have in teacher induction and development. It was just such a seminar that Larry, Nancy, Marilyn, Barbara, Heidi, and Kay participated in during their first year of teaching. As noted previously, our aim was essentially that of providing a safe place for them, a place where they could come to be unconditionally supported and within which they could discuss virtually any issue they wished together and with us, members of the wider educational community. In addition, we provided them with copies of the transcripts of the interviews we conducted with them and with copies of drafts of the case studies, which were discussed and criticized, believing that they would be useful for thinking about themselves and their development as teachers. Uniformly, the beginning teachers said this was so. For the most part, the agendas for our meetings were set in consultation with the group and in response to their concerns; we had no intention of attempting to direct their development.

In retrospect, at times our interest in better understanding the process of becoming a teacher interfered with other possible seminar outcomes. Not wanting to muddy up or complicate the experience of the first year of teaching too much, we took a somewhat passive stance toward the teachers and their development in contrast to the kind of interactive relationship deemed most desirable by Young (1990). Had we played a more active role, we may have been able to help ameliorate some of their difficulties, especially those encountered by Larry, Nancy and Marilyn, although each claimed that our listening to them discuss their problems and our occasional offering of suggestions were very helpful. Perhaps the most useful aspect of the seminar had nothing to do with our presence at the meetings or absence but rather with simply being with other first-year teachers who could empathize with what was being experienced and who could draw upon their experiences to offer suggestions and support. Marilyn's comments suggest this was so:

> It's wonderful to hear that other people have the same [problems] and that it's okay . . . . [As first-year teachers] we are in the same boat . . . we have the same things happen. We have the same feelings; we're all thinking, 'Oh brother, what a lousy teacher I am.'

Ethically, we have struggled with what we could and should have done, given our purposes. We are not, at this point, certain about what role we should play in future seminars but we believe a more active stance is clearly called for, even while recognizing that there are severe limitations to how far we can become involved, given fiscal and other institutional and professional constraints. Inevitably and unfortunately, once in the school, the burden of teacher induction and development shifts away from the university, thus confirming the false and foolish theory/practice dualism embedded in training orientations to teacher development. And yet, it is our view that the university needs to continue to be actively involved and that this is essential to building the wider professional community as a community based upon an ethic of caring and a commitment to student learning and development. Moreover, such involvement is essential to the vitality of university-based teacher-education and research.

SCHOOL ACTION

Within the first year or two of teaching much can be done within schools to assist the beginning teacher negotiate a productive and satisfying role along the lines we have suggested. Briefly, and again drawing on our experience in schools (Bullough, 1989a) and especially from our work with the first-year teachers included in *Emerging as a Teacher*, we will note a few of the many positive actions that can be undertaken particularly by principals who 'In many ways . . . shape the organizational conditions under which teachers work and the definitions of teaching they come to acquire' (Rosenholtz, 1989: 427), and by experienced teachers.

Teaching assignment

Obviously, the inappropriateness or appropriateness of a teaching assignment does much either to hinder or facilitate role negotiation, as Heidi and Larry discovered shortly after the start of the school year. And it is equally obvious that beginning teachers generally get the worst teaching assignments (Rosenholtz, 1989). Before Heidi and Larry stepped into the school a cluster of problems were awaiting them that would complicate and make more difficult their struggle to become teachers. Both teachers took the jobs aware of some of these problems but were in need of work and no other positions were forthcoming. Moreover, the principals who did the hiring found themselves in the position of not being able to obtain, at least from the pool of new applicants, better candidates. This said, we question the tendency among some building administrators to think of making assignments bureaucratically, in terms of filling slots with bodies, rather than humanely and intelligently to include consideration of all of the resources in the school. For example, to avoid facing the complicated discussions that would be required within departments in order to have experienced teachers fill some, perhaps less desirable secondary-school teaching assignments, the tendency is to take advantage of the vulnerability of beginning teachers in order to fill them.

All beginning teachers need some reduction in load to allow time to learn to teach, including time to observe other teachers within the building. Only Nancy, among the six first-year teachers, had a reasonable teaching assignment and that was because of teaching in a private school. For beginning teachers who step into an assignment for which they are more than ordinarily un-prepared – they are all to some degree unprepared – a significant load reduction is called for. In order to do so it may be necessary for there to be a slight increase in other teachers' loads but it has been our experience that when these teachers understand the situation and are part of the decision-making process, as members of the school community and having been first-year teachers themselves, they respond positively and empathetically.

Mentoring

Mentoring – at least in the sense of being supervised – is rapidly becoming part of teaching in America. Unfortunately, as the case studies illustrate, even when mentoring is legislatively mandated, it is of uneven quality and effectiveness, varying from the outstanding support and concern shown toward Marilyn to the neglect experienced by Heidi and Barbara.

The reasons for Heidi's neglect are of particular interest. The mentoring programme in place in Heidi's school was based upon a training view of teacher development. From this view, as noted, emphasis is placed on skill development, narrowly conceived, and represented on a rating sheet. Since Heidi had no obvious skill deficiencies and the classes were under control, her mentor and the building administrators were not concerned about her. As Heidi remarked at year's end, they had no conception of the struggle she experienced coming to terms with being a teacher. Indeed, they had stopped thinking of her as a first-year teacher in need of care and of assistance:

> My principal ... told me that he was talking to the vice-principal ... about his surprise at my success in the classroom as a first year teacher. The vice-principal told him he could see that any day he walked by my room. They concluded I was not a first year teacher [at all]. That comment meant a lot to me [but] the administration didn't see the things I went through .... They were not usually aware of my stresses and personal conflicts .... To them, I was successful where it really mattered ... in the classroom.

Obviously, mentoring is only as good as the mentors, and beginning teachers desperately need good mentors able to help them become oriented to the school, a major problem faced by beginning teachers (Odell, 1986), manage their work-loads, and learn about teaching. Heidi certainly would have appreciated such assistance. But more than this, they need mentors they trust, and who are able and willing to help them discover and come to terms with who they are as teachers, a struggle that takes place internally, behind the scenes, witnessed from the hallway when glancing through an opened classroom door.

Among the variables affecting the quality of the mentoring received was how highly the building administrators valued the work of the mentors; mentors also need to be cared for. If they were little interested in mentoring themselves, and made few efforts to honour the work of effective mentors, little was accomplished as illustrated by both Barbara's and Heidi's experience. Generally speaking, it is unreasonable to expect school-building administrators to function as mentors, but it is reasonable and essential for them to take an active interest in mentoring, as did Marilyn's principal, and openly to acknowledge their appreciation for work well done. Moreover, an active interest in mentoring will allow adminstrators to respond with resources if and when difficulties arise. Without this interest problems may be discovered only after they have become very serious and immediate action is required as with Larry. On the other side, beginning teachers must take advantage of the opportunities afforded by willing and able mentors, a lesson Nancy needed to learn.

Access to decision making

An essential aspect of fostering school community is for teachers to be significantly, albeit reasonably, involved in the various levels of decision-making. From the start of their experience in school, beginning teachers should be included in deliberations affecting the school. Through participation they will encounter teachers who are model community members who demonstrate the value of collaboration to personal development. And it is through participation that beginning teachers may learn that their views are valued and matter, and that others are interested in them. Moreover, through participation they will gain important insights into how their school works and what resources are available to assist them in their quest to become a teacher. Generally speaking, none of the first-year teachers were significantly involved in school decision-making although the elementary-school teachers participated in more significant ways than did the secondary-education teachers.

Feedback and evaluation

Each of the teachers, excepting Nancy, was evaluated formally at least twice during the year by school-district policy and state law. None of them, with the exception of Marilyn, reported that the evaluations were of any use. Kay's experience was fairly typical; like the other teachers she avoided risk and manipulated the situation to obtain the desired positive assessment of her classroom performance. Ongoing, well-informed, formative evaluation, for the purposes of providing feedback, can play a significant part in helping the beginning teacher negotiate a productive and satisfying teaching role. There are several benefits to ongoing evaluation, we will mention only a few: beginning teachers are frequently poor judges of their own performance, reacting in overly sensitive ways, for example, to student and parent opinions. Thus, evaluation and feedback can be a means for helping the beginning teacher keep events in a useful perspective, as well as a source of ideas. In addition, knowledge of good performance is very important to role negotiation and to feeling successful in teaching, especially during the survival stage of learning to teach when so many beginning teachers are tortured by self-doubts. For example, as discussed in chapter 5, beginning teachers frequently have difficulty accepting that what they have done is the source of success or failure. Instead, they will look outside themselves to a 'good' or a 'bad' class, for instance, as the cause. Confidence and power come from recognizing and accepting the results of actions undertaken. Additionally, peer evaluation is a promising avenue for giving and receiving feedback and can be an important means for becoming connected with others within the school community, as Marilyn's experience indicated. Moreover, through partici-pation in peer evaluation, the beginning teacher not only has the opportunity to observe others teaching, but also to engage in meaningful conversations about teaching (Gitlin and Bullough, 1987).

Support and encouragment

All the teachers from time to time felt at least a modicum of support and received some encouragement from their school administrators and from other teachers. Only Kay and Marilyn felt continuously and appropriately supported, but even they did not feel secure enough to take curricular and instructional risks openly. Indeed, Marilyn, despite the remarkably high degree of help offered and accepted, continued to feel vulnerable and avoided virtually all risk taking. This is extremely important when viewed in the light of the trial-and-error approaches to learning how to teach that beginning teachers use. Inevitably learning to teach involves frequent failures (Bullough, 1989a; Wildman, Niles, Magliaro and McLaughlin, 1989) and an unwillingness to risk may retard teacher development and unnecessarily limit student opportunities learning. On his part, Larry felt a great deal of support from two teachers within the school and a friend who was a teacher, but that was all. Generally speaking, especially during the first few months of school, these beginning teachers kept their problems to themselves, in part believing that to have problems was to admit failure. Like other teachers they sought to protect themselves (Blase, 1988) and generally withdrew into the security of their classrooms in order to maintain a level of self-esteem (Rosenholtz, 1989).

In the face of a lack of encouragement and support, the teachers' reactions were sensible but, from the perspective of becoming a teacher, unfortunate. Ultimately, a very different view of learning to teach, one associated with participation in the school and the wider professional community, needs to prevail. As Rosenholtz observed:

> if teaching is collectively viewed as an inherently difficult undertaking, it is both necessary and legitimate to seek and to offer professional assistance. This is exactly what occurs in instructionally successful schools, where, because of strong administrative or faculty leadership, teaching is considered a collective rather than an individual enterprise; requests and offers of assistance among colleagues are frequent; and reasoned intentions, informed choices, and collective actions set the conditions under which teachers improve instructionally.
>
> (Rosenholtz, 1989: 430)

From our own experience, perhaps the most simple and useful approach an administrator can take to nudge along collegiality, and to combat the tendency among first-year teachers to withdraw into their classrooms, is to hold periodic meetings for first-year teachers only, and to have the good sense to not be present during all of their discussions! A further step would be to establish employee-assistance programs that would include access to counselling services when needed for beginning as well as for experienced teachers (Pajak and Blase, 1989: 307).

CONCLUSION

Recognizing that over 30 per cent of all beginning teachers who assume teaching positions do not make it to their second year of teaching, the challenge of improving the process of teacher induction and socialization is grimly insistent. To make matters worse, it appears that the most able teachers are those most likely to leave teaching (Schlechty and Vance, 1983). This is not only a horrendous waste of the time and energy expended to educate short-term teachers, it is in many respects a sad tale of lost opportunities, of insensitiviy to suffering, and of individual intellectual blindness and institutional rigidity. There are, however, many hopeful signs on the horizon, one of which is the growing interest in teacher education generally, and in the problems of beginning teachers specifically. It is our hope that *Emerging as a a Teacher* will contribute to an understanding of the problems associated with negotiating a teaching role and of how and in what ways these problems may be addressed productively. Furthermore, we hope that *Emerging as a Teacher* will serve as a reminder that teaching is a collective responsibility and that the interests of all citizens, but especially of children, are at stake in how well or how poorly the beginning teacher negotiates a teaching role, and set of professional relations, and in the kind and quality of understandings about self-as-teacher that are eventually produced. It is self-evident that the key to educational renewal is the development of a cadre of satisfied, committed, caring, critically intelligent, and dedicated teachers who feel they are part of vital school and professional communities. It is also quite apparent that much that goes on during teacher induction encourages just the opposite set of qualities with often devastating results. Under such circumstances it is something of a miracle, fostered by extraordinary human effort and will power, and perhaps by a measure of luck, that a teacher like Heidi emerges. While miracles do happen, we ought to be about making them unnecessary.

NOTES

CHAPTER 1

1 'Certification' refers to the course of study that teacher-education students pursue and that leads upon successful completion to a licence or certificate to teach.

CHAPTER 2

1 The American public-school system is typically divided into three levels and twelve grades. The elementary school, divided into six grades, serves students age 5 to 12; the junior high, divided into three grades, serves students age 12 to 15; and the high school serves students to age 18 in three grades.

2 A cooperating teacher is an experienced teacher in whose classroom a student teacher practises teaching. The cooperating teacher is responsible for helping to provide professional education and to mentor novice teachers.

3 A description of the Rockers and other American youth subculture groups is contained in chapter 9.

CHAPTER 4

1 American colleges and universities typically require for graduation both a major and minor area of study. A major represents roughly a year or more concentrated fulltime study in a discipline, while a minor represents approximately a half year of fulltime study.

2 Intern teachers, in this instance, are university students who have completed all of their teacher education except practice teaching. In lieu of practice they assume a fulltime teaching position but for half pay. Thus, by having two interns in a single school, it becomes possible to free an experienced teacher in the building from teaching in order to assume the responsibility of mentoring the interns.

CHAPTER 6

1 A description of these subculture groups is presented in chapter 9.

CHAPTER 7

1 Descriptions of the student subcultural groups are presented in chapter 9.

CHAPTER 9

1 A 'letter jacket' is a jacket that students wear upon which is attached a large letter that stands for the school the student attends. Letters are earned by students through participation in a variety of school activities, most notably sports.

REFERENCES

Anderson, R. C. (1977). 'The notion of schemata and the educational enterprise: General discussion of conference.' In R. C. Anderson, R. J. Spiro, and W. E. Montague (Eds.), *Schooling and the acquisition of knowledge* (pp. 415–31). Hillsdale, NJ: Lawrence Erlbaum Associates, Publishers.

Aspinwall, K. and Drummond, M. (1989). 'Socialized into primary teaching.' In H. De Lyon and F. W. Migniuolo (Eds.), *Women teachers: Issues and experiences* (pp. 13–22). Milton Keynes: Open University Press.

Ball, S. J. and Goodson, I. F. (1985). 'Understanding teachers: Concepts and contexts.' In S. J. Ball and I. F. Goodson (Eds.), *Teachers' lives and careers* (pp. 1–26). London: The Falmer Press.

Bardman, B. (1967). *The place of reason in education.* Columbus, OH: The Ohio State University Press.

Belenky, J. F., Clinchy, B. M., Goldberger, N. R. and Tarule, J. M. (1986). *Women's ways of knowing: The development of self, voice, and mind.* NY: Basic Books, Inc.

Berliner, D. C. (1986). 'In pursuit of the expert pedagogue.' *Educational Research, 15*(7), 1–23.

Beynon, J. (1985). 'Institutional change and career histories in a comprehensive school.' In S. J. Ball and I. F. Goodson (Eds.), *Teachers' lives and careers* (pp. 158–79). London: The Falmer Press.

Blase, J. J. (1988). 'The everyday political perspective of teachers: Vulnerability and conservatism.' *Qualitative Studies in Education, 1*(2), 125–42.

Bloom, A. (1987). *The closing of the American mind.* NY: Simon and Schuster.

Blumer, H. (1969). *Symbolic interactionism: Perspective and method.* Englewood Cliffs, NJ: Prentice-Hall, Inc.

Board, J. C. (1991). *A special relationship: Our teachers and how we learned.* Wainscott, NY: Pushcart Press.

Boyer, E. L. (1983). *High school: A report on secondary education in America.* NY: Harper and Row.

Broudy, H. S. and Palmer, J. R. (1965). *Exemplars of teaching method.* Chicago, IL: Rand McNally.

Bullough, R. V. Jr. (1981). *Democracy in education: Boyd H. Bode.* Bayside, NY: General Hall, Inc.

Bullough, R. V. Jr. (1987). 'Accommodation and tension: Teachers, teacher role, and the culture of teaching.' In J. Smyth (Ed.), *Educating teachers: Changing the nature of pedagogical knowledge* (pp. 83–94). London: The Falmer Press.

Bullough, R. V. Jr. (1988a). 'Evaluation and the beginning teacher.' *Education and Society,* 6(1 & 2), 71–0.

Bullough, R. V. Jr. (1988b). *The forgotten dream of American public education.* Ames, Iowa: Iowa State University Press.

Bullough, R. V. Jr. (1989a). *First year teacher: A case study.* NY: Teachers College Press.

Bullough, R. V. Jr. (1989b). 'Teacher education and teacher reflectivity.' *Journal of Teacher Education,* 40(2), 15–21.

Bullough, R. V. Jr. (1990a). 'Personal history and teaching metaphors in preservice teacher education.' A paper presented at the annual meeting of the American Educational Research Association, Boston, April.

Bullough, R. V. Jr. (1990b). 'Supervision, mentoring, and the discovery of self: A case study of a first year teacher.' *Journal of Curriculum and Supervision,* 5(4), 338–60.

Bullough, R. V. Jr. (1991). 'Exploring personal teaching metaphors in preservice teacher education.' *Journal of Teacher Education,* 42 (1), January, February, 43–51.

Bullough, R. V. Jr. and Gitlin, A. (1985). 'Beyond control: Rethinking teacher resistance.' *Education and Society,* 3(1), 65–73.

Bullough, R. V. Jr. and Gitlin, A. (1989). 'Toward educative communities: Teacher education and the quest for the reflective practioner.' *Qualitative Studies in Education,* 2(4), 285–98.

Bullough, R. V. Jr., Gitlin, A., and Goldstein, S. (1984). 'Ideology, teacher role, and resistance.' *Teachers College Record.* 86(2), 339–58.

Bullough, R. V. Jr., Holt, L. and Goldstein, S. (1984). *Human interests in the curriculum: Teaching and learning in a technological society.* NY: Teachers College Press.

Bullough, R. V. Jr., Knowles, J. G. and Crow, N. A. (1989). 'Teacher self concept and student culture in the first year of teaching'. *Teachers College Record,* 91 (2): 209–34.

Butt R. L. and Raymond D. (1987). 'Arguments for using qualitative approaches to understanding teacher thinking: The case for biography.' *The Journal of Curriculum Theorizing,* 7(1), 62–93.

Cherryholmes, C. H. (1988) *Power and criticism: Poststructural investigations in education.* NY: Teachers College Press.

Clark, C. M. (1988) 'Asking the right questions about teacher preparation. Contributions of research on teaching thinking.' *Educational Researcher,* 17(2), 5–12.

Cole, M. (1985). 'The tender trap? Commitment and consciousness in

213

entrants to teaching. In S. J. Ball and I. F. Goodson (Eds.), *Teachers' lives and careers* (pp. 89–104). London: The Falmer Press.

Cremin, L. A. (1988). 'George S. Counts as a teacher: A reminiscence.' *Teaching Education* 2(2), 28–31.

Crow, N. A. (1987). 'Socialization within a teacher education program: A case study.' Unpublished doctoral dissertation, University of Utah, Salt Lake City.

Cusick, P. A. (1986). 'Public secondary schools in the United States.' In T. M. Tomlinson and H. J. Walberg (Eds.), *Academic work and educational excellence: Raising student productivity* (pp. 137–52). Berkeley, CA: McCutcheon Publishing Corporation.

Denscombe, M. (1985). *Classroom control: A sociological perspective.* London: Allen & Unwin.

Dickmeyer, N. (1989). 'Metaphor, model, and theory in education research.' *Teachers College Record, 91*(2), 151–60.

Dreeben, R. (1970). *The nature of teaching.* Glenview, IL: Scott, Foresman.

Duckworth, E. (1986). 'Teaching as research.' *Harvard Educational Review, 56*(4), 481–95.

Eckert, P. (1989). 'Jocks and burnouts: Social categories and identity in the high school.' NY: *Teachers College Press.*

Elbaz, F. (1983). *Teacher thinking: A study of practical knowledge.* London and Canberra: Croom Helm.

Florida Coalition for the Development of a Performance Measurement System. (1983). *Domains: Knowledge base of the Florida Performance Measurement System.* Tallahassee, FL: Office of Teacher Education and In-Service Staff Development.

Freedman, S. (1987). 'Teachers' knowledge from a feminist perspective.' In J. Smyth (Ed.), *Educating teachers: Changing the nature of pedagogical knowledge* (pp. 73–81). London: The Falmer Press.

Friere, P. (1970). *Pedagogy of the oppressed.* NY: Herder & Herder.

Gehrke, N. J. (1981). 'A grounded theory study of beginning teachers' role personalization through reference group relations.' *Journal of Teacher Education, 32*(6), 34–8.

Gitlin, A. and Bullough, R. V. Jr. (1987). 'Teacher evaluation and empowerment: Challenging the taken-for-granted view of teaching.' *Educational Policy, 1*(2), 229–47.

Giroux, H. A. (1983). *Theory and resistance in education: A pedagogy for the opposition.* South Hadley, MA: Bergin and Garvey, Publishers, Inc.

Goodson, I. F. (1981). 'Life histories and the study of schooling.' *Interchange, 11*(4), 62–76.

Goodson, I. F. (1988). *The making of curriculum: Collected essays.* London: The Falmer Press.

Gould, S. J. (1983). *Hen's Teeth and Horses Toes.* NY: W. W. Norton, Inc., chapter 8.

Grant, C. A. and Sleeter, C. E. (1988). 'Race, class and gender and abandoned dreams.' *Teachers College Record, 90*(1), fall, 19–40.

Grumet, M. (1988). *Bitter milk: Women and teaching.* Amherst, MA: The University of Massachusetts Press.

Hargreaves, A. (1986). 'Whatever happened to symbolic interactionism?'

In M. Hammersley (Ed.), *Controversies in classroom research*, (pp. 135–52). Milton Keynes: Open University Press.

Harper, C. A. (1939). *A century of public teacher education.* Washington, D. C. : National Education Association.

Hebdige, D. (1979). *Subculture: The meaning of style.* London: Methuen and Company, Ltd.

The Holmes Group. (1986). *Tomorrow's teachers: A report of the Holmes Group.* East Lansing, MI: Michigan State University College of Education.

The Holmes Group, (1990). *Tommorow's Schools: Principles for the design of professional development schools.* East Lansing, MI: Michigan State University College of Education.

Huberman, M. (1989). 'The professional life cycle of teachers.' *Teachers College Record, 91*(1), 31–57.

Hunt, D. (1987). *Beginning with ourselves: In practice, theory and human affairs.* Cambridge, MA: Brookline Books.

Hunter, M. (1984). 'Knowing, teaching, and supervising.' In. P. L. Hosford (Ed.), *Using what we know about teaching* (pp. 169–92). Alexandria, VA: The Association for Supervision and Curriculum Development.

Jackson, P. W. (1987). 'Facing our ignorance.' *Teachers College Record, 88*(3), 384–9.

Jewett, R. E. (1988). 'H. Gordon Hullfish: Master teacher.' *Teaching Education, 2*(2), 40–2.

John-Steiner, V. (1985). *Notebooks of the mind: Explorations of thinking.* Albuquerque, NM: University of New Mexico Press.

Johnston, P. (1989). Constructive evaluation and the improvement of teaching and learning. *Teachers College Record, 90*(4), 509–28.

Kemmis, S. and McTaggart, R. (1988, 3rd edition). *The action research planner.* Victoria, Australia: Deakin University.

Kliebard, H. M. (1988). 'Fads, fashions, and rituals: The instability of curriculum change.' In L. Tanner (Ed.), *Critical issues in curriculum: Eighty-seventh yearbook of the National Society for the Study of Education, Part I* (pp. 16–34). Chicago, IL: The National Society for the Study of Education.

Knowles, J. G. (1989). Biography and coping strategies: A case study of two beginning teachers. Unpublished doctoral dissertation, University of Utah, Salt Lake City, Utah.

Kotarba, J. A. and Wells, L. (1987). 'Styles of adolescent participation in an all ages rock n'roll nightclub: An ethnographic analysis.' *Youth and Society, 18*(4), 398–417.

Lacey, C. (1977). *The socialization of teachers.* London: Methuen.

Lakoff G. and Johnson, M. (1980). *Metaphors we live by.* Chicago, IL: The University of Chicago Press.

Lamy P. and Levin, J. (1985). 'Punk and middle-class values: A content analysis.' *Youth and Society, 17*(2), 157–70.

Lashley, T. J. (1989). 'Teacher education reform: The road less traveled. *Action in Teacher Education, 11*(1), 2–4.

Leming J. S. (1987). 'Rock music and the socialization of moral values in early adolescence.' *Youth and Society, 18*(4), 363–81.

215

Liston, D. P. and Zeichner, K. M. (1987). 'Reflective teacher education and moral deliberation.' *Journal of Teacher Education, 38*(6), 2–8.

Littlewood, M. (1989). 'The "wise married woman" and the teaching unions.' In H. De Lyon and F. W. Migniuolo (Eds.), *Women teachers: Issues and experiences* (pp. 180–90). Milton Keynes: Open University Press.

Livingston, C. and Borko, H. (1989). 'Expert–novice differences in teaching: A cognitive analysis and implications for teacher education.' *Journal of Teacher Education, 40*(4), 36–42.

Lortie, D. (1975). *Schoolteacher: A sociological study.* Chicago, IL: The University of Chicago Press.

Mattingly, P. H. (1975). *The classless profession: American schoolmen in the nineteenth century.* NY: University Press.

Messerli, J. (1972). *Horace Mann: A biography.* NY: Alfred A. Knopf.

Miller S. I. and Fredericks M. (1988). 'Uses of metaphor: A qualitative case study.' *Qualitative Studies in Education, 1*(3), 263–76.

Mishler, E. G. (1979). 'Meaning in context: Is there any other kind?' *Harvard Educational Review, 49*(1), 1–19.

Munby, H. (1986). 'Metaphor in the thinking of teachers: An exploratory study.' *The Journal of Curriculum Studies, 18*, 197–209.

Nias, J. (1989). *Primary teachers talking: A study of teaching as work.* London and NY: Routledge.

Noddings, N. (1984). *Caring: A feminine approach to ethics and moral education.* Berkeley, CA: University of California Press.

Noddings, N. (1991). 'Stories in dialogue: Caring and interpersonal reasoning.' In C. Witherell and N. Noddings (eds.), *Narrative and dialogue in education* (157–170), NY: Teachers College Press.

Odell, S. J. (1986). 'Induction support of new teachers: A functional approach.' *Journal of Teacher Education, 37*(1), 26–9.

O'Loughlin, M. and Campbell, M. (1988). 'Teacher preparation, empowerment and reflective inquiry.' *Education and Society, 6*(1 & 2), 54–70.

Oram, A. (1989). 'A master should not serve under a mistress: Women and men teachers 1900–1970. In S. Acker (Ed.), *Teachers, gender and careers* (pp. 21–34). London and Philadelphia: The Falmer Press.

Pajak, E. (1986). 'Psychoanalysis, teaching, and supervision.' *Journal of Curriculum and Supervision, 1*(2), 122–31.

Pajak, E. and Blase, J. J. (1989). 'The impact of teachers' personal lives on professional role enactment: A qualitative analysis.' *American Educational Research Journal, 26*(2), 283–310.

Peterson, H. (Ed.). (1946). *Great teachers: As portrayed by those who studied under them.* New Brunswick, NJ: Rutgers University Press.

Pinar, W. (1980). 'Life history and educational experience.' *The Journal of Curriculum Theorizing, 2*(2), 159–212.

Polanyi, M. (1958). *Personal knowledge: Towards a post-critical philosophy.* Chicago, IL: University of Chicago Press.

Pollard, A. (1982). A model of coping strategies. *British Journal of Sociology of Education, 3*(1), 19–37.

Progoff, I. (1975). *At a journal workshop.* NY: Dialogue House Library.

Provenzo, E. F. Jr., McCloskey, G. N., Kottkamp, R. B. and Cohn, M. (1989). 'Metaphor and meaning in the language of teachers.' *Teachers College Record*, *90*(4), 551–73.

Riseborough, G. F. (1985). 'Pupils, teachers' careers and schooling: An empirical study.' In S. J. Ball and I. F. Goodson (Eds.), *Teachers' lives and careers* (pp. 202–65). London: The Falmer Press.

Rosenholtz, S. J. (1989). 'Workplace conditions that affect teacher quality and commitment: Implications for teacher induction programs.' *The Elementary School Journal*, *89*(4), 421–39.

Rumelhart, D. E. (1980). 'Schemata: The building blocks of cognition.' In R. J. Spiro, B. C. Bruce, and W. F. Brewer, (Eds.), *Theoretical Issues in Reading Comprehension: Perspectives in Cognitive Psychology, Linguistics, and Education* (pp. 33–58). Hillsdale, NJ: Lawrence Erlbaum Associates, Publishers.

Russell T. and Johnston, P. (1988). 'Teachers learning from experiences of teaching: Analyses based on metaphor and reflection.' Unpublished paper, Faculty of Education, Queen's University, Kingston, Ontario, Canada.

Ryan, K. (1983). 'Forward.' In J. Greenstein, *What the children taught me* (pp. vii–xiii). Chicago, IL: University of Chicago Press.

Ryan, K. (1986). *The induction of new teachers.* Bloomington, IN: Phi Delta Kappa Educational Foundation.

Schlechty, P. C. and Vance, V. S. (1983). 'Recruitment, selection, and retention: The shape of the teaching force.' *Elementary School Journal*, *83*, 469–87.

Schon, D. A. (1983). *The reflective practitioner: How professionals think in action.* NY: Basic Books.

Schon, D. A. (1987). *Educating the reflective practitioner: Toward a new design for teaching and learning in the professions.* San Francisco, CA: Jossey-Bass.

Shulman, L. S. (1986). 'Paradigms and research programs in the study of teaching: A contemporary perspective.' In M. C. Wittrock (Ed.), *Handbook of research on teaching*, 3rd. ed. (pp. 3–36). NY: Macmillan.

Sikes, P. J., Measor, L. and Woods, P. (1985). *Teacher careers: Crises and continuities.* London: The Falmer Press.

Snow R. P. (1987). 'Youth, rock'n'roll, and electronic media.' *Youth and Society*, *18*(4), 326–43.

Soder, R. (1988). 'Studying the education of educators: What we can learn from other professions.' *Phi Delta Kappan*, December, 299–305.

Van Til, W. (1988). 'William Heard Kilpatrick: A memoir.' *Teaching Education*, *2*(2), 36–9.

Veenman, S. (1984). 'Perceived problems of beginning teachers.' *Review of Educational Research*, *54*(2), 143–78.

Walker, R. (1986). 'The conduct of educational case studies: Ethics, theory and procedures.' In M. Hammersley (Ed.), *Controversies in classroom research*, (pp. 187–219). Milton Keynes: Open University Press.

Waxman, H. C., Feiberg, H. J., Vaughan, J. C. and Weil, M. (Eds.). (1988). *Images of reflection in teacher education.* Reston, VA: Association for Teacher Educators.

Weinstein, C. S. (1988). 'Preservice teachers' expectations about the first year of teaching.' *Teaching and Teacher Education,* 4(1), 31–40.

Weinstein, C. S. (1989). 'Teacher education students' preconceptions of teaching.' *The Journal of Teacher Education,* 40(2), 53–60.

Wildman, T. M. and Niles, J. A. (1987). 'Reflective teachers: Tensions between abstractions and realities.' *Journal of Teacher Education,* 38(4), 25–31.

Wildman, T. M., Niles, J. A., Magliaro, S. G. and McLaughlin, R. A. (1989) 'Teaching and learning to teach: The two roles of beginning teachers.' *The Elementary School Journal,* 89(4), 471–93.

Winetrout, K. (1988). 'Boyd H. Bode: A mission but no blueprint.' *Teaching Education* 2(2), 32–5.

Woods, P. (1977). 'Teaching for survival.' In P. Woods and M. Hammersley (Eds.), *School experience* (pp. 271–93). NY: St. Martin's Press.

Woods, P. (1987). 'Life histories and teacher knowledge.' In J. Smyth (Ed.), *Educating teachers: Changing the nature of pedagogical knowledge* (pp. 121–35). London: The Falmer Press.

Yin, R. K. (1984). *Case study research.* Beverly Hills, CA: Sage Publications.

Young, R. (1990). *A critical theory of education: Habermas and our children's future.* NY: Teachers College Press.

Zeichner, K. M. and Gore, J. (1989). 'Teacher socialization.' East Lansing, MI: National Center for Research on Teacher Education.

Zeichner, K. M. and Liston, D. P. (1987). 'Teaching student teachers to reflect.' *Harvard Educational Review,* 57(1), 23–48.

Zeichner, K., and Tabachnick, R. B. (1981). 'Are the effects of university teacher education washed out by school experience?' *Journal of Teacher Education,* 32, 7–11.

Zeichner, K. M., Tabachnick, R. and Densmore, K. (1987). 'Individual, institutional, and cultural influences on the development of teachers' craft knowledge.' In J. Calderhead (Ed.), *Exploring teachers' thinking* (pp. 21–59). London: Cassell Educational Limited.

Zumwalt, K. K. (1988). 'Are we improving or undermining teaching?' In L. Tanner (Ed.), *Critical Issues in Curriculum: Eighty-seventh yearbook of the National Society for the Study of Education, Part I* (pp. 148–74). Chicago, IL: The National Society for the Study of Education.

SUBJECT INDEX

AUTHOR INDEX